MARCH 28,

to WEST CHES

Library

From

Bill Warner

W. LLOYD WARNER: SOCIAL ANTHROPOLOGIST

W. LLOYD WARNER
Social Anthropologist

by Mildred Hall Warner

Publishing Center for Cultural Resources
New York City   1988

Library of Congress Cataloging-in-Publication Data

Warner, Mildred Hall.
   W. Lloyd Warner, social anthropologist.

   Bibliography: p. 217.
   Includes index.
   1. Warner, W. Lloyd (William Lloyd), 1898—1970.
2. Anthropologists—United States—Biography. I. Title.
GN21.W37H35   1987   306'.092'4 [B]   87-20756
ISBN 0-89062-234-5 (cloth)
ISBN 0-89062-230-2 (paper)

Cover: W. Lloyd Warner with Murngin tribesmen, ca. 1928.
Frontispiece: W. Lloyd Warner, 1939.

Produced by the Publishing Center for Cultural Resources,
New York City.
Manufactured in the United States of America.

CONTENTS

INTERVIEWS are not only time-consuming but strenuous if they require searching files and searching memories. They can also be exciting in stimulating recall of events and people long forgotten. Alice Chandler, who was associated with my husband's work from early days at the University of Chicago and is now administrative assistant to the president of the university; Burleigh Gardner, president of Social Research Inc.; Robert J. Havighurst, who worked closely with Lloyd on many projects and is now Professor Emeritus of Education and Behavioral Sciences, University of Chicago; Solon T. Kimball, Graduate Research Professor of Anthropology, University of Florida until his death in 1985; Flora Rhind (now deceased), retired secretary of the board of the Rockefeller Foundation; and Ralph Tyler, formerly dean of social sciences, University of Chicago, and later director of the Center of Advanced Studies, Stanford—all contributed to the content of this book and read the manuscript. To Helen MacGill Hughes, my gratitude for her able editing of an earlier draft. Charles Baldwin, retired as U.S. Ambassador to Malaysia; Hilda Carter, at one time secretary to Lawrence U. Henderson at Harvard University; Meyer Fortes, Professor of Social Anthropology at King's College, Cambridge University; Everett Hughes, Professor Emeritus, Boston College; Amelia Little, of Old Newbury, Massachusetts; David Moore, late of the Conference Board; Harriett Moore, consultant in social research; Leone Phillips, consultant in social research; Lee Rainwater, Professor of Sociology, Harvard University; David Riesman, Professor at Large, Harvard University; and Leo Srole, College of Physicians and Surgeons, Columbia University—all have added importantly to this book.

I hold a special place for Theodora Kroeber Quinn, who reminisced with me about the old days, gave unstintingly of her time, and arranged for my unrestricted use of the Kroeber and Lowie files in the Bancroft Library archives. She died July 4, 1979.

In organizing the data for Big Farmers and Ranchers and having it typed for deposit in archives, I had the use of research funds remaining in my husband's name at the Carnegie Corporation. In a limited way I have called upon a memorial fund to my husband at the University of Chicago for the present project.

The archives of the Rockefeller Foundation, of the Baker Library and the Houghton Library at Harvard, of the Bancroft Library at the University of California at Berkeley, and of the Regenstein Library at the University of Chicago have been most valuable resources.

AFTER MY HUSBAND'S DEATH in May 1970, many people approached me for information about his personal life. Ironically, with the best source no longer available there seemed to be an urgency to learn what this person was like, about the people and experiences that had molded his life and about his thinking and his professional career. When Lloyd Fallers agreed to write a biography for publication by the University of Chicago Press in its Heritage of Sociology Series, I was pleased because he was so able; I could turn over to him whatever material I had or could recall. Lloyd Fallers died.

When I went to my husband's offices at Michigan State University to remove his files in early fall of 1970, nothing remained—banks of files accumulated through forty years had disappeared. The dean and the president instigated and supervised a search of the building, the archives, and Lloyd's first offices. When I began to accept the fact of this loss, I realized that it should be my responsibility to record what I could recall, assisted by limited personal files. This led to interviewing people who had been important in his life and his work and to archives where I might find records and correspondence. During this period, I heard a recurrent theme of how Lloyd Warner had changed the lives of people who had studied with him, expressions of gratitude for the way he had led them in a direction that brought excitement and fruition to their professional careers. Other themes were his gaiety and wit, his humanity, his empathy with the feelings of others, his ability to appreciate special qualities in a great variety of persons. I hope I have caught some of this.

Since I had taken some part in my husband's work in relation to research, preparation of manuscripts for publication, and at times correspondence, I wanted to add what I could to knowledge of his professional as well as his personal life. To someone else falls the task of the development of his theories, his scientific contribution.

Lloyd thought of himself always as a social anthropologist, a comparative sociologist, a behavioral scientist, with strong interests in the motivations of individuals and the significance of symbols.

I have tried to keep family on the periphery. Had I let us in as we lived our lives, this would be quite a different book with a different purpose. This book must be accepted with its limitations. I hope that, for some, it will bring insights into Lloyd Warner as a person.

For

Ann Warner Arlen
Caroline Warner Hightower
William Taylor Warner

CHAPTER I

IN LATE MAY 1926 the Anthropology Club of the University of California was marking the end of the academic year with a dinner meeting at a Berkeley restaurant. Among those present was Bronislaw Malinowski, who was to teach at the university that summer as a visiting professor. A. R. Radcliffe-Brown, the honored guest, had been visiting in the United States while on his way to fill the newly created chair of anthropology at the University of Sydney. Suddenly he called down the table to Lloyd Warner, then a graduate student, "I say, Warner, how would you like to come to Australia with me?" Warner, uncertain of the intention of the question, replied facetiously. But Radcliffe-Brown insisted, "No, no. I'm serious. If you are interested let's get together and talk."

The Rockefeller Foundation had for some time been considering an integrated long-range program for the study of the Australian aborigines.[1] The Australian Association for the Advancement of Science, the Australian National Research Council, and the Australian universities had agreed upon the urgent need of a chair of anthropology at one of the universities and of the immediate study of the native tribes of Australia. The foundation had received a brief report on the location and general characteristics of some of the native people from the explorer G. H. Wilkins, who was making natural history collections for the British Museum along the coastal area from Sydney to Port Darwin.

At the suggestion of Vilhjalmur Stefansson, the Arctic explorer and ethnologist who had spent some time in Australia, Wilkins wrote to Clark Wissler, head of the Department of Anthropology of the American Museum of Natural History, specifying accessible places in Queensland where the aborigines had not been in close contact with civilization. One such location was the Cape York Peninsula, whose natives might safely be approached through interpreters at the mission station. One or two natives with a slight knowledge of English could be found in each tribe. Certain points in the Northern Territory and east of Port Darwin were recommended as locations for profitable study though they were not readily accessible through the regular lines of communication afforded by the stations of the Methodist Missionary Society. The Northern Territory mainland opposite the station on the Crocodile Islands was described by Wilkins as a virgin field for the ethnologist. "The natives," he reported, "are friendly but some still practice promiscuous cannibalism. (Within the last two months two bodies have been eaten by natives who are at present about my camp.) Several white men have been killed in these districts, but it has usually been due to their own indiscretion. So far as we know the natives have never killed a white man for food. .... The people East of Arnhem Bay and North of Caledon Bay in Arnhem Land are credited with aggressive hostility toward white men."[2]

To learn what plans Australian authorities and scientists might be making for teaching and for doing field work among the aborigines, Edwin R. Embree, director of the Rockefeller Foundation's Division of Studies, and Clark Wissler had gone to Australia and New Zealand in the fall of 1925. Learning of the interest of the Australian scientific organizations and of the foundation, Vilhjalmur Stefansson had offered Edwin Embree his cooperation.[3] Both Embree and Stefansson were to play continuing roles in Lloyd Warner's personal life and professional career.

Plans did not proceed smoothly, however. The foundation wanted the participation, including financial, of all the Australian governments. A university had to be chosen for the proposed chair. A professor of anatomy of the University of London protested the filling of a chair of anthropology at the University of Sydney before an incumbent for the chair of anatomy had been appointed. Apparently Davidson Black, the anatomist and anthropologist, had been offered the post but declined because he was reluctant to leave China.

Upon the resolution of these problems—which did not take very long, considering the many factions involved—it was agreed to base the chair at the University of Sydney and to offer it to A. R. Radcliffe-Brown of Oxford University, who was then in South Africa. Embree, on behalf of the Foundation, invited him to visit the United States and possibly Europe before assuming his new post. He accepted and arrived in this country in April 1926. Under the guidance of Embree, the Foundation's Division of Studies showed itself increasingly concerned with the study of primitive societies, especially of disappearing cultures. Radcliffe-Brown was an excellent authority to counsel anthropologists on the status of current and proposed work and on the areas most urgently in need of study before the cultures—and indeed the people—might disappear.

In writing to Embree from shipboard after his visit, Radcliffe-Brown summarized his American experiences with warmth and satisfaction. He was convinced that the University of Chicago was becoming one of the most important centers of anthropology. There he had seen Fay-Cooper Cole, chairman of the Department of Anthropology, and Edward Sapir, the linguist, and had a few days at Berkeley with Alfred Kroeber, who had just returned from an archaeological dig in Peru. Radcliffe-Brown went on to Nevada, where he apparently did some fieldwork and met Robert Lowie of the Berkeley faculty at Reno. He found another protagonist of the importance of anatomy at Stanford in its president, Ray Lyman Wilbur, who stoutly supported the proposed work at Sydney.

Edward Winslow Gifford, who headed the Lowie Museum of Anthropology at Berkeley, and some of his students were his last contacts in America. Warner was one of the latter. Radcliffe-Brown wrote:

> There is at Berkeley a graduate student, William Lloyd Warner, whom I judge to have in him the makings of a first-class anthropologist. He is willing to come to Australia for eighteen months and take up the study of the aborigines in the field. Lowie and Gifford both speak highly of his work and I think Kroeber would do the same. I am myself so strongly impressed that I would have no hesitation in recommending that he should be offered the opportunity to do research in Australia.
>
> I am not quite clear what should be the procedure in this instance. It would save time if the Foundation would itself consider the case and, if my suggestion were approved, provide a sum for his expenses. If this cannot be done I will propose to the Australian National Research Council that they should invite him to come to Australia for this research. . . .
>
> If Warner were given a fellowship he might profitably spend a short time with Hooton at Harvard and have some talk with Wissler. He would have to spend a month with me in Sydney getting a proper grasp of the nature of the Australian field and its problems. He could then spend twelve months with a native tribe.
>
> You see, I am very keen on getting the work started as quickly as possible, and this seems to me to afford us an excellent opening.[4]

Warner's record at Berkeley had not conformed to convention. In his third year of undergraduate work as an English major he had taken off with a friend for an interlude in New York. When he returned to Berkeley a few months later he had difficulty in being reinstated. At this time he had the great good fortune to meet the anthropologist Robert Lowie, who interceded for him. Warner was so impressed by Lowie that he changed his major to anthropology in order to work under him, completed the course requirements for his bachelor's degree in one year with straight A's, and had completed the equivalent of two years of graduate work when Radcliffe-Brown flung wide the door that Lowie had opened to his future career.

Notes to Chapter I

1. Rockefeller Foundation Archives, August 1924.
2. G. H. Wilkins to Wissler, 29 December 1924, Rockefeller Foundation Archives.
3. Vilhjalmur Stefansson to Rockefeller Foundation Archives, 16 April 1924.
4. Radcliffe-Brown to Rockefeller Foundation Archives, 31 June 1926.

Randsburgh, looking east, early 1900s

WILLIAM LLOYD WARNER was a native Californian. His mother, who was a Carter, was also born in California, and the Warner family arrived when his father was young. Lloyd's uncle, Arthur Carter, wrote a family history covering four generations.

Lloyd's maternal grandparents were both born in Calhoun County, Mississippi—James Richard Carter in 1843 and Martha Elvira Covington in 1849. James was a sick child, who developed tuberculosis, and defiantly decided he would cure himself by military service in the Civil War. He returned home on furlough in 1864, a healthy young man who had sustained no war injuries. He fell in love with Martha Covington, the sister of his war buddy Billy Covington. She was the eldest of thirteen children of a prosperous farm owner. When the war ended in 1865, James and Martha married. He worked in his father's tanning factory and lumber mill. Three children were born (one died) before they left for Redlands, California, where some of Martha's brothers and sisters had already gone.

In 1870, James and Martha arrived in San Francisco, and then endured a stormy voyage of two days and two nights to Wilmington. Everyone on board was sick except Martha; James became very ill and it seemed to take him years to recover fully. From Wilmington they then traveled by stagecoach to San Bernardino, about eight-five miles distant, stopping to change the four horses at a halfway house in what is now Pomona. James was advised to settle on a ranch in San Mateo Canyon (San Timoteo Canyon), where in the course of the following nine years a son and three daughters were born. Redlands was designated the birthplace of Lloyd's mother, Belle.

It was not a peaceful life. James had to fight to keep Indians from taking everything he raised. He had no firearms but used a hoe handle very effectively. The ranch house had a verandah on three sides; the Indians rode their horses up and around the verandah, infuriating James, who could only run them off. In spite of the raids and James's terrible temper, the Indians respected him, calling him "The Boss Man from Mis-sip."

In 1883 James and Martha took charge of the ranch the latter's parents had acquired upon their arrival to join their children. Hortons, Martha's mother's family, were also there, and the Covingtons and Hortons married into the Dunlap and Cook families, whose members were old settlers. In a generation this close kin group numbered about one hundred. Reunions were frequent and continued for many years. Martha and James had ten children, including the daughter who died as a baby.

After several years on the Covingtons' ranch in San Mateo, Martha and James leased a ranch in Yucaipa, where they lived in an adobe house built in 1785. There they raised cattle and hogs, fruit, and vegetables, and did some dry farming. They had a smokehouse and sold hams and bacon to a grocery in San Bernardino and to the cooks feeding the workers, mostly Chinese, digging the ditch for the pipeline from Big Bear (now Lake Tahoe) to Redlands. In 1887 they built a six-room house, which was torn down in 1920. The adobe was acquired by the California State Historical Society.

A few years later they returned to Colton and bought ten acres; James and Billy Covington cleared the cactus, built a house, and planted an orange grove. In 1897 they rented a fifty-acre ranch eight miles east of Redlands, where they raised chickens and turkeys as well as fruit.

In 1897 their daughter Belle married William Taylor Warner, whose family had come from the East and settled in the Redlands area when he was a boy. The young couple lived in Redlands, but Belle went home to her parents in Colton for Lloyd's birth in 1898.

Will's family had come from England in one of the early migrations and settled in Connecticut. When his grandparents started west they stayed for a while in Kansas, where Lloyd's father was born. They later came by covered wagon across the Oregon Trail to Colton where they settled and raised peaches. His parents and brother and sister all died at an early age. Lloyd adored both of his grandfathers and enjoyed hearing them recount stories of the Civil War, one fighting for the North and the other, of course, for the South. His grandmother Carter was an extraordinary lady. Living and working as she did under difficult conditions while raising a large family, she was always, as Lloyd remembered her, properly dressed, always in gloves when the occasion demanded, formal in speech and manner, yet warm and loving.

Lloyd spent much of his early childhood at the Carter ranch. He remembered the slaughtering of the hogs and how all parts of the animal were used and enjoyed in the southern tradition—carried on by his mother, who was imaginative too in Spanish cooking. Lloyd's appreciation of a great variety of foods and interest in new ones was a resource to him when he was living with the aborigines in Australia. Scornful of anthropologists who went into the field supplied with tins of dull food, he ate with the natives and learned to enjoy almost everything from kangaroo to roasted ants and grubs.

When Lloyd was only a few years old his father took a job with the Yellow Aster gold mine in Randsburgh. In those boom days the town had one street with thirteen saloons and at least that many houses of prostitution. Life was meager, but his mother was a pioneer who coped, helping the teacher of the one-room school, supporting the work of the Methodist Church, cooking good meals where no fresh foods were ever available, fashioning a Christmas tree of the branches of greasewood. Randsburgh was in high desert country and a long distance from anywhere.

However, there were always things to keep a boy busy. Lloyd and other boys rounded up the miners' burros; which were allowed to run wild in the desert, and tamed and rode them. No one claimed the burros; the miners would catch them as they were needed, calling them desert canaries. There were always rattlesnakes to kill, especially in houses that his parents owned and rented. And there were tarantulas and scorpions to avoid.

When Lloyd was five his happy life as an only child was disrupted by the arrival of his sister Madge. (A son had died soon after birth two years before.) The family returned by train to the Carters for the birth. Here Lloyd could be spoiled by his grandparents and enjoy his many cousins. Redlands attracted many early settlers because it is such fine citrus country.

When Madge was almost four and Lloyd nine, his parents returned to the Colton-Redlands area for better schooling and social environment for their children. Here his father managed one hundred acres for growing oranges and grapes for a group of bankers. A little six-grade country school nearby was in trouble because it lacked the minimum of fifteen students. So Madge was recruited at age five to hold the school. Accustomed to an afternoon nap, she slept every day after lunch, her head on her desk, an embarrassment to Lloyd. The next year he went to school in Colton, a little over a mile away, first walking, later riding a bicycle.

When Lloyd was fifteen his sister Marjorie was born. Lloyd took the surrey and drove Madge to stay with neighbors, then went to San Bernardino for the woman who was to help. When they returned, the doctor had arrived and so had the baby. He was permitted to name her after his current girlfriend.

Except for a fire in the gasoline stove that burned out the kitchen only a month before Marjorie was born, this was a happy period. The fire might have taken the entire house, but everyone living near enough to see the smoke came at once and confined it to the kitchen. Later they returned to help rebuild and had completed the new kitchen before Marjorie was born.

For Lloyd this was a time of visiting with friends and relatives, trips to the mountains, hunting birds' eggs in the eucalyptus grove at the rear of the ranch, swimming in a big reservoir. Lloyd blew out eggs and had quite a collection for display at school.

His father also taught him to shoot doves, rabbits, and squirrels, which his mother knew well how to prepare. This kind of hunting was a sport. One day it abruptly stopped. Lloyd was in the vineyard one beautiful morning when he saw a jack rabbit preening himself in the sunlight. He raised his gun and sighted him, and the rabbit suddenly looked to him not like quarry but like a beautiful living creature enjoying the pleasure of grooming. He lowered the gun and did not use one again until he went to Australia, where a shotgun and rifle were helpful in obtaining food not only for himself but for the Murngin with whom he lived.

Vacations were usually spent in the mountains at Gail's Ranch owned by the Dunlap family above San Bernardino. Lloyd always loved the mountains and the desert.

He kept a diary in 1914 when he was going to Colton High School. In it are frequent mentions of grandparents, aunts, uncles, and cousins visiting. He records playing football and basketball; being a member of the glee club and elected class president; picking oranges and suckering the trees; trapping gophers, work for which he was paid; buying a pig for $6.50; being pinched for throwing oranges and getting a talking-to from the judge; and being sent out of English class for laughing but readmitted after writing a poem. He went to Sunday School and Christian Endeavor; played cards with friends and stayed up until three; hitched the mules or horses to haul fertilizer and sand to repair the walks; painted the chicken house with crude oil; hauled lumber, ice, and hay; hoed weeds and mowed; took music lessons; and helped with the birth of a colt.

He usually had animals. He built a rabbit pen and bought a pair of rabbits; soon he was able to give a rabbit to his girlfriend Marj.

Many complaints were recorded in his diary that spring when rain confined him to the house, though often there would be a club meeting or he read books and magazines which he had bought or borrowed in Colton. He was also writing stories. There are frequent comments about having a swell time—going to shows, having friends visit, and a truck ride that was quite exciting, and he enjoyed buying clothes.

It would seem that in the course of that school year Lloyd worked more closely with his father than at any other time. His father had many skills and could take care of all of the maintenance of the ranch and the house. Lloyd learned all of these skills, but he had no interest in them.

When Lloyd started high school the family bought a large and comfortable old house in Colton and his father worked in the cement plant at Mount Slover, a mountain composed entirely of cement rock, or hydraulic limestone. The cement dust damaged Will's lungs, and he developed tuberculosis and had to stop all work until he was cured.

In the summer of 1914, after the close of school, Lloyd worked in the local cannery. Another summer he worked with a county road-repair crew. Meanwhile, he was growing very fast—all up, not out—and reached six feet three by the end of the year, when he was sixteen.

His interest in sports from early days continued throughout his life. At first it was baseball, basketball, and football; he kept in his diary an elaborate score system for the Colton and San Bernardino teams.

In the fall of 1915 he was hired as a reporter for the Colton Courier; he covered sports, including the automobile races in Corona. For the Colton paper and the San Bernardino Sun he reported an official race with some of the famous drivers of all time—Barney Oldfield, Ralph DePalma, Bob Berman—and took photographs of them and their cars.

After a year in Colton High School, Lloyd transferred to San Bernardino, where the school was larger, the teaching staff better, and where they had an excellent English department; the study of English interested him more than anything. The head of the department and teacher of junior and senior English was a smiling, gushing sort of person whom Lloyd did not like. Her exact opposite was the teacher of the two lower years who perhaps overcame her frustration by training the debating team. Jenny Y. Freeman, precise, always beautifully and simply dressed, had a keen intellect and an interest in training young minds in precision, facts, verification, presentation with no flourishes—effective because substantiated. Under her tutelage Lloyd became a member of the debating team; she was the first teacher to have a strong influence on him.

Lloyd was a graduating senior when the United States entered World War I. He enlisted on Mar. 30, 1917, a few days before the formal declaration. He had his basic training at Camp Kearney, and then a series of assignments such as guarding a railroad tunnel in Los Angeles. He was given leave to go home to graduate from high school. At Camp Kearney he started to have all of the childhood diseases to which he had not been exposed—measles, mumps, and whooping cough. Scarlet fever and diphtheria together put him in the hospital. He was too ill to care much about anything. The orderly drew the curtain around the boy next to him, who had just died, turned to Lloyd, and said, "Well, your turn tonight, slim." Perhaps this aroused enough spirit to give him the determination to recover, but not completely; while his unit was shipped overseas he was still hospitalized—with tuberculosis. He was given a medical discharge and sent home to recover.

Treatment for tuberculosis at that time was rest, of course, fresh air and sun, and egg nogs. Lloyd recovered from the tuberculosis but never did recover from the egg nogs—milking the family cow had turned him against milk and the egg nogs were intolerable.

The doctor gave him permission to attend college provided it be near enough to permit him to live at home and receive the necessary care. The University of Southern California met these requirements. After one year there he transferred to the University of California at Berkeley. His family moved to Moneta to be near his Warner grandparents and later to Whittier, where his parents died many years later. His sister Madge remarked that after Lloyd went to Berkeley he rarely came home, and it was always as a kind of visitor. He had indeed left home.

How he supported himself is something of a mystery. He had a small disability allowance from the Veterans' Administration; he tutored a young student in English and for some time lived with the family. Repeatedly he is described as well groomed and well dressed, but there is no doubt that he and his friends were usually broke and in debt.

Another student at Berkeley was Frances Farmer. She had graduated from San Bernardino High School and gone to Pomona College before Lloyd transferred to San Bernardino from Colton. Their lives had been connected tangentially. Their mothers were friends, and her family lived in Rialto near the places where Lloyd's family lived. Like Lloyd's family, hers were pioneers—her mother endlessly resourceful with a remedy for every need or ailment, a kind of folklore which she transmitted to her daughter. Frances was majoring in English at Berkeley; this was Lloyd's field, although he did not select a major for another year. Here they came to know each other well for the first time and became friends—a close friendship which continued until his death.

Lloyd's high school years had given him good grounding in traditional subjects: four years of English and of history, and one year each of algebra, plane geometry, chemistry, physical geography, Latin, Spanish, debating, spelling and penmanship (which left him largely untouched), and public speaking. During his first year at Berkeley he had a general program: three two-semester courses in English and the second semester of another; a year of political science and of economics and the second semester of another which he dropped; and in general paleontology, the demonstration course of which he dropped the second semester. He was impatient about the use of his time and when he did not like a course he stopped attending classes, not bothering with the formalities of altering his registration. This habit was later to cause difficulties.

Lloyd joined Sigma Chi fraternity at USC but soon realized that this was not his kind of life and left the fraternity house. Meanwhile, he had made a number of close friendships that were to continue through his life: with Frances Farmer, Morris Ankrum, a drama major, and Harry Tucker, a mathematics genius who took all comers at poker and thereby financed his university career. Another close friend was Stokeley Fortson, perhaps the most brilliant of them all who, within a few years, was to become an alcoholic and die tragically drinking sterno.

Lloyd married Billy Overfield, an attractive girl, as immature and little prepared for marriage as he. It was a brief and stormy experience, disturbing and disillusioning. In the fall of 1921 when Morris suggested that he and Lloyd go to New York to try their talents in the theater, Lloyd welcomed the opportunity to get away.

In New York both of them had walk-on parts with George Arliss in *The Green Goddess.* They took rooms near the old Lafayette Hotel, and

In uniform, 1917

Broadway, 1921

Morris went on with the theater. Lloyd got a job with Fred Fisher in the music-publishing business, arranging for name bands to introduce new song publications. He had fun, and he did well. Fred Fisher was as tough as they come in that business, yet he and Lloyd were friendly. Fisher had done well with "I'm Always Chasing Rainbows"—a direct steal from Chopin, of course—and decided that Chopin was his and was ready to sue another publisher who brought out "I'm Forever Blowing Bubbles" with equal success.

The New York experience could not last. It was an interlude in which Lloyd made enough money to buy some good clothes and to resume his academic career, to which he now understood he was completely committed.

Frances Farmer had a little apartment up in the Berkeley hills and was working for her master's degree in English. One rainy night she answered a knock at the door and there stood Lloyd. He put down his suitcase and said, "I can't take New York any longer. I want to get back in the university and I don't know how I am going to do it." He had impulsively left the university without regard for the formalities demanded by the registrar, and his record showed "Disqualified." Frances was a friend of Robert Lowie, who was acting head of the department of anthropology while Alfred Kroeber was doing field work in Peru. She telephoned Lowie, he joined them, and Frances left him with Lloyd to discuss the situation. Lloyd was impressed with Lowie as a person and in his philosophy. When Lowie succeeded in having Lloyd reinstated, Lloyd wanted to change his major to anthropology. Frances always thought that Lloyd went to New York in frustration over his English major—that he had a scientific mind not satisfied by the subjects he was studying. Not long after Lloyd's return she went to China with a family whose children she was tutoring, and Lloyd had already become Lowie's protégé. He had found his field and his mentor.

Having made the decision to enter anthropology, he must have been impatient in filling the requirements for readmission—the removal of three incompletes in English courses, one in Semitics, and one in philosophy—requirements he filled almost completely in summer session. Officially, he was reprimanded by the university president, placed on probation, excluded from student activities until the first day of the month in which he would become a candidate for the A.B. degree, and lost library privileges until the end of the calendar year. Actually, he was readmitted officially in October.

Later, when Kroeber had a conference with the dean about Lloyd's acceptance as a graduate student, the dean said, "Look at his undergraduate record, what can you do with it?" There were straight As and then a flat F, and when Kroeber asked Lloyd about the latter he said, "It was a terrible course. It bored me stiff. I went twice and never went back." But he did not drop it.

Theodora Kracow Brown (Krak), a young widow with two small sons, had received her A.B. cum laude at Berkeley in 1919 and her M.A. in psychology in 1920. She was living in northern Berkeley with her mother-in-law, who had strongly urged her to return to the university for graduate studies. She changed her field to anthropology and thus came to know Lloyd.

Krak remembers Lloyd's taking in one year every course required for the A.B. degree in anthropology—perhaps every course offered in the field at that time—as well as some hangover courses required for reinstatement. He made straight As. The registrar's record confirms this. In his final year as an undergraduate Lloyd took a course called Oceania under Edward W. Gifford. It covered the origins, traditions, and customs of the native races of Oceania. He also took Outlines of Culture Growth from Kroeber (human origins and classification, beginnings of culture, growth of civilization in the great centers of Egypt, Europe, and Asia, diffusions in Africa and Oceania, related and marginal peoples, world religions and international contacts), Chapters in Culture History from Lowie (the history of the cultivation of plants, domestication of animals, fire-making, the evolution of the alphabet, and history of metalwork), another course from Lowie, Primitive Society (rules and forms of marriage among the ruder peoples of the world, kinship customs, the position of women, social groups, property and its inheritance), and a course in the archaeology of Egypt and Babylonia.

As a graduate student Lloyd had a seminar with Lowie in applied methods, and took Kroeber's course in culture processes and a course from both Kroeber and Lowie in field, library, and museum research. Probably Gifford, as the museum man, would have participated in the last-named course as well. He also took a history course in modern colonization covering the history of the growth of colonial empires after 1492; motives, rivalries, and policies of expansionist nations in the occupation and exploitation of dependent areas; and the growth of administrative ideals in the control of backward peoples.

This course anticipated some of the experiences he would have in Australia. He had considerable contact with Malinowski, who was in residence that year and was one of a group of anthropologists who made up the North Berkeley Little Bohemia, as Krak called it—Duncan Strong, Ralph Beals, Jean and Matt Sterling, Julian Steward, Bob Lowie, and others. Their locus was the home of Jaime D'Angoulo, a colorful character. Krak wrote an unpublished paper about the group called "An Innocent Bohemia," in which she sees their parties and escapades as terribly innocent but, like many incidents of the 1920s, made into something sophisticated, quite the opposite. Bob Lowie, in writing to Malinowski in 1929, after the latter's departure from Berkeley, talks of Pitt-Rivers's arrival in Berkeley, and Lowie's putting him in touch with the "hyperarboreans of North Berkeley."

Lowie married in 1933 a psychologist he had known for some time, Louella Winifred Cole (Cy to her friends). Born in Vienna in 1883, Lowie had a gentle, warm, old-world manner even though his family came to this country when he was only ten. He received his A.B. degree from the City College of New York in 1901 and his Ph.D. from Columbia, under Boas, in 1908. From then until 1921 he was in the Department of Anthropology of the American Museum of Natural History. There were intervals in 1917–1918, when he taught at the University of California, and in 1920–1921 at Columbia while retaining his association with the museum. He then returned to the University of California as an associate professor of anthropology and became a full professor in 1925, at times being acting chairman of the department until his retirement in 1950.

In spite of the fact that Cy cut off Bob from his friends, of whom she apparently was quite jealous, they seemed happy together and she introduced him to many activities that gave him great pleasure—we would often swim together at an indoor pool, an activity which neither Bob nor Lloyd had ever cared about, and we all enjoyed it. Cy was a remarkable teacher, excelled at demonstration, illustrating, making everything seem simple. Under such circumstances, she and Lloyd were very friendly; but on other occasions her jealousy of the close friendship and love that Lloyd and Bob had for each other was a barrier that made our visits awkward and strained. Her choice of home was a symbolic gesture of dissociation from life in the Berkeley hills where most of the faculty enjoyed living for the beauty, the charming old homes, many, like the Kroebers', designed by Maybeck, the magnificent views of the bay. She chose a large, plain house in the flats and rented rooms. Bob did not seem to mind although he had spent his Berkeley days living with his hyperarboreans of whom there remained a small cadre around whom we would rally on our frequent visits. We enjoyed Bob most when he saw him alone as on the occasion of his receiving an honorary degree from the University in Chicago in 1941.

Lowie's research was primarily among the North Plains Indians, the Assiniboine, Crow, Athabaskans, and Hopi. Of his many publications, probably the best known are landmarks in anthropological theory— *Primitive Society,*[1] originally published in 1920, and *Primitive Religion,* in 1924.[2] In later years, during World War II, which troubled him deeply, and thereafter, he talked increasingly about the German people, their history, culture, nature. In 1945 he wrote *The German People*[3] and, much later, in 1954, *Toward Understanding Germany.*[4]

The other person who touched Lloyd's academic life closely in Berkeley days was Alfred Kroeber.[5] As Boas, under whom Kroeber received his Ph.D. in 1901, had introduced anthropology as a study at Columbia in 1896, Kroeber did so at the University of California in 1900. A native New Yorker, he received all of his schooling there, and like many easterners, had never been west of the Hudson. He went west, however, on trips arranged by Boas to study American Indian languages, as a result of the urgency Boas felt for studying aboriginal peoples before their cultures were forever altered through the inexorable process of acculturation. Kroeber held his first academic appointment as an assistant in English at Columbia before he came fully under the influence of Boas and became a fellow in anthropology in 1899. The Academy of Sciences in San Francisco in 1900 needed a curator for a rapidly growing ethnographic collection from California Indian cultures, and Boas recommended Kroeber. Soon after, Benjamin Ide Wheeler, president of the University of California, offered Kroeber the post of instructor in the soon-to-be-created Department of Anthropology and of curator of the associated museum. Both were housed in a corrugated iron building, which for the ethnographic material was a kind of storage warehouse, divided from the classrooms. Here Lloyd studied anthropology twenty years later. It was replaced subsequently by the very handsome Kroeber Hall with the Lowie Museum, a stunning memorial to two great scientists who worked together closely for so long a period of time and created one of the great departments of anthropology in the world.

Kroeber's primary interest was in the California Indians, and here I refer you to Theodora Kroeber's *Ishi*,[6] an eloquent account of a Yana Indian whom Kroeber befriended and who became a most important informant on California Indian language and culture. Kroeber spent periods in Europe, taught at Columbia, Harvard (which offered him a permanent appointment), and the University of Chicago, and worked at the Smithsonian and the American Museum of Natural History. He did fieldwork in New Mexico and Mexico, Peru, and the Philippines. Although his interests seemed to focus on ethnography rather than ethnology, he studied the nature of culture and its processes and during all of his professional life was a student of linguistics—the historical relationship within and between languages and the structure of language. With Roland B. Dixon of Harvard, he grouped California Indian languages; he also studied the relationships among Australian languages, and this probably helped Lloyd in preparing for field work among the Murngin.

Of his many publications, which reveal the great range of his interests, perhaps the most influential was *Anthropology*,[7] the first textbook in the field, published in 1923.

Another important publication was *Configuration of Culture Growth*,[8] which he had spent many years planning and, at intervals, writing. Comprehensive in detail and length, it represents Kroeber's "historic line of inquiry"—"an historical archaeological expedition into the areas of highest achievement of the principal civilizations of the world through time." Kroeber had been psychoanalyzed, and his thinking was affected by studies in this field, but he kept those interests quite separate from his work in anthropology. Lloyd, on the other hand, became a student of Freud, Jung, Horney, and others, and incorporated some of their concepts into his own intellectual analyses.

Kroeber lost his first wife after a prolonged illness in 1913. He met Theodora Brown (Krak) as a graduate student in anthropology in the early 1920s and they were married in 1924. They had a son and a daughter, who—with Krak's two boys—made a delightful family. We visited them at Kishamish, their retreat in the Napa Valley, one summer when Lloyd was teaching at the university, and were warmed by the relationship we experienced among them, Alfred being as close to his stepsons as to his own children. We enjoyed visiting the vineyards of this famous wine country, sampling wines, and deciding which we would like to have shipped by keg to Chicago—not realizing that state tax laws made this impossible.

I first met Alfred Kroeber when he was a member of the Social Science Research Council in New York and I was on the staff working with Robert S. Lynd. Kroeber seemed to awe almost everyone there, certainly the staff. When I came to know him later as a warm, witty, outgoing, affectionate person, I wondered how he gave this impression at the council. Certainly he was a distinguished scholar, but not uniquely so in that setting. When he gave a series of lectures at the University of Chicago he often came to our home—we quickly realized that it was as much to see our children as their parents. He had a treasure of games to play with them—one a sleight-of-hand sort of thing in which a crow, a bit of black tape on the end of a finger, would disappear and reappear in most unexpected places. Obviously he was lonely for his own children.

Frances Farmer Stevens talks about their college days, the group that gathered over coffee at a little Greek restaurant on Shattuck Avenue for talk sessions that lasted into the night. Often none of them had enough money for a meal. Sometimes Barney, who had a little place near Sather Gate and later became famous as the owner of Barney's Beanery on Santa Monica Boulevard, would lend them money to go to San Francisco, where they knew an Italian speakeasy that served red wine in coffee cups. Morris Ankrum, Harry Tucker, and Lloyd comprised a triumvirate with others moving in and out of the larger group. Lloyd was always interested in English literature, contributed poetry and stories to the campus paper, and was considered ultraliberal in politics—he was a member of the Socialist Party at the university. He helped to organize a campus group for the march to Washington to demonstrate for Eugene Debs, making his fifth try for the presidency as the nominee of the Social Democratic Party. Lloyd was expelled for this. In the hearing for reinstatement the dean asked him how he had developed such liberal ideas. Lloyd replied, "Why from you, sir, in your course in political science." He was reinstated.

Frances also talks of the influence of George Boas, who gave a course in public speaking, which in fact was a course in philosophy, art, history, humanities—everything but public speaking. He became interested in Lloyd and felt that he needed intellectual development in the arts, that this was a gap that should be filled. He took Lloyd to all of the area museums and gave him an intensive course in the history of art.

Lloyd was fortunate in the support he elicited from professors who, like George Boas and Robert Lowie, felt they recognized ability they wished to help nurture. Boas had done graduate work at Harvard and Columbia and received his Ph.D. in philosophy at the University of California and his LL.D. at Washington and Lee after leaving Berkeley and going to Johns Hopkins. He developed a great range of interests. His paper on the fixation of symbols is revealing of the source of Lloyd's fascination with symbolic meanings. Lloyd's interest in the arts continued through his studies in later years, and was reflected in his work in symbolism in church art especially as well as in more abstract symbols.

One year when he was recovering from surgery he read extensively in the arts and planned a trip that would take us to every great art museum in the world, or at least in the western world. With my interest in the development of Romanesque and Gothic cathedral architecture, I had learned that there comes a point when one cannot look at one more cathedral; not only does the law of diminishing returns come into play but one's experiences become one grand exhausting fusion. I suggested to him that he start with the Chicago Art Institute, visit it every day or perhaps every few days to have something of the experience of the trip he planned. He realized that what he had proposed was not realistic, but the prospect had led him into extensive abstracting of volumes on art history, art as symbolism, etc., which certainly increased our pleasure in the museums we did visit. I never knew what was going to attract him—the fragile transparency of the veils of Fra Lippo Lippi or the lush figures of Rubens' Catherine de Medici series.

A word about some of Lloyd's peer group in anthropology at Berkeley: Duncan Strong became professor of anthropology at Columbia; Ralph Beals, chairman of the department at the University of California, Los Angeles; Matt Sterling, director of the Smithsonian Institution; Julian Steward, professor of anthropology at Columbia. Lloyd enjoyed telling about his experience as a reader in anthropology when he received a paper from Matt Sterling which he graded A with a notation that he could give it no less since he had written it himself.

Theodora Kroeber was also a member of that group. She and Lloyd had a course with Gifford in which he assigned a crossword puzzle as a midterm exam. They both walked out. No one could finish the puzzle in one session so it was continued until the following class two days later. That night and the next Krak and Lloyd worked until twelve or one o'clock devising unexceptionable answers with the wrong number of letters—far more work than correct answers would have been; Lowie or Kroeber, whoever was acting chairman, felt that they should be given a pass. There were many escapades, many friends and good times, and much hard and serious work, even though Krak says that both she and Lloyd always got As without half trying. He surely received comprehensive grounding at Berkeley in North American Indians for he could use their cultures for comparative illustration unerringly throughout his career.

In recalling Lloyd's anthropological training, Lowie spoke of his imbibing at the University of California the brand of theory dispensed by himself and Kroeber that included the belief that tribal contacts and chronological relations are matters of scientific concern, a tenet germane to his purposes when Lloyd reached the Murngin. When Malinowski lectured in Berkeley during the summer of 1926 Lloyd experienced a consistently functionalist philosophy of culture. The work in Australia with Radcliffe-Brown gave him still another outlook "intensifying his nascent devotion" to kinship systems and introducing him to the French sociologists Émile Durkheim, Marcel Mauss, Lévy-Bruhl, and Levi-Strauss.

Notes to Chapter II

General sources: Registrar's Office, University of California Berkeley; Lowie Kroeber Papers, Archives of Bancroft Library, Berkeley.

1. Robert H. Lowie, *Primitive Society* (New York: Liveright, 1947).
2. Lowie, *Primitive Religion* (New York: Liveright, 1952).
3. Lowie, *The German People,* A Social Portrait to 1914 (New York: Farrar and Rinehart, 1945).
4. Lowie, *Toward Understanding Germany* (Chicago: University of Chicago Press, 1954).
5. Theodora Kroeber, *Alfred Kroeber, A Personal Configuration* (Berkeley: University of California Press, 1970).
6. Theodora Kroeber, *Ishi in Two Worlds* (Berkeley: University of California Press, 1961).
7. Alfred Kroeber, *Anthropology* (New York: Harcourt Brace, 1923, 1948).
8. Kroeber, *Configuration of Culture Growth* (Berkeley: University of California Press, 1944).

In Australia, ca. 1928

RADCLIFFE-BROWN'S invitation to Lloyd to join him in Australia and his recommendation to the Rockefeller Foundation that Lloyd's work there be financed by them produced a grant for field work. He first, however, undertook preliminary studies with Earnest Hooton at Harvard that prepared him to take measurements of the native people later worked up, under Hooton's direction, by W.W. Howells.[1]

The concentrated program at Harvard formed the basis of a lifelong friendship with Hooton. Writing to Bob Lowie, Lloyd spoke of how much he was learning from Hooton in anatomy, bones, measurement of bones of skeletons and of the living, statistics, and interpretation. He felt he was being qualified to do physical anthropology in the field and some digging on the side. Perhaps it was his youth speaking when he speculated that he might be able to accomplish something in clearing up the boundaries between the sociological and physiological branches of anthropology. He commented that Hooton thought Lowie the best ethnologist in the country—even in the world—which made Lloyd feel that Hooton must be a great anthropologist. However, he complained about the Harvard attitude of superiority. He then told Lowie that his was the greatest and finest mind that he had contacted in anthropology. "You have an attitude, too, that is superior to all others, so for God's sake, please turn out a rounded out library in the whole field of culture. You owe it to the rest of us. . . . I just read this over and know it sounds curiously uncritical, but it is the result of cold evaluations." In contrast he comments that Dixon's *Race History of Man* is terrible—almost naive—"figures, figures, and all of them leading him astray." He felt that he was doing much more work because he was away from Berkeley and would continue to do more and more—but acknowledged that he was homesick for friends—Harry Tucker, Krak, Harold Luck, and, of course, Bob Lowie. Edwin Embree wrote to Radcliffe-Brown about meeting Lloyd and finding him enthusiastic about his studies with Hooton and looking forward eagerly to working with Radcliffe-Brown in Australia.

Lloyd enjoyed the work at Harvard but hated the New England winter. Years later he would still speak with indignation of crossing the Harvard Yard and slipping off the boardwalks into the snow. The climate certainly did not agree with him; his sister Madge describes Lloyd's arriving with a heavy cold, thinner than usual, certainly in need of medical care. But the doctor was reassuring that a month's ocean voyage, with leisurely stops at tropical islands, would be excellent therapy. He sailed soon after from San Francisco, arriving in Sydney in January 1927.

This was not Radcliffe-Brown's first experience with Australia. He had been there in 1910–1913 doing fieldwork as Anthony Wilkin Student in Ethnology from Cambridge. English born and educated, he was the first student in anthropology of W.H.R. Rivers and studied with A.C. Haddon at Cambridge, where he held a scholarship at Trinity College from 1901 to 1906. His scholastic interests were wide-ranging, and his encyclopedic mind brought many disciplines into the background of his anthropological studies. His first field work was with the Andaman Islanders; the draft of his report became the thesis for his Fellowships at Trinity, which he held until 1914, but the book was not published (by Cambridge University Press and, in New York, Macmillan) until 1922. He was also a reader in ethnology at the London School of Economics during 1909–1910, lecturing on the potlatch of the northwest coast American Indians and on the Australian aborigines, whom he would study in the field during the following several years. Comparative sociology held great interest for him—he wanted to see the study of anthropology and sociology combined in many universities. In the U.S. the trend was contrary—combined departments were separating. The social structure of primitive societies was one of his great interests and led him into close intellectual ties with Durkheim, Mauss, and other French sociologists. Australian kinship was another primary interest of his. He looked upon human society as the product of natural law and social institutions as the result of certain principles that could be ascertained and studied.

He was in Australia at the time of World War I as one of a number of anthropologists presenting papers at the meetings of the British Association for the Advancement of Science. In his paper[2] he gave a definition of totemism that is important in understanding Lloyd's work: "a special magico-religious relation between an individual or a social group . . . and a class of natural objects . . . ." He analyzed the variables within the institution of totemism by regional types according to the ways in which these variables are combined. Meyer Fortes, of Cambridge University, compares Radcliffe-Brown's analytical paper and its proposal for classifying totemism with Malinowski's theoretical and polemical paper discussing the distinction between the sacred and profane according to Durkheim in the *Elementary Forms of the Religious Life*,[3] concluding that the division is not an essential and fundamental feature of religion. He became director of education in Tonga in 1916, and Charles Baldwin (a close friend of Radcliffe-Brown's and of Lloyd's in Sydney) recalls that the Queen of Tonga—6 feet 4 inches and 300 pounds—took a great fancy to this cultivated English scholar and gave him some kind of title with the status of economic adviser. He returned to Sydney very full of himself and of anecdotes about the queen. The Tonga interlude, which put him in touch with Polynesian society, strengthened his interest in applied anthropology.

Radcliffe-Brown went to South Africa in 1923, where he became ethnologist at the Transvaal Museum in Pretoria. Then, with the rapid changes in South Africa to an industrial society, and when the need for scientific study of the native peoples led in 1920 to the establishment of a chair of anthropology at the University of Cape Town (the first full-time professorship of anthropology in any British university), he became its first incumbent. His inaugural lecture discussed emerging social changes of the society, the need for systematic study, the approach of theoretical anthropology to these issues, and then he stated—something basic in his thinking, "all the various customs, institutions, and beliefs of a society formed together a closely connected system ... change one part of the social system and you inevitably produce a far-spreading movement . . . ."

He became widely known throughout South Africa. He advocated the systematic study of Bantu social life, history, and languages by trained field workers, asking for a greater understanding of the effects of English law on the social organization of these people. He left South Africa in 1925 to take the new chair of social anthropology at the University of Sydney. He was visiting the United States on his way to assume this chair when he stopped in Berkeley, met Lloyd, and invited him to join him in the Australian experience.

In writing informally from Australia to Edwin Embree in February 1927 on the status of work conducted under the aegis of the Australian National Research Council, Radcliffe-Brown comments[4] that it had been difficult to find competent people for the required research. He was working within certain guidelines: for example, the agreement between the federal government of Australia and the governments of the Australian states in jointly funding the Department of Anthropology at Sydney specified that the first task would be providing training in anthropology and in native administration for cadets entering the service of the Mandated Territory of New Guinea. Radcliffe-Brown expressed the hope that they would soon have the qualified people necessary to make full use of the research opportunities under the foundation grant. He then commented on Warner's arrival on January 6 and notes that Warner would leave at the beginning of March to spend six months in the Northern Territory and then return to Sydney to work on the results of the field trip. With renewal of his research grant, he would return to the field to check his first results and continue his research.

"I am much impressed with Warner's abilities and his enthusiasm," Radcliffe-Brown wrote. "His work here and, so far as I can judge of it, the work he did at Harvard, are excellent. He has managed, in the seven weeks with me, to get a thorough grasp of Australian culture and to prepare himself quite adequately for work in the Australian field. I am convinced that he will do a very valuable piece of research and that he will become a first-class, all-round anthropologist. . . . I hope that it may be possible later on to find students of anthropology, such as Warner, who could come and assist us in research, and I shall keep in touch with the various Departments of Anthropology in America with that end in view. Such cooperation would, I hope, benefit not only Australia but also America, in that it could afford American Anthropologists an opportunity of making studies of races and types of culture other than American and also of getting an intimate knowledge of methods and ideas of anthropology which are somewhat different from those current in their own country."[5]

Here Radcliffe-Brown might have been referring to the fact that, under the strong influence of Franz Boas at Columbia, the pattern had developed of limiting fieldwork to North American Indians.

In commenting on the status and progress of work in a more formal report to the Foundation, Radcliffe-Brown lists others concerned with the natives of the interior; fieldworkers included Chapman and Priestley from the University of Sydney in New South Wales and students of anatomy at Sydney in North Queensland making anthropological observations and securing casts of teeth. Ursula McConnell of the University of Queensland and of London (sister-in-law of Elton Mayo, who had gone to the University of Pennsylvania, then Harvard) was receiving special training in anticipation of a year's study of the aborigines of the Cape York Peninsula. Camilla Wedgwood, the British anthropologist, was in Sydney as a temporary lecturer from 1928 to 1929. Raymond Firth, of the Universities of New Zealand and London, lectured and was doing field work in the Cape York Peninsula. Among other visiting professors or investigators working from October 1926 to June 1930 were A.P. Elkin, of the Universities of Sydney and London, working in the northern part of West Australia; Reo Fortune, a graduate of the University of New Zealand with a Cambridge diploma of anthropology, working among the Tewara and in other parts of the D'Entrecasteaux Archipelago; H.I. Hogbin, the first student of anthropology trained at the University of Sydney; C.W.M. Hart of the University of Sydney, working in the Melville and Bathhurst Islands; and Ralph Piddington of the University of Sydney, working in Western Australia.

On February 1, 1927, Lloyd wrote to Lowie from Sydney trying to give a full report of his life there. He was very happy—happier than he could remember. "Brown has been very decent to me. We have a very nice relationship. We eat together and play around considerably. He lectures to three of us every day which is rather considerate because this is the summer session in Australia and the University is closed. The other two are going to Queensland and the Solomons. If you will look at the map of the Northern Territory's seacoast you will find the outlines of the headwaters of two rivers—the Roper which flows into the Gulf of Carpentaria and the

Katherine, flowing into the Indian Ocean. I shall be somewhere north of there, working with some people who are not in touch with white civilization. There has been no anthropological work done in that area. Farther North, in the country of the tribes neighboring to mine, the work of exploration has yet to be done. If luck and God, at all, go with me I am going to take a fling at them. The nearest people studied are those along the coast near Darwin and the Katherine River in the West and South of me (Spencer and Gillen)[6] and the tribes north of the Arunta, also by Spencer. By now I think I have a fair grasp of the Australian culture, clan systems, totemism, kinship system etc. The work is fascinating. I am lucky as hell." The letter to Lowie continues: "I shall leave Sydney on the second of March by boat to Brisbane in Queensland. There I shall either go inland by airplane to Darwin or continue by boat to Darwin. If the air accommodations can be had I'll take that transportation north since it is faster and almost as cheap as the water route."

He then comments upon how well he was being treated in Sydney, entertained, elected to honorary membership in various clubs, written up in feature articles in the newspapers. Radcliffe-Brown introduced him at many social functions, including those given at Government House by the vice-regent of New South Wales and his wife, Sir Dudley and Lady de Chair. He was under contract to two of the newspapers to write special articles on his fieldwork that he welcomed as a way of paying off ever-present, horrible debts. Articles Lloyd wrote for the *Sydney Sun* were printed in six successive editions beginning Sept. 19, 1927, upon his return to Sydney from his first seven months in the field. They present a different point of view related to a non-scientific audience.

He went by boat from Brisbane to Darwin, then by lugger to the Crocodile Islands, where there was a mission station in the charge of the Reverend and Mrs. Theodore Webb, whose views in almost every field of human interest diverged from Lloyd's, yet they were most helpful. There he had the great good fortune to meet Mahkarolla, a Murngin who could speak some English. Lloyd was able to explain to him the purpose of his trip, and Mahkarolla agreed to take him to his own people, of whom he was an elder member although only about forty-five. Lloyd believed firmly in traveling unencumbered by tinned food and a lot of gear. He had a Brownie box camera with which he took photographs of ceremonies that qualified for special exhibit at Sydney and many of which are at the Peabody Museum of Harvard and have been published widely. He took with him a tent, a rifle, some cooking utensils, a few clothes, a kerosene lantern, salt, pepper, sugar—minimum essentials—and had reluctantly included a revolver. The general area to which he was going had seen several murders of whites recently, and his advisers felt it only prudent that he should have a weapon for self-protection. It almost caused his death.

With Mahkarolla's help, Lloyd tried to gain the confidence first of the old men of the tribe by explaining to them that he had been asked to live among them by the old man of his people (i.e. the Rockefeller Foundation) in order to learn about their way of life. He tried, of course, not to be intrusive, to follow along with the men's group when that seemed appropriate, and to eat what the Murngin ate, which was not always easy. Most of the food he learned to like, although tree grubs, raw or lightly roasted in the ashes of a small fire, were among the last. He found them similar to snails.

The aborigines of Arnhem Land may be divided into four large cultural groups, with few differences among them, and these groups are subtypes of a larger culture. These four groups (the Murngin are one of them) are divided among the eight tribes living in the country from Cape Wessel in the northeast along the islands and coast of the eastern side of the Gulf of Carpentaria and east from Blue Mud Bay to the upper reaches of the Goyder and Glyde rivers; on the west, from Cape Stewart along the coast of the Arafura Sea. West of that area the social organization is Kariera, south of Blue Mud Bay, the Mara-Anula, and in the islands of that region, the Arunta.

The basic organization is the patrilineal clan, whose members marry outside of the clan (exogamic). Each clan averages forty or fifty individuals possessing a common territory of about 360 square miles, whose most important focus is the totemic water hole, from which all members of the clan are born and to which they return at death. Here live the totem's spirits, the mythological ancestors, the souls of the dead, and the unborn children. This sacred water hole is the most important unifying concept in the whole clan ideology, the fundamental symbol of clan solidarity. Clans are divided into exogamic moieties or halves. The tribe is a larger group of much less significance except in warfare, which usually occurs around blood feuds. The clan is a war-making group; but a clan's land cannot be taken from it by act of war. No violent conflict occurs within a clan. The clan is comprised essentially of ego's father's father and father's father's sister, father, father's sister, older brother, younger brother, sister, son and daughter, and son's son and son's daughter—all in ego's brother's lineage. Sometimes other kin are included but never from the opposite moiety.

Of course all members of a clan do not live on the clan's land since marriage is patrilocal, requiring sisters and daughters to move to the husband's clan territory to live and to rear their families. Since these people move according to food supply, having no cultivation or domesticated animals, it is difficult to place them demographically. When food is plentiful during the dry season, friendly clans come together.

When in recent times important mineral deposits were found in North Australia it was extremely disruptive to the native population. It was not the taking of land that was of such importance but the taking of the sacred water holes, the repositories of all of their history, mythology, sacred ceremonies, and spiritual life.

The rainy season—weeks or months of torrential rain—produces lush tropical growth, but there is little activity then since movement is often almost impossible. It is followed by a period of drought lasting six or seven months when some water holes and much of the food supply disappear.

Two theories have held the interest of anthropologists for many years and have been the subject of prolonged and emotional arguments. One involves the opinion that the natives of central and north Australia have no knowledge of physiological conception, based on the fact that the father always dreams his child, who then emerges from the totemic water hole and enters the mother's womb. Sometimes the father tells the dream to his wife; sometimes he waits until she tells him that she is with child, whereupon he says, oh yes, I knew that because I dreamed it. This opinion goes back to the studies of Spencer and Gillen, reported in 1898, in which they concluded after much interrogation that the idea is firmly held that the child is not the direct result of intercourse.

During the first eight or nine months of Lloyd's life with the natives of North Australia he too was convinced they had no understanding of physiological conception but believed the woman was impregnated by a totemic child spirit, the child appearing in a dream as a totemic soul and asking that its mother be pointed out to him so that he could enter her vagina. Yet there were clear indications that the natives understood the true nature of the father's physical function.

After a rest and study period in Sydney working with Radcliffe-Brown on his field notes, Lloyd determined to pursue the subject further since his people were an extension of the central tribes studied by Spencer and Gillen. Writing to Lowie in November 1927 he said that at first he could only find that the native man was interested in the fact that the "little fish spirit" entered the woman from his well. "But after going through all of the more intimate details of what positions they used in coitus etc., I found that the native understood full well 'that white stuff belong man make baby' but it did have to have the spirit for help." Lloyd felt that when these men realized the thrust of his questions they thought them rather silly.

Their sex life was important to them and feelings about their women very possessive. Since most of the killings of whites that had occurred in the area were the direct results of breaking the law of the natives concerning their women, Lloyd was circumspect in his behavior. The people to the west had a custom of offering wives to visitors, but the Murngin did not—though wives were exchanged during certain high ceremonies, especially those pertaining to fertility rites. However, after Lloyd had been with them for awhile, some of the men offered him one of their wives. He wrote to Lowie from Sydney after his first field trip that he followed Malinowski's advice and "kept pure." Or, as his black interpreter said, he was a "bloody proper yoo-elk." "Truly, Lowie, it was funny to see me gravely refusing the offer of the wives of my various friends for varying reasons given by me—the true one being that every white man killed in the north (and there have been an impressive number) have been guilty of breaking the law of the natives concerning their rights over their women." So Lloyd, "valuing my life, valuing the information I was collecting by bucketfulls, stayed pure."

He talked about how much he had enjoyed the seven months of fieldwork in spite of fever, dysentery, mosquitoes, sand flies, and many other pests. He had gone into the interior of Arnhem Land with blacks who had a reputation for being treacherous and cruel, had been in the center of many spear fights, and had seen a couple of scores of totemic corroborees.

The other theory that has roused the interest and emotions of anthropologists through the years—sometimes called the Murngin controversy—involves the Australian kinship system, on which a number of publications have appeared since Lloyd's "Morphology and Functions of the Australian Murngin Type of Kinship, Part I."[7] Lloyd wrote to Lowie that he had fifty genealogies and eleven kinship systems, three of the Type I variety (mother's brother's sister marrying father's sister's son) with a four-class system, and seven of a type that is Type I and II—"one (or ego) marries his mother's mother's brother's daughter's daughter and at the same time marries his mother's brother's daughter" (traditional cross-cousin marriage). He found an eight-class system working as a four-class system "to fit, of course, into the Type I and Type II Hybrid relationship system."

One reason for collecting so many genealogies was that Radcliffe-Brown stressed their importance in understanding a kinship system based on marriage defined in terms of kinship based on genealogical relations. In "Murngin Social Organization" (reprinted from *American Anthropologist*, Vol. 53, No. 1 January—March 1951), Radcliffe-Brown discusses this and analyzes other types of kinship systems in Australia besides the Murngin—the Kariera, Kumbaingeri, Aranda, Karadjeri. "Everywhere in Australia the fundamental basis of social organization is a system of patrilincal local groups or clans of small size. A man belongs to the clan of his father and father's father, and his nearest patrilineal relatives are the members of that clan. Each individual has genealogical connections with other clans, for example with his mother's clan, and the clans of his father's mother and his mother's mother. Thus, for each individual the

Sydney caricature, 1928

SEMPER INEBRIATUS

WARNERII

FORN   BARST

To all to whom these presents shall come :—

GREETING —

Know Ye, all men that our Trusty and well Beloved

— LLOYD WARNER —

whose signature is appended hereto, has —

1. been duly initiated into the O.B.E. and is entitled to all the Privileges pertaining thereto ;

2. taken upon himself the Freedom of the City of Darwin, to the general Disgust of the Mayor and Council ; and has

3. by his Unseemly Behaviour, Unquenchable Thirst, Raucous Singing, and General Bonhomie, proved himself worthy of being received into the Order of Absorbers ;

And wherefore it has pleased the GRAND SPONGE, and his Council of Hums to confer the signal honor of SPONGER, with its attendant privileges on the aforementioned person, the same was conferred to the accompaniment of much Noise, Singing, Drinking, and Fighting, in accordance with the Ancient Traditions of the ORDER, on the Rosebed at the Botanical Gardens, at midnight on the 12th. October, 1928.

Given under our hands and seal,
This Next day, in the First Year of our ORDER.

William Lloyd Warner. His Mark

_____ Grand Sponge
C.C.Fenton_____ Grand Bluff
C.H. Allan_____ Grand Soak
_____ Grand Noise
_____ Grand Slam

Certified as Darwin Sponger, 1928

social organization is presented in a perspective that is particular to him, a set of personal relationships in which he stands to a number of other persons. The classificatory kinship terminology enables him to classify his relatives into a certain limited number of kinship classes, and among those included in one class he distinguished between nearer and more distant relatives. His behavior towards any particular person is determined very largely by the genealogical relationship, which fixes not only the class to which that person belongs, but also the degree of nearness or distance of the relation. This arrangement of persons in personal relationships based on genealogical connections will be here spoken of as the 'kinship system' of any tribe or region." In the original manuscript for this article which deals with the results of Lloyd's work on the Murngin as well as his own theories and those of other anthropologists who had not done fieldwork in Australia, Radcliffe-Brown concluded, "There is this to be said. Warner's account of the Murngin is making anthropological history."

During his first seven months in the field Lloyd filled eight notebooks, each averaging 27,000 words, covering social organization, totemism, rituals, and mythology in addition to observations on, for instance, modes of daily life, accounts of black and white magic, and warfare. The notes were supplemented by photographs of corroborees and preparations for them. Radcliffe-Brown subsequently wrote a paper verifying Lloyd's findings, and the Berndts, in later researches on the Murngin, added further validation. When the Berndts visited England in 1954 while Lloyd was teaching at Cambridge, a seminar was held in Meyer Fortes' rooms at King's College. It was agreed in advance that the subject of Australian kinship would be avoided if possible, but of course this could not be. Edmund Leach attacked the Berndts with such force that everyone mustered to their defense. Australian kinship systems had lost none of their emotion.

Some earlier writers on Australia had concluded that the family system as it is generally known did not occur on that continent. Lloyd found that the larger kinship organization is built around the elementary families of orientation (into which the individual is born) and procreation (which he establishes in marriage). "The simple reciprocal of the son and father ties him by a set of organized attitudes and behaviors to one-half of the tribe and, more immediately, to his clan. The direct mother-son reciprocal is the foundation on which is built his entire set of relations by affinity, since it is the mother's brother's daughter who becomes the son's wife." The spiritual affiliations organized around the father-son reciprocal place the individual in the totemic ceremonies, give him his spiritual identity, including totem and power names, and identify his sacred well, to which his soul will return, and all of the ritual surrounding these events.

The underlying basis of the families of orientation and procreation is the incest taboo: any direct contact with the sister is forbidden.

"The marriage of a male ego to his wife is something more than the modern marriage contract to any woman out of a general group. He marries into his wife's family of orientation, a group of four personalities who are his mother's brother, his mother's brother's wife (who is also part of another family), his wife's brother, and his wife's sister, who is also mother's brother's daughter. Ego, then, is constantly looking to his mother's people for his wives while he is a member of his own family of orientation and while forming his family of procreation, and when he has a son he still seeks the father of his mother's group to obtain wives for his male offspring."

Lloyd found in the entire kinship system, based on the elementary family, seventy-one kinds of relations, seven lines of descent, with five generations in each lineage.

In later years, the Berndts, who have done extensive work in Arnhem Land, commented that Lloyd's basic conclusions structured the whole anthropological picture in Australia and solved the very knotty problem of kinship, "which is so a-typical that no one had ever figured it out."

One impressive characteristic of the kinship system is that the North Australians not only developed a system so complex, but they lived with it in ordering their daily lives. Every individual must have contact that fits into this system—Lloyd, for example, had to be given a place in order for him to be part of their social group. The family is the basis of social organization, and no family unit ever lacks a member: if the father dies his younger brother takes over his wives and children; if a mother dies the other wives take over—in fact, the wives look after each other's children in usual daily life. Equally impressive is the precise recall of their history as told in myths and represented in their ceremonies, which are an important part of Murngin life. The males in the society are age-graded and pass from one period to another through rites of passage in which they learn increasingly higher secrets of the society and the myths—all of which are kept from the women, who are considered profane. The artifacts for these ceremonies are made by the men and, though they require much effort and a high degree of artistry, are buried after each ceremony rather than re-used. There are practical reasons, of course—the rainy season and the need for frequent, unencumbered movement. All of the men contribute to the preparation of these ritual objects, and no one person was identified as artist.

Lloyd did not approve of an anthropologist's keeping for his own pleasure ethnographic objects collected on field trips. He gave all of his collection to the museum in Sydney and to the Peabody Museum at Harvard. He retained only one bark painting,[8] which is said to be the oldest example brought out of Australia, a woman's ainmara, the woven mat used for carrying things and also to cover the most important part of her body when a stranger approached—her face; a stone with a chipped edge that had once been hafted to a shaft for use as an axe; a ceremonial object of egret feathers attached to a stick with beeswax; and a huge oyster shell.

There was sexual dichotomy in the gathering of food. The men hunted kangaroos, wallabies and emus with spears, harpooned turtles, dugong, porpoises, sharks, and crocodiles and captured oppossum and snakes; they also hunted cockatoo, egret, duck, ibis, and other water birds. They often cooked and ate part of the quarry in the field, the cooking varying with the catch: turtles, for example, were cleaned and heated stones put inside to create an oven. The women gathered many varieties of bivalves along the shore, pandanus fruit, the small cabbage palm, cycad palm nuts, eggs of both sea and land birds. Men and women gathered honey and usually ate it on the spot; both gathered tree grubs, which were usually washed and eaten raw.

Death, illness, any untoward event or lack of adjustment within the community were believed to be caused by magic. Rarely when an old man died was it accepted as caused by old age. A black magician could kill by stealing a soul, and Lloyd collected a number of accounts of such killings, especially from a famous black magician named Laindjura. He had difficulty judging the extent to which the magicians believed their own stories but concluded that Laindjura, at least, believed many of his. When someone became ill a white magician was called and if he decided that the man's soul had been stolen, then everyone knew he would die, and they withdrew from him and treated him as if he were dying. The power of the community action was great; the man died.

White magicians were called to cure illness, to say whether it had been caused by a black magician, to name him, to heal wounds, and to give the individual a sense of well-being. They got their power from two "familiars" who lived in a little bag fastened to a string around the head, the bag dropping near the ear. When Lloyd was on a trip with some of the Murngin men they heard that members of a hostile clan were preparing to ambush them, and they had to return by forced march over a long distance. This reactivated a back injury Lloyd had received in a motor accident as a teenager. When the group returned to camp, Willidjungo was called to treat him because he was in great pain. He performed the accustomed ritual, then sucked at the site of the pain, and spat out a wad of bush cotton which had caused the pain. And so it had because—fortunately for the fieldwork—the pain was gone.

In every community there were a few bad characters. When the Murngin old men, as leaders, decided that one of their people was incurably asocial, a "bad guy," they decided that he should be eliminated. This was usually agreed to by everyone because the group could not tolerate the recurring embroilments and trouble, the disruption to community solidarity. Often it would be arranged with a neighboring clan to accomplish the killing. Black magicians were not used in this way, but were hired by individuals to kill or make someone ill. Jealousies about women—assignations were not infrequent—were usually resolved by the individuals.

The incident in which Lloyd was almost killed began with trouble started by a young man who was "no good." Lloyd was incensed by what was happening and went into his tent for his revolver. Several of the men said "Yes, go get him" and Lloyd started into the bush with Mahkarolla and some others, one of whom suddenly called out just in time for Lloyd to see what he thought was a throwing stick hurled at him. He sucked in his stomach and the weapon—not a throwing stick but an iron killing stick—missed him by an inch. He realized, of course, that he had allowed himself to become involved, not the role for the detached observer, and that the revolver could get him into trouble rather than protect him. His rifle he lent to trusted individuals for hunting since the food supply was always marginal. This increased his solidarity with the group.

Warfare between hostile clans of opposite moieties was the main killer of young men and caused enough deaths to make the system of polygamy almost a social necessity. Sometimes fights started during large ceremonies, when emotions were high and certain acts would make the totem angry. Lloyd was called in one day by one of the old men to participate in a conclave to consider trouble with a neighboring clan. They had committed an unforgiveable act, killing a courier who was holding high an amnesty symbol, a large piece of white birch bark. All of the friendly clans were contacted, and all agreed that war and killing were bad and should be stopped so they decided to fight. They were planning a war to end all wars. What did Lloyd think?

Upon returning from the field, Lloyd wrote Lowie that "Brown told some scientists here in my presence that I had done the best piece of field work ever done in Australia. I think not true, but it shows his belief. I must say I was highly flattered."

He and Radcliffe-Brown had started working on a general book on Australian culture made possible by the renewal of his fellowship by the Australian National Research Council, hoping to finish it before Lloyd would go north again in April for another year. Lloyd described Radcliffe-Brown to Lowie "as a most brilliant person, with knowledge of the whole of Australian and African anthropology, an almost unbelievable grip of Australian culture enabling him to contribute greatly to interpreting the traits and material found here. I admire him greatly and like him tremendously, as I believe he likes me. He is now scheming to get me sent to London for my doctorate (quiet on this) through dear Laura's generosity when I leave Australia." Laura was the Laura Spelman Rockefeller Memorial, soon to be merged into the Rockefeller Foundation.

For methodology in reconstructing the history of the Murngin, Lloyd agreed with Lowie, who had said, "My position, then, towards oral tradition, may be summarized as follows: It is not based, in the first instance, on a universal negative unjustifiably derived for a necessarily limited number of instances but on the conviction that aboriginal history is only a part of that hodgepodge of aboriginal lore which embraces primitive theories of the universe generally, and that its a priori claims to great respect on our part are nil. Such claims must be established empirically, if at all; but, so far as my experience, the empirical facts are diametrically opposed to such claims."[9]

Lloyd's studies were based on observation of the culture for intrusion from other areas. The culture-area method, giving spatial facts an interpretation in time, which (when combined with archaeological evidence, for example) he used in reconstructing the possible history of Murngin burial customs; documents of earlier explorers; the archaeological method to determine how long the Murngin had possessed certain objects; and the tree ring method, examining the growth rings of tamarind trees brought to the shores of the Arafura Sea and the Gulf of Carpentaria by Malay traders.

The Malays had been in contact with North Australia for a long period, coming first probably by accident of storm but returning for native pearl shell, pearls, tortoise shell, trepang, and sandalwood. They brought rice, dugout canoes with mast and pandamas sail (no outriggers), molasses, tobacco, cloth, belts, knives, tomahawks, gin, pipes, and other articles. The sailing canoe made it possible for the Murngin to make longer journeys, passing hostile territory where they would have been forced to land had they used their bark canoes. But the bark canoes were lighter, more adaptable to forays for spearing fish and turtle, easily made, and easily abandoned in the frequent seasonal migrations. The rice, of course, was never planted. Coconut palms might very well have grown from nuts washed ashore. In the records Lloyd took of the physical measurements of large numbers of people in Northeast Arnhem Land, he found little evidence of miscegenation—only two "hybrids" with lighter skin color than the darker Australoid (but no darker than the pure Australoids of the interior where there was no opportunity for racial mixture), who were brachycephalic (round-headed) rather than dolicocephalic (long-headed) as the pure aborigine. Lack of evidence of miscegenation was probably due to several factors: the insistence of the people east of the Goyder River that females remain monogamous whereas the people to the west practiced wife lending; and the Malay system of guards to prevent contact with the native women.

Nails in planks that came ashore were used as fish hooks. Metal objects brought by the Malays were used, but stone spears were still ground and used as well as metal ones. There was, in fact, a strong resistance to outside influence. The Murngin traded with other tribes for objects they lacked, but this type of exchange had a large element of social reciprocity, enforcing a social bond and enlarging the social periphery of each group. This is illustrated by the fact that the trade was ritualized and sometimes involved the exchange of like objects.

The contribution of the Malays to the material life of the North Australians was not extensive, but it exceeded their effect on the social life. A pidgin Malay language spoken by most of the older men along the Arafura coast became a kind of lingua franca among the various linguistic groups so that a man traveling from Cape Don, in the far west, could be understood by people of Groote Eylandt, stimulating intertribal communication. Locations touched by the Malays carried their names as well as native, and almost all of the people along the Arafura Sea were given Malay personal names, which were passed on through generations. There was some Malay influence in mythology and ritual, as in the burial rites, when the body was raised symbolizing departure of the spirit of the dead as the raised sail symbolized the departure of the Malay traders.

On trips to the mission station Lloyd met some of the government men working in the Northern Territory, including Dr. Cecil Cook, protector of aborigines, New South Wales, and North Australian mounted policeman "Johnny" Walker. They invited him to Port Darwin, and these visits were a welcome break in fieldwork. Dr. Kirkland and Mr. Harsborough entertained him and the government men often had parties for him; the official document given him when he left after his second field trip testified to their congeniality. Lloyd found them able, well trained for their work with the aborigines, intelligent dedicated people.

Back in Sydney after his first field trip, Lloyd stayed in the same hotel as Radcliffe-Brown, a congenial arrangement that allowed them to spend more time working together on his notes and continuing his training. He become rather in demand as a speaker because at that time people in Sydney did not know much about the back country. At an American Society lunch one day, a member of the audience, Charles Baldwin, was impressed by Lloyd's talk and somewhat astonished that this well-groomed, urbane, rather handsome young man could have lived as he did among the Australian blackfellows, and he invited him to have drinks. The question of living quarters came up. Chuck, living alone, learned that Lloyd and Radcliffe-Brown were looking for a place to share. They thought they could all live together, and when Radcliffe-Brown agreed, found an apartment, and within a few weeks moved in—the older, distinguished professor of anthropology, his young protégé, and a self-described scientifically complete outsider.

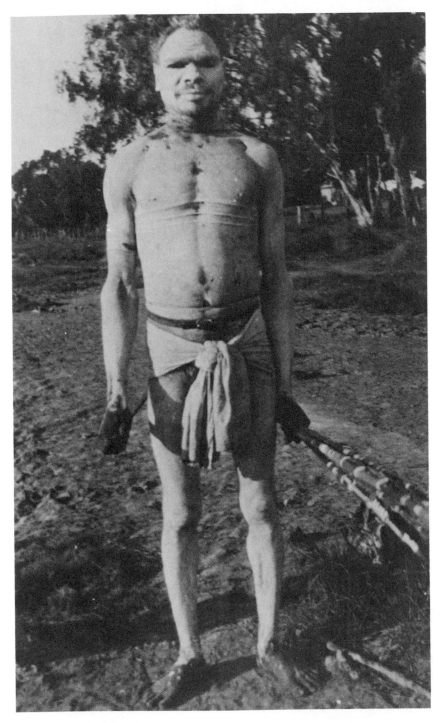

Murngin painted for ceremony

Radcliffe Brown by Aletta Lewis, 1928

Chuck and Lloyd were at about the same place in their careers. Chuck was twenty-four when he joined the foreign service of the Department of Commerce—a service started by Herbert Hoover as secretary of commerce to stimulate American exports and improve foreign economic reporting. The State Department was so conservative and conventional, looking upon trade as something rather dirty, that Hoover felt his department should undertake some responsibility in the area. Chuck went to Australia for three years as assistant trade commissioner, a government official in the foreign service but not in *the* Foreign Service. Later the State Department became more progressive and absorbed the program with its personnel, so Chuck went into the proper Foreign Service "through the back door." At first Chuck had the impression that Radcliffe-Brown, essentially a conservative person, viewed him with some concern as to whether he belonged in the household. It was only after about six months that he called him by his first name rather than Baldwin, and from then on they developed a congenial relationship.

Theirs was an interesting and understanding menage. Each pursued his own interests and career, Chuck establishing himself in the Foreign Service, Radcliffe-Brown involved with his work at the university and supervising Lloyd's work, training, and counseling, and Lloyd transcribing and interpreting his field notes. Also at this time Radcliffe-Brown became concerned about Lloyd's obtaining his Ph.D. The University of Sydney did not grant graduate degrees. Moreover, he really wanted Lloyd to go to a university in England or on the continent and began to explore various sources of funds to make this possible. Meanwhile, he arranged for Lloyd to be tutored in French in order to fill the usual language requirement. Lloyd had shown great aptitude in learning and recording the language spoken by the Murngin and some of the surrounding tribes—variations of Austro-Dravidian—and the French lessons did not take too much time from his primary work of transcribing and interpreting his field notes.

Both Lowie and Kroeber tried to procure for Lloyd a fellowship grant for graduate study abroad and for writing the book on his Australian research, but without success since most foundation programs for European study were for postdoctoral work. Lowie especially felt that the importance of European study had been exaggerated in Lloyd's mind by Radcliffe-Brown's orientation, that travel abroad would be helpful, but that a European degree would not be as important as a degree in the United States. "The days are past when doctorates from abroad counted for more than the home product." He also urged Lloyd to write, stressing the importance of a publication record in academic recognition, and that his academic achievement would depend upon the opinions of anthropologists in this country, not abroad. Lloyd, during his second field trip, had recorded the life story of Mahkarolla as the native told it to him; it was a truly unique document told with the simplicity and lack of dissembling of someone talking to a close and trusted friend. Lowie wanted this account and others on kinship for publication in *The Anthropologist*. Meanwhile, he was in touch with universities in this country for possible teaching fellowships. He spoke enthusiastically about the status of anthropology in this country, with new jobs being created and at very decent salaries. For example, a full professorship brought $4,000.

But it was not all work. They worked hard, and they played hard. When Lloyd put on an old coolie jacket that came to his knees, Chuck knew that it was work time, and he would tiptoe around the apartment. But again he would come home and find Lloyd and Rex, as Radcliffe-Brown was called, mixing a pitcher of martinis, another indicator. Rex was something of a gourmet, sometimes bringing home a thick steak or other delicacy and a couple of bottles of excellent wine. On occasion Lloyd invited some of the characters he had encountered who engaged his interest. All of his life he enjoyed and appreciated people of highly varied backgrounds who happened to have a special attraction for him, a special appeal.

Aletta Lewis, the English artist, was a friend of all of them. She did a very perceptive portrait of Lloyd and one of Radcliffe-Brown that he absolutely rejected. She had a way of catching certain characteristics and what Rex saw he did not like. Her manner was always straightforward and direct. Margaret Mead was there. She and Aletta went to Samoa together— Aletta to paint and Margaret to do the fieldwork she wrote up first as a scientific monograph and later as *Coming of Age in Samoa*, a more popular version. Aletta returned first, bringing portraits of chieftains and babies and a gift of a tappa cloth for Lloyd and for Chuck.

One day Chuck stayed in bed with a cold and called the doctor. Lloyd was on his bed, in his coolie jacket, working on field notes. He let the doctor in and returned to his work. The doctor, carrying a black bag and stethoscope, asked a few questions and listened to Chuck's chest, all with the usual highly professional manner. Lloyd began to laugh, astonishing both Chuck and the doctor. He apologized and asked them to pay no attention. After the doctor's departure Chuck asked for an explanation and Lloyd began to read from his field notes an account of his being unobtrusively present when a medicine man was called to minister to a native who had severe pains in his stomach. The white magician, with his familiars in a bag at his shoulder, kneeled and asked the man where he had pain. The medicine man took some things out of the bag and, turning away from the sick man, then leaned down and sucked on the man's body. Again turning, he put the things he had been holding into his mouth, faced the patient and blew. Out of his mouth came some feathers and sticks he said had made the man sick. He assured his patient he would be well again.

Lloyd was fortunate in meeting someone he liked very much—Midge, the young widow of a British army officer who had been stationed in India. She was an extremely nice person, attractive, cultivated, popular, the mother of two small children. Rex liked her too, but she and Lloyd formed a strong relationship that Chuck thought very constructive, and they expected to marry.

When I first met Lloyd—in Paris, in 1929—plans had become uncertain, largely because neither Lloyd nor Midge was sure they were really suited, and he was there to meet her and resolve the differences or separate. Before leaving to return to the states and to his new post at Harvard, he tried to persuade me to return too, felt that I was wasting my time living abroad (though certainly I had no intention of becoming an expatriate). When I later did return it was not so much because of his persuasion but because the friend with whom I was living, in the household of a French family, was assistant fellowship secretary at the Rockefeller Foundation in Paris and was returning to take the corresponding position with the Social Science Research Council in New York, where the Foundation's fellowship program had been transferred.

Chuck in describing Radcliffe-Brown said in part, "He was a man of the world, Rex. He was a gourmet. He was sought after socially. Sydney in those days was not a primitive society, God knows, but it was far from sophisticated and certainly not well developed culturally. People frowned upon artists and writers. It was a he-man's country like the pioneer west. To the hostesses of Sydney, this very distinguished British scientist, good-looking and unattached, was quite a catch. Rex went out a good deal socially and rapidly acquired a reputation for being something of a snob—certainly he dealt brusquely with people he didn't like or who bored him. One of his techniques was to turn to a dinner companion suddenly and say, 'Do you like string?' He had a whole coterie of devices to terminate a conversation either because the person was bright enough to know that it was rude or not quite bright enough and would be left wondering. But these devices extricated him from a boring conversation."

When he left Australia, Chuck returned to the Department of Commerce in Washington, worked with E.R. Stettinius, Jr. and Averill Harriman during the depression organizing the Business Advisory Council, and then left government service for a number of years to operate the Washington office of the Credit Men's Association. He had a naval commission during the war and then entered Foreign Service work with the State Department as an auxiliary officer—"I came in legitimately the second time"—in Chile as commercial attache; Oslo as economic councilor, handling trade matters and turning over millions of dollars worth of cargo vessels to replace the ships sunk in the war; Trieste as U.S. political adviser, 1948–1949— a hot spot then, and he was the officer in charge. He was then transferred to London as economic councilor to our embassy, the biggest economic job in the Foreign Service, and while there became a Class I officer. There in 1950 he and Lloyd met again when Lloyd was on his way to give the Munro Lectures at the University of Edinburgh.[10] Theirs remained a close friendship even though they saw each other infrequently through the years. Chuck married Helen Friendly, a charming, intelligent person, and together they would drive across the country when they had leave to come home from foreign posts every three years. They would always stop to visit us. Through these trips they were in closer touch with events, attitudes, social and political changes in their homeland than most homebound residents. Chuck's last position with State was as our ambassador to Kuala Lampur. They built a retirement home in Charlottesville, Virginia, housing the treasures which they had gathered worldwide through many years, and Chuck became "ambassador in residence," a unique post, at the University of Virginia.

In reminiscing about Lloyd recently, Chuck spoke of the impressions he had of him as a human being which I am including here because one of his comments especially has been made by so many others: Lloyd's capacity to relate to, and appreciate special qualities in, such a variety of people—a capacity which certainly enriched his own life. "He was an emotionally turbulent sort of person with a tender, gentle quality which isn't always found in the male of the species. He was completely masculine. He endured his life in Arnhem Land—very masculine, very hardy—yet he would appear in Sydney, dapper, beautifully dressed. When we lived together I had the opportunity to see his gaiety, his fun-loving proclivities, but throughout his character were this gentleness, tenderness, reflecting a solicitude for human beings, not a cold clinical interest in mankind but a warm feeling, which, incidentally, often expressed itself in some amusing ways. One night he proudly brought home a cabbie that he had found somewhere who, he thought, was a remarkable human being and he wanted me to meet him. Between the time he hailed the cab and reached the apartment, he had engaged the man in conversation and decided he had found a rare person, as he later explained to me scientifically—what made the taxi driver tick, in what segment of human society he was, and how Lloyd had pigeon-holed him. It was his gregariousness and gentleness that made it possible for him to make friends very quickly with a great variety of people; the cabbie didn't know quite what to make of him, I am sure, but he had developed a great fondness for this curious American who had tucked him under his wing and brought him home. He also developed a close friendship with a curious character—an Australian aviator, a fighter pilot, of considerable distinction. Short, very tough, not too much education though he had been through one of the

Australian universities, had a fine war record—an ace—and he was flying old planes to New Guinea with mining equipment—very hazardous over the mountains, very high wages. He later worked for Qantas and took me across the country on a commercial flight in a crotchety old European plane, and that was the last I saw him.

"Lloyd had latched onto him because he too displayed certain societal characteristics that intrigued him. An unusual interest in human beings both for the human being but also for what makes his mind tick, how does he fit into society, is the society better or worse or not affected by what he does. This I think was tied to his respect for the emotions, the integrity of the individual—everybody has his place, perhaps not what we would want, but it should be respected. He had receptivity to people completely outside of his intellectual area but within his area of curiosity about society as a functioning organism. We talked once about religion, and he spoke of the Catholics as the only Christian sect unashamed of the influence of emotions—they cater to them, sometimes even pamper them. Their sacerdotal ceremonies and robes and incense and tinkling of bells seemed to him to be derived from the primitive tokenism of the kind he had found among the aborigines. But they do it unashamedly—whereas other religions are somewhat ashamed to be emotional. I think in a way this was almost a cardinal principle of Lloyd's—he was not ashamed of his emotions, he knew that he had them, and that they moved him very strongly. And he would talk about them openly—and in doing this exposed a very sensitive person, but he was willing to do it. He had courage, guts."

Chuck then spoke of meeting, during the past ten years or so, possibly fifteen people who had been colleagues or students of Lloyd's, and consistently all of them remarked about Lloyd's ability, his capacity for humor and fun, his teaching skills, and how he could do all of these things without seeming to take himself so seriously.

When Lloyd took the lugger at Darwin beginning the long journey home, his friends had a party to see him off. Lloyd knew that Mahkarolla was there but could not find him. At last, as the boat was pulling away, he saw him at the far edge of the crowd, his head bent, crying. He was one of the closest friends Lloyd ever had. Through the years he had word of him: he was working in Darwin, he had contracted tuberculosis. The Murngin were having the problems of all aborigines with the intrusion of white culture—their territory with its totemic waterholes, the very basis of their social organization and sacred life, was being overrun; they were on the route of the American and Australian planes during the Second World War; later bauxite deposits were found. Many of the Murngin drifted to Darwin, took menial jobs. Lloyd never wanted to return, feeling that he could not tolerate the effect of the many changes, but in one way and another, especially through anthropologists, he kept in touch. Fritz Goro was there doing the photographs of the Great Barrier Reef for the outstanding story in *Life* magazine and wrote Lloyd that he had seen Mahkarolla and would like to stop to meet Lloyd and talk about his experience. He had been impressed by Mahkarolla as the very special individual he was and wanted to meet the man who had meant so much to him—Fritz Goro had found Mahkarolla's account of his relationship with this person from such a totally different culture almost impossible to believe, leaving him with questions and wonderings, which he had to resolve by meeting Lloyd. Soon after this visit we received word of Mahkarolla's death.

Recently I had a letter from a doctoral student doing fieldwork in educational anthropology at Millingimbi Island written on behalf of Mahkarolla's son, Banguli, asking for copies of articles on Australia published by Lloyd and copies of photographs of aborigines not printed in *Black Civilization*. Banguli was teaching school on Millingimbi. I was able to send him some reprints and photographs, in some of which Mahkarolla was pictured quite clearly. It would have pleased Lloyd to have this contact and to know that Mahkarolla's son is doing well and holds a respected position in his altered world.

Notes to Chapter III

All correspondence with Kroeber and Lowie is from the Archives of the Bancroft Library, Berkeley.

W. Lloyd Warner, *Black Civilization*, is the source of the Murngin material. See bibliography of Warner books and articles.

1. W. H. Howells with W. Lloyd Warner data, "An Anthropometry of Natives of Arnhem Land and the Australian Race Problem," *Papers of the Peabody Museum of Archaeology and Ethnology*, Harvard University, 16:1, 1937.
2. A. R. Radcliffe-Brown, "The Definition of Totemism," *Anthropos*, 9: 622–30; "The Sociological Theory of Totemism," *Proceedings*, Fourth Pacific Science Congress, 3:295–309, 1929.
3. Emile Durkheim, *The Elementary Forms of the Religious Life: A Study in Religious Society*, Trans. J. W. Sevrin (London: Allan and Unwin, 1915).
4. Rockefeller Foundation Archives.
5. Rockefeller Foundation Archives.
6. Spencer and Gillen, *Native Tribes of Central Australia*.

7. W. Lloyd Warner, "Morphology and Functions of the Australian Murngin Type of Kinship, Part I," *American Anthropologist*, 33:2, 1972, 198.
8. Now with Chicago's Field Museum of Natural History.
9. Robert H. Lowie, "Oral Tradition and History." Address of the retiring president at the Annual Meeting of the Americal Folk-Lore Society, New York City, Dec. 27, 1916.
10. W. Lloyd Warner, *The Structure of American Life* (Edinburgh: University Press, 1952). Published in the United States as *American Life: Dream and Reality* (Chicago: University of Chicago Press, 1957).

Portrait by Aletta Lewis, ca. 1929

BEFORE RETURNING to the United States, Lloyd discussed with Rad-cliffe-Brown his dream of applying to the study of a contemporary American community the techniques of research and analysis he had used among the Murngin. He had first brought up his ideas with Chuck when, in discussing what each would do after Australia, Chuck asked what meaning his work there would have when he returned home.

Lloyd wanted to use his knowledge of Murngin social organization to obtain a better understanding of how men in all groups, regardless of place or time, solve the problems confronting them. His investigations of a simple society, he hoped, would equip him to analyze more complex forms of social organization. He also wanted to use it as a kind of screen through which to pass American contemporary industrialized society to ascertain what, if anything, he could find that would be analogous to the primitive, or what he had observed in the primitive, the detail of which might be discernible in the American society. He was quite excited about this research concept and eager to pursue it.

Radcliffe-Brown, however, was a little less enthusiastic since it seemed to him like a practical application of his science to which he was opposed. Chuck wondered whether the difference in attitude was due to Lloyd's being a product of an aggressive, pragmatic American society and Radcliffe-Brown's coming from the conservative British culture, or whether it was that Rex, an older scientist, was more interested in science for science's sake and Lloyd for what it could do for human society. I doubt the validity of the latter conjecture since in later years, when asked what practical application his researches would have, a question often asked by the people of a community under study, he would reply that the purpose of the research was the discovery of knowledge and understanding of society, the advancement of learning, that practical application was not a goal.

The efforts of Radcliffe-Brown, Kroeber, and Lowie were rewarded through contacts they made with Harvard's Alfred Tozzer. Radcliffe-Brown had cabled him about Lloyd's qualifications for a teaching fellowship at a time when by chance the Department of Anthropology at Harvard was "left high and dry suddenly in the middle of summer," as Tozzer phrased it in a note to Bob Lowie. Earnest Hooton's experience with Lloyd as a student was important in the department's decision to offer him an appointment as tutor since, as Tozzer wrote to Kroeber in 1915, Earnest Hooton was a great success in the department and his course in physical anthropology was to be a possible requirement for those going to medical school: "He is a corker and fits into the family." His role in the department was to become of growing importance when, as the years went by, Tozzer and Roland Dixon became increasingly estranged until, at the time of Lloyd's arrival, their communication was entirely by notes and memos.

Before leaving Australia Lloyd heard of the Middletown study by the Lynds and decided that they had preceded him in the type of research he wanted to do on his own. He could hardly wait to obtain a copy and was relieved that the Lynds had used a sociological approach rather than the anthropological techniques Lloyd wanted to apply. He was well received at Harvard, had a pleasant office in the Peabody Museum, and found comfortable living quarters at the Faculty Club. He gave a course in introductory anthropology at Harvard and at Radcliffe, and made plans to pursue his work for the Ph.D. He had only to meet residence requirements, take a language exam, and write his dissertation which would be, of course, the monograph on his Murngin research.

The University had recently completed many of the units of a new house plan, fashioned after the colleges of Cambridge and Oxford. Lloyd became a tutor at Kirkland House, where he made friends with another tutor, Kitchener Jordan, of the history faculty, whose wife Frances was dean of Radcliffe College. She was the sister of Beardsley Ruml, who as director of the Laura Spelman Rockefeller Memorial, which had participated in financing of the Australian National Research Council, had expanded its program into the social sciences, with anthropology as one segment. Carleton Coon was teaching physical anthropology. He and his beautiful, able wife, Mary, soon became friends of Lloyd's, their home a frequent gathering place for the students and younger faculty members of the department. Anthropologists tend to be a clannish group within each university and throughout the country, and, indeed, throughout the world. Joe Brew, later to become director of the Peabody Museum, had his archaeology laboratory on the floor below Lloyd's office. Here he was occupied gluing potsherds from recent digs, teaching, and training. Hallam Movius, a graduate student in that field who later moved into faculty status, was part of the group.

News of Lloyd's arrival soon reached Elton Mayo, an Australian by birth, who had come to this country in 1922 on leave from the University of Brisbane, where he was professor of philosophy. He had lectured across the continent and then accepted a three-year appointment at the University of Pennsylvania under a grant from the Carnegie Corporation. Elton's academic background was first in medicine, in his family's tradition. He studied at the University of Adelaide and, later, Edinburgh. But when he returned to Adelaide he came under the influence of a professor of philosophy who encouraged him to study psychology, and this led to collaboration with Dr. Mathewson of Brisbane in the treatment of shell-shocked soldiers using psycho-therapeutics new to Australia that effected some remarkable cures. He came to feel that modern industry might be the cause of similar problems in individual adaptation resulting in many of the social and moral ills of industrial civilization. Mayo also came under the influence of Émile Durkheim, the French sociologist whose *Division of Labor in Society*[1] had first appeared, in French, in 1893.

Leaving Adelaide to accept the newly established chair of philosophy at the University of Queensland, Mayo continued his research in the problems of social unrest and morale. In applying the clinical methods of the French psychologist Pierre Janet, he concluded that the roots of social maladjustment were usually in obsessive thinking and that social problems were basically the individual's problems. At the University of Pennsylvania he met Beardsley Ruml, who recommended to John D. Rockefeller, Jr., then interested in research on the alleviation of conflict and distress in industry, that a grant be given to Mayo for three months' work at the Wharton School — successful research that led to his receiving a further grant for three years from the Laura Spelman Rockefeller Memorial, of which Ruml had become director in 1922. He had felt intellectually constricted in Australia, where university studies seemed to be regarded as professional training, and looked to American universities, where it was considered on the other hand important to study social and industrial problems in order to understand society.

His schedule at the University of Pennsylvania required only informal meetings with students; the rest of his time was free to pursue his research interests. He made contacts with various Philadelphia firms, and, using his training in psychopathological analysis, consulted on problems they were encountering in their organizations.

In 1925 Mayo met Wallace D. Donham, dean of the Graduate School of Business Administration at Harvard since 1919, who invited him to give a lecture there. This was followed by an invitation to join the faculty for five years as associate professor of industrial research, a position funded by the Laura Spelman Rockefeller Memorial. There he collaborated with Lawrence J. Henderson, a theoretical biochemist and physiologist, in the organized study of the psychological problems of industrial personnel. During this period Henderson was on the faculty of the Harvard Medical School as a full professor. Through the collaboration and interstimulation of Henderson and Mayo, whose continued intellectual training and interests ranged through the anatomical, physiological, pathological, psychological, and sociological fields, emerged the now famous Fatigue Laboratory,[2] at the business school. Here studies were made of biochemical changes, including those that occur in the bloodstream during active muscular exercise, in both human and nonhuman subjects. The Fatigue Laboratory had the active support of Dean Donham, a classmate of Henderson and personal friend of President A. Lawrence Lowell, and of Dean

Edsall of the Medical School, who was one of the original sponsors. Financial support for the initial work of both Mayo and Henderson and of the Fatigue Laboratory came from the Laura Spellman Rockefeller Memorial and the Rockefeller Foundation.

The studies were well timed because industry had recently come to realize that it could not ignore the human factor if it were to prosper. This was the social context of the basic premise of the laboratory, that group psychology, social problems, and the physiology of fatigue of normal man must be studied, not only as individual factors in determining physical and mental health, but more especially to determine their interrelatedness and effect upon work. Mayo's function was as consultant director of psychological investigation in large industrial establishments. An iconoclast and innovator, like Henderson, he had learned during World War I that he wanted to study the adaptation of the normal individual to industry, and it was to this end that he studied with Janet in Paris—"in order to state more precisely the personal and social maladies of our modern industrial civilization."

In 1927 Mayo gave a lecture to the National Industrial Conference Board and here met George Pennock of the Western Electric Company, the manufacturing subsidary of A. T. & T., an engineer who was directing researches on the effect of illumination on the production of workers. Three years old, these researches were a joint effort of the company and the National Research Council. Since the results were somewhat baffling, Pennock asked Elton Mayo to visit the Hawthorne Works, in Cicero, Illinois, to observe the research as leader of a research team that included Western Electric personnel and, from the Harvard faculty, Fritz Roethlisberger and T. North Whitehead, the statistician, son of the famous Harvard philosopher Alfred North Whitehead.

As the research progressed, a program of individual interviewing was introduced that revealed the relation between output, morale, and personal preoccupation, spreading the focus of the research out from the individual to the social environment in which he lived. Mayo then asked Lloyd if he would take part in this phase of the research, the individual worker in his social context. "A representative of the Harvard Department of Anthropology had called attention to the logical insufficiency of a merely psychological study of the individuals in a department. Laboratory and clinical psychological studies are interested in the individual . . . but they do no more than touch the fringe of human inquiry."[3]

Lloyd was intrigued with the possibilities of the research and working with Mayo, whom he found intellectually exciting and a sophisticated, sensitive companion. The research was concentrated in two test rooms where the workers and their performance were observed under controlled conditions. Lloyd wrote a memorandum suggesting methods for studying the social situation that existed within the test rooms.

> An important problem before us at the present time in the Western Electric research is to study and understand the total social organization of each of the test rooms. This includes not only the formal industrial structure which the company has created but also the organizations formed by the employees in their conscious or unconscious attempts to form themselves into a group of their own. . . . The first step necessary is to itemize the number of social personalities found in each place—by this I mean the types of occupations performed by the workers found in the two test rooms. . . . All of these social personalities are integrated by a set of primary and secondary relationships which can be analyzed into separate parts. [Sixteen categories are listed] . . . Following the analysis of the social situation into its primary reciprocals, it will be necessary then to combine the various reciprocals into secondary association to see how these various social bonds react on each other and finally to integrate the social situation in the test rooms on the basis of social relationships which exist there.

Mayo's interest had been in the individual worker in his response to various pressures as manifest in Janet's studies of obsessive thinking, Freud's compulsion neuroses, and Durkheim's anomie. "Durkheim's modern representative and critic, Professor Maurice Halbwachs, thus expresses his view: 'Social life offers us the spectacle of an effort eternally renewed by human groups to triumph over the causes of disintegration which threaten such groups. The weapons of society in this struggle are collective beliefs and customs.' As breaks in the social group appear, increase, multiply, or disappear, the structure of the collective organism is transformed accordingly as its vitality is diminished or increased. The simpler the community, the more easily does it maintain the integrated character of its activities. The more complex it becomes, the more necessary is it that explicit attention shall be given to the various problems involved in the maintenance of social integrity."[4] Dr. J. S. Plant had earlier pointed out to his colleagues the dangers in psychiatry of concentrating upon the individual to the neglect of the high significance of social changes (Mayo, p. 136). Halbwachs on this point: "The most important problem for a complex and rapidly changing society is the contrivance of means that will assure the preservation of social integrity of function side by side with the development of function. It is probable that the work a man does represents his most important function in the society; but unless there is some sort of integral social background to his life, he cannot even assign a value to his work. Durkheim's finding in nineteenth-century France would seem to apply to twentieth-century America."[5]

In *The Social Problems of an Industrial Civilization*,[6] Mayo referred to William James' observation that every civilized language except English has two commonplace words for knowledge—for example, in French, *connaitre* and *savoir*—the English equivalents, knowledge-of acquaintance and knowledge-about. He deplores the presumption that meetings of eminent specialists, even in great universities, could devise a method by which non-logical problems could be resolved and urges following the path of all the sciences—first, patient, pedestrian development of "firsthand knowledge" (knowledge-of acquaintance) and then intimate acquaintance with the facts (knowledge-about) on the part of the administrator. "When one turns from the successful sciences—chemistry, physics, physiology—to the unsuccessful sciences—sociology, psychology, political science—one cannot fail to be struck by the extent of the failure of the latter to communicate to students a skill that is directly useful in human situations. . . . The so called social sciences encourage students to talk endlessly about alleged social problems . . . of sociology in the living instance, sociology of the intimate, nothing at all."

Mayo observed that the lack of collaboration, of communication, between workers and administrators has been caused by defining it in economic terms rather than social and human terms.

> If we study the simplest situation, as among primitive peoples studied by Malinowski, A. R. Brown, Lloyd Warner we can inspect collaboration in work. Amongst the Australian aborigines their method of living involves an almost perfect collaboration drilled into members of the tribe in such a fashion that a kinship relation, a social ceremony, an economic duty become signals or commands to act or respond in a certain manner. I say 'drilled into' members of a tribe, because although individual actions, as with a regiment of soldiers, are intelligently related to the actions of others and to the situation, yet no member of the tribe can expound the system and its grounds as a logic. The tribe responds to situations as a unit; each member knows his place and part although he cannot explain it . . . primitive collaboration is rather the effect in action of a primitive social code. From the point of view of its simple effectiveness, however, it is more like a 'drilled' and military evolution than like our civilized inter-relationships.

He comments that the symptoms they found of social disorganization would be charactisteric of modern communities in Europe as well as in the United States, a result of the disturbance of community integrity by exceedingly rapid economic growth.

My colleague Warner has pointed out that industrial methods have been rapidly developed of late years in a logical or scientific direction, and internationally rather than nationally. The consequence is that the imposition of highly systematized industrial procedures upon all the civilized cultures has brought to relative annihilation the cultural traditions of work and craftsmanship. . . . It would seem that one of the important problems discovered by the research division at Hawthorne—the failure of workers and supervisors to understand their work and working conditions, the widespread sense of personal futility—is general to the civilized world and not merely characteristic of Chicago.

Cicero is part of the larger Chicago community, aspects of which had been studied by the sociologists at the University of Chicago, Robert E. Park and Ernest Burgess and their colleagues, by Clifford Shaw (*Delinquency Areas*, 1929), Ruth Cavan (*Suicide*, 1929), and others.

Not only was a study of the total community of Chicago beyond possibility, it would not have yielded what the research wanted to know about "total personalities." It was here that Lloyd's desire to apply anthropological techniques to a contemporary American community came into focus for Mayo. Rather than study certain social segments or geographical areas of a large community the study as conceived would involve a community small enough to be encompassed in one multifaceted research, a community which would indeed comprise the social context of the work to be undertaken. In a later report on the researches sponsored by the Department of Industrial Research, through its Committee on Industrial Physiology (financed by the Memorial), the distinction is made between a type of inquiry about human beings that could be made in a laboratory and a type that could not—where the total situation of the individual had to be studied. The studies that became known as Yankee City were seen as focusing on the determinants of cooperation in a modern community in its widest sense. The point of view of the studies is expressed in brief quotations from the first volume: ". . . society is a group of mutually interacting individuals. Hence, if any relationship of a given social configuration is stimulated, it will influence all other parts and in turn will be influenced by them . . . most, if not all, societies have a fundamental structure or structures which integrate and give characteristic form to the rest of the society . . . and determine the basic outlook of an individual"[7]—that is, his adjustment or maladjustment to society.

It is difficult to discuss research in the social sciences during this general period without frequent reference to Beardsley Ruml. When the funds of the original Laura Spelman Rockefeller Memorial, augmented by additional contributions from John D. Rockefeller, Sr., and wise investments, exceeded the needs of the projects and causes in which Mrs. Rockefeller had been interested, the trustees first turned to the welfare of women and children but found this still too narrow an objective. In 1922 Beardsley Ruml, a psychologist then in his late twenties and associated with James R. Angell, president of the Carnegie Corporation, was appointed director. He submitted a plan for the Memorial to move into the social sciences— economics, sociology, political science, psychology, anthropology, and history. He urged that the Memorial's work in social welfare clearly showed the need for the development of the social sciences—human capacities and motives related to the behavior of human beings as individuals and in groups. The social sciences were young, facilities meager, university instruction limited, precluding the possibility of contact with social phenomena. Research in these areas was largely deductive and speculative, based on secondhand observations, documents, and anecdotes. One result of his efforts was the Institute of Human Relations at Yale, financed by the Memorial, the General Education Board, and the Foundation. Major research centers were started at the University of Chicago, Harvard, Columbia, Yale, Virginia, Texas, North Carolina, Stanford, Vanderbilt, and universities abroad.

Ruml felt that research could not be confined to university departments but must be involved with the processes which would give it practical effectiveness. The Social Science Research Council (SSRC) was organized in 1923 to correlate and stimulate research and promote easy flow of men and ideas between institutions—the famous cross-fertilization of ideas. The administration of the Memorial's fellowship program was transferred to the SSRC. Research was financed at the University of Chicago in sociology, social anthropology, and psychology; projects of the local Social Science Research Committee were also funded.

In 1929 the Memorial was merged into the Foundation. The International General Education Board, its funds spent according to plan, was liquidated and the Foundation reorganized into five major divisions: International Health, Medical Sciences, Natural Sciences, Social Sciences, and the Humanities. Ruml left to become dean of the Social Science Division at the University of Chicago, and his place in the new division of the social sciences was taken by Edmund E. Day, professor of economics at Harvard and later dean of the School of Business Administration at the University of Michigan, his alma mater. He had been associated with Ruml in various projects. His emphasis, like Ruml's, was on the university and university research. By 1935 Day felt that the social sciences had developed to a point where there was less theorizing, less dispute about method, "more reasoning on the basis of extensive evidence regarding real situations. Rigorous theoretical training is now more securely upheld by a richer supporting documentation. This change in the character of research activity is reflected in the research training of the oncoming generation.

They are better equipped technically at no apparent loss of basic theoretical training."[8]

Soon after assuming the presidency of the University of Chicago, Robert Maynard Hutchins expressed appreciation of the work of the Memorial in promoting the social sciences in the United States. It is an intriguing comment since at this time Hutchins was denigrating the social sciences and doing his best to deter their progress, or so it seemed.

To avoid possible confusion it should be said that the Spelman Fund, the only independent entity to emerge from the consolidation of the Memorial with the Foundation, had as its purpose to carry on certain programs considered incompatible with Foundation plans. For example, under the guidance of Charles E. Merriam, chairman of the Political Science Department at the University of Chicago, Beardsley Ruml, and Guy Moffett, it financed the creation of the Public Administration Clearing House at the University of Chicago (though not part of the University), always known by its address on the Midway "1313." This clearinghouse for government agencies included the Council of State Governments, "a monument of permanent usefulness," considered to be its most important contribution.

Meanwhile, at Harvard, the Hootons very graciously had open house every day for tea, which gave the students an opportunity to talk informally with Earnest and his wife, with other faculty members who often dropped in, and with visiting anthropologists whom they might never have had the opportunity to meet. I think there was a bit of feeling among some of the students that attendance with some regularity was expected and not a privilege alone, but certainly no one could have felt that attendance was de rigueur. Conversation ranged widely; many of these students must now look back upon those occasions and appreciate the privilege they enjoyed in contrast to the social situations at many universities where the student has no informal contact with faculty and indeed may never be invited to a faculty home.

These were busy, full days for Lloyd—teaching anthropology at Harvard College and Radcliffe, writing the monograph on his Australian research, performing some tutorial duties at Kirkland House, trips to Chicago to consult on the Western Electric research, conducting seminars, making friends—Frances and Kitch Jordan, Helen and Talcott Parsons, members of his own department, Dorothea and Elton Mayo, many others in Boston as well as Cambridge—and finding a community for the new research. Lloyd also made fairly frequent trips to New York where he had many friends including his old childhood friend, Frances Farmer, who had gone to Harbin as a tutor with an American family, and there married Bill Stevens, who was with Standard Oil in China and Manchuria. When they returned they settled in New York City where I met them with Lloyd.

For the community research, the first task was to define the criteria that would control the selection of a community, select possible communities meeting these criteria, study them in a process of elimination, and then make an intensive study of those remaining. A brief summary of the criteria established by Warner in collaboration with the research committee: a well-integrated community where the various parts of the society functioned with comparative ease rather than in confusion and conflict; a population predominantly old American in order to observe how the stock that is thought of as the core of modern America organizes its behavior when not overpowered by other ethnic groups; one with a long tradition, where the social organization has become firmly organized and the relations of the various members of the society exactly placed and known by the individuals of the group; and one that has not undergone such rapid social change that disruptive factors would dominate those which maintain balanced groups. It was hoped to avoid a society where several ethnic traditions were equally dominant and, therefore, total-community integration low and subcommunity integration high, possibly resulting in ethnic conflict. A few industries and several factories were necessary in order to see how workers related to the larger community. It was also important to the research that the community not be an aberrant one.

Since the research was to be done by Harvard students and faculty it should be located within easy commuting distance of Cambridge.

When Newburyport was tentatively selected, detailed surveys and maps were made and interviews conducted to test the findings about the qualifications of the community for the proposed project. Members of the research committee saw key figures in the town to explain the plan and goals of the research, the sponsorship, who would be doing the work, methods to be employed, the basic principles—and to ask for their cooperation. Eliot Chapple, an anthropology student whose family lived in Salem, became field director, moving to Newburyport with his wife in the fall of 1931 and remaining into 1934. Other fieldworkers came up from Cambridge, usually spending a weekend, sometimes longer during reading periods and vacations. Each was given for expenses $2.50 a night for room and $2.00 a day for meals. They stayed in rooms in a big house in the business district, owned by a couple who had a diner next door—and still complain over the lack of amenities and the dull evenings. Four fieldworkers started the research, the number gradually increasing to ten and, at the maximum, fifteen. Those with special aptitudes or other qualifications were put in charge of appropriate phases of the work: Leo Srole, who later collaborated in writing Volume 3, Allison and Elizabeth Davis, Conrad Arensberg, and Buford Junker, the only undergraduate. Burleigh Gardner and Solon Kimball joined a year later, then J. O. Low, who had received his

A. B. degree from Harvard long ago and sold his partnership in a successful securities business in New York, feeling that he wanted to return to académe as a serious student of his society. He started taking courses from Lloyd, joined the research team, helped with the study of factories, and collaborated in the writing of Volume 4. Paul Lunt, a member of an old Newburyport family, had received his preparatory schooling at Brown Nichols in Cambridge, joined the research team out of interest, and became an important member, serving as catalyst, opening many doors, and contributing insights that possibly could not have been obtained otherwise. He studied at Harvard and later participated in the writing of the first two volumes of the research report. Eliot Chapple, Solon Kimball, and Conrad Arensberg all later received their Ph.D. degrees from Harvard; Allison Davis, Burleigh Gardner, and Leo Srole from the University of Chicago, having followed Lloyd in his move to Chicago in 1935. Joe Low and Paul Lunt also came. Marion Lee and Dorothea Mayo, trained in the history of art and architecture, made the study of Newburyport houses. Osgood Lovekin, of the Harvard Business School, brought his family for a year, renting a charming old home on High Street, and Joe Brew, the archaeologist, helped, as did Gwen Harrington and Bess Haughton. During the first year Lloyd too was a commuter.

Of the research methods and procedures of most importance was the research interview; then various types of sustained observations; printed documents and newspapers; case histories, biographies, and autobiographies; photographs of houses and other significant objects; and surveys, including aerial.

During the first year especially, frequent research seminars were held at the Harvard Faculty Club, usually attended by Elton Mayo and Fritz Roethlisberger, often L. J. Henderson, and others. Fritz, who, with William J. Dickson of the Western Electric Company, had developed the interviewing technique used, counseled the research team on the eight rules they had developed for the control of the immediate relations of the interviewer to his informant: the interviewer should listen to the informant in a patient and friendly, but intelligently critical, manner; not display any kind of authority; not give advice or moral admonition; not argue; talk or ask questions only in order to help the person talk and relieve any fears or anxieties he may appear to have in relation to the interviewer; offer praise for reporting thoughts and feelings accurately; direct the conversation to a neglected topic; and discuss implicit assumptions if this seems advisable. Roethlisberger and Dickson acknowledged the necessity for the interviewer's having a guiding hypothesis in order to avoid the conversation's becoming possibly incoherent, but they cautioned against fixed and preconceived ideas that would prevent the interviewer from being alert to something new.

In the course of a conversation, the interviewer should follow certain simple rules of interpretation: keep what is said as an item in a context rather than treat everything as manifest content, or as either fact or error, or as being at the same psychological level; listen not only to what a person wants to say but also to what he does not want to say or cannot say without help; treat the mental contexts as indices, seeking through them the personal reference that is being revealed; keep personal reference in its social context.

The seminars stressed the importance, in a community research, of the interviewer's maintaining friendly, pleasant relations, guiding the conversation, without seeming to do so, to the foci of the research. Interviewing is an art requiring discipline and control—some people can do it while others fail, some can succeed in certain situations but fail in others. However, most respondents talk rather freely and regard the interview as a social conversation.

The research needed to cover all social situations in the community and study intensively the several types. So interviewing had to be carried out systematically and in a way that would obtain the detailed analysis ultimately required. Verification of facts was accomplished through repeated and varied interviews, through checking official and other printed source materials, observation, and cross-checking with materials gathered by other fieldworkers, each of whom would present to the seminar material he had gathered since the previous session.

There were sessions in Newburyport, often over breakfast at O'Connell's Grill. An article in the local paper would be read and Lloyd would ask, "What is this telling us about the culture? Mrs. Jones entertains certain guests—what is that telling us? With its vast intense involvement, this paper is symbolizing the nature of the culture to which it is addressed—how do we understand both the newspaper and the culture it represents?" All issues of the paper were clipped and indexed.

Early in the research it became apparent that, in order to achieve the goal of studying everyone in the community, a technique would have to be developed to record and analyze this vast amount of data. With computers it would have been a simple task; but the researchers were working with Hollerith punch cards. It was decided to code activities and record the interactions of all individuals in social context. For example, the "personality cards" would yield information about the social composition of each club, church congregation, formal and informal social groups and so forth. "The Yankee City research on the whole, has been inspired by the belief in a scientific collection of facts not for their own sake, but for the purpose of later scientific generalization in an effort to understand their nature. Although our emphasis has been on the group aspects of social behavior, we have attempted to avoid the conventional dichotomy of the individual and the society by a restatement of the problem of individuals in interaction.

"A well-stated hypothesis of the general nature of society was advanced by George Simmel, who said, 'Society exists whenever a number of individuals enter into reciprocal relations.' He maintained that society 'is an objective unity, judged by the one valid criterion of unity, namely, the reciprocal activity of parts.' He further clarified this statement: 'The group is a unity because of . . . processes of reciprocal influencing between the individuals.'[9]

"Throughout our research we have employed the concepts of interaction between two or more individuals and the social interrelationships within which these interactions take place. The explicit, overt behavior of individuals, verbal or bodily, as well as 'mental attitudes or psychological occurrences within the minds of individuals' studied, have been understood by us 'as a product of mutual determinations and reciprocal influences.' Although our interest has centered on the aspect of the individual's behavior in a group, it must be obvious that there has been no attempt to view such phenomena, including collective representations, as beyond the individual or as manifestations of the so-called group mind. The larger systems of interrelations which compose the extremely complex and highly elaborate society of Yankee City were studied in specific detail. As were the interactions, direct and indirect, of the individuals who constituted the biological units."[10]

The discovery of the social meaning in the local paper, census tracts, and assessor's records was exciting to the students, as one comments: "[Warner] was the great conceptualizer, bringing together theories and concepts from many sources and applying them to understanding people in social organizations whether the Murngin or the modern community. He was devoted to research, not theories alone—let's go out and look at the practical world in the light of this theory (Malinowski, Durkheim, Ogden and Richards, Piaget, Radcliffe-Brown) and try to make sense out of it. His impact on his students was not as a brilliant lecturer in the classroom but as an exciting person to work in the field. He never was enthusiastic about giving a course or lecturing—his enthusiasm was for the interplay of ideas and stimulation—as in a seminar where there was a lot of give and take. It was through research that he built students and real anthropologists." Because of the original conception of the Newburyport research and his relations with Elton Mayo, he was also bringing understanding of the world he was finding back to the people who have to act in it—a bridging of two worlds, the academic and the practical world of business where men have to make decisions and act on them.

In the flowing together of many threads of talent into the research, Lawrence J. Henderson was a stimulator as well as an active participant. With Mayo, he had become a firm believer in the importance of the study of the behavioral sciences. He was a proselytizer, respected, highly influential, whose interests ranged widely. After receiving his A. B. degree from Harvard in 1892 and his M. D. in 1902 he spent two years in chemical research at the University of Strasbourg, where he met Robert E. Park, whose thinking may very well have helped direct him into his interest in sociology. When he returned to Harvard he taught courses in biochemistry—something of an innovation in associating chemistry and biology—in the medical school which was based in both Cambridge and Boston. He developed a close friendship with A. Lawrence Lowell, president of Harvard from 1909 to 1933; they often walked together between Boston and Cambridge; they were part of a little group that included Nielson, later president of Smith College, who was teaching English at Harvard at that time, and they met periodically to exchange ideas.

Henderson took part in seminars in philosophy at Harvard, gave the first course there on the history of science, and wrote two general books on the relationships between the organism and its environment. It was William Morton Wheeler, the Harvard expert on insect societies, especially the social organization of ants, who suggested to Henderson that he read Vilfredo Pareto, whose *Trattato di sociologia generale*, published in 1916, had been translated into French, with an English translation in preparation. Henderson was something of a Francophile and read the language easily.[11]

Vilfredo Pareto—engineer, turned economist, then sociologist—who had engendered considerable hostility in the academic world by joining the Mussolini government, came close to satisfying Henderson's demand for an orderly way of looking at human behavior. Using the galley proofs of the English translation of Pareto's work (published as *The Mind and Society: A Treatise on General Sociology* in 1935), Henderson conducted a seminar in Pareto in 1932–1934 attended by twelve to fifteen people from a number of fields, including Mayo and Robert Lamb, the economist. When Lamb joined the faculty of MIT, he asked Lloyd to counsel on the broadening of the curriculum from a narrowly based scientific-engineering one to include courses that would give an understanding of society to those students whose work would have such a strong—and at times dire—effect on their social world.

Lloyd urged his students to attend the seminar. Most of them knew Henderson from his attendance at the conferences on the Newburyport research. The procedure of the seminar was for Henderson to read from the galley proofs and then discuss in a way that scattered gems of wisdom. Lloyd had cautioned his students not to attempt to engage Henderson in argument or discussion, which was sound advice, as one of them was to discover when he attempted to involve Henderson in academic argument and was torn to bits.

Others attending the seminars included Talcott Parsons and George Homans, sociologists, Hans Zinsser, a bacteriologist, a lawyer named Curtis, Robert Merton, then a graduate student in sociology, Joseph Shumpeter, an economist, Crane Brinton and Bernard DeVoto, both historians, and Elton Mayo. DeVoto had first met Henderson in Morgan Center, Vermont, where Henderson had a group of cottages; here he gathered fellow intellectuals each summer for work and discussion and to enjoy good food and wine, and good conversation. It is possible that Henderson was attracted to Pareto because he had such an orderly mind and wanted human behavior to come to him in orderly scientific patterns, and Pareto's writing came closest to achieving these concepts. It troubled him that people did not act in an orderly, logical way.

Discussions between Lowell and Henderson led in 1933 to forming the Society of Fellows, which Lowell funded when he could not interest a foundation. He thought that the Ph. D. program was too rigid, that there should be some other way for a young man to work in his field of specialization without having to be in the lockstep Ph. D. program. In the Society of Fellows, the junior fellows were elected for three years, during which they could follow a free program with complete access to Harvard departments, faculty, libraries, and laboratories. It was understood that three additional years might be granted to fellows of proved qualifications. But Lowell's hope that this program would replace the Ph. D. program, that it would become a symbol well understood and accepted in the academic world, was not fulfilled because other institutions did not acknowledge it as evidence of Ph. D.-level achievement. The University of Chicago was at the same time moving into an undergraduate program that granted a terminal degree after completion of the requirements of the college, which combined the last two years of high school with the first two of college. This degree was not recognized by other institutions as qualification for graduate work.

Henderson became chairman of the society; among the senior fellows were Alfred North Whitehead, John Livingston Low, Samuel Eliot Morrison, and Crane Brinton. All of the fellows met every Monday night for dinner, de rigueur, at Eliot House, where they had rooms. There were also meetings of the senior fellows to interview possibilities for junior fellowships. Hilda Carter, recently director of public information at the University of Wisconsin, Eau Claire, worked for Henderson and Mayo at that time and attended these meetings to take notes. A full record was kept of the interviews.

With these ideas of Lowell's as background, it is easy to understand how he encouraged Lloyd not to take time out to get his Ph. D. Because of Henderson, Lloyd had frequent contact with Lowell, who was thoroughly familiar with Lloyd's work and felt that it was foolish for someone now sitting on faculty committees examining Ph. D. candidates to take time from his research to complete the requirements for his own degree. Involved as he was in research, writing, and teaching, Lloyd happily accepted Lowell's advice and, to my knowledge, never regretted having done so—especially since he was soon drawn into plans for an anthropological study of Ireland even as fieldwork and analysis of the Newburyport research were continuing and the writing had begun. He had completed the first draft of the monograph, *Black Civilization*, on his Australian research and had meanwhile published a brief research report in the *Australian Geographer*, "Morphology and Functions of the Australian Murngin Type of Kinship."

Notes for Chapter IV

Note sources: Archives of Baker Library, Graduate School of Business Administration, Harvard University.

1. Émile Durkheim, *De la division du travail social—étude sur l'organisation des societés superieures*, 1893. Translated by George Simpson as *Division of Labor in Society* (N.Y.: Macmillan, 1933).
2. Steven M. Horvath and Elizabeth C. Horvath, *The Harvard Fatigue Laboratory, Its History and Contributions*, Institute of Environmental Studies (Englewood Cliffs, N.J.: Prentice-Hall, 1973), p. 21.
3. Elton Mayo, *Human Problems of an Industrial Civilization* (Boston: Graduate School of Business Administration, Harvard University, 1933), pp. 115–16.
4. M. Halbwachs, *Les causes du suicide* (Paris: Felix Alcan, 1930), p. 448. Quoted by Mayo, *Human Problems*, pp. 134–35.
5. Ibid., p. 136.
6. Elton Mayo, *The Social Problems of an Industrial Civilization* (Boston: Harvard University, 1945), p. 19.
7. W. Lloyd Warner and Paul S. Lunt, *The Social Life of a Modern Community*, Yankee City Series, Vol. I (New Haven: Yale University Press, 1929).
8. Raymond B. Fosdick, *The Story of the Rockefeller Foundation* (New York: Harper and Bros., 1952) for this section.
9. Nicholas J. Spykman, *The Social Theory of George Simmel* (Chicago: University of Chicago Press, 1925), p. 27.
10. Yankee City Series, Vol. I, pp. 35–36.
11. Vilfredo Pareto, *Tratto di sociologia generale*, 1916. Edited by Arthur Livingston and translated by A. L. and Andrew Borgiorno as *The Mind and Society* (New York: Harcourt Brace, 1935).

THE IRISH RESEARCH, undertaken under various sponsors, had a number of goals. Having learned at Western Electric that the workers had to be viewed in their social as well as physical context, the Committee on Industrial Physiology set the research task of putting aside preconceived logics and examining each particular study to discover the simple obvious facts of human situations. The early exploratory period included studies of the personal adjustment of nearly four hundred students at the Harvard Business School as well as early phases of the Yankee City research, which viewed society as a group of mutually interacting individuals.

But concepts of cooperative phenomena between individuals or groups and their society had to be related to any type of society, not an industrial one alone. Therefore, researches were planned for the study of a community in the Deep South, with its caste-class system, for the Norfolk Prison colony, for an extension of the study of an individual's social adjustment as reported in Elton Mayo's paper "Frightened People,"[1] and for studies of unemployment and of the human and social problems of a nonindustrial community.

During general discussions over tea at the Hootons and in the smoking room of the Peabody Museum, the idea was suggested of studying a small country from the total anthropological perspective—archaeology, physical anthropology, perhaps linguistics, and social anthropology. Earnest Hooton became interested and thought it might be possible to raise research funds among the members of the large Irish community in Boston. There were a number of meetings that the Irish seemed to enjoy for the status this Harvard interest gave them, and Lloyd became enthusiastic about the symbols revealed, as in the dominant role of the female in the Irish community, but only a token sum was raised for the research.

The Committee on Industrial Physiology supported the project because Ireland met their criteria for a community primarily not industrial. Not only was it an agrarian society but small enough in geographic size and population to be encompassed in one study.

Thus the ideas for a research that came to be known as the Harvard Irish Survey were developed, with Hooton the director of the archaeology and physical anthropology studies and Lloyd of the work in social anthropology. The goal was to involve three fields of anthropology in the study of the origin and development of the races and cultures of Ireland.

Lloyd was asked to go to Ireland in the summer of 1931, while the Newburyport research was in progress, to explore the possibilities and feasibility of these proposals. At that time there were two acceptable hotels in Dublin—the Shelburne and the Gresham. Lloyd stayed at the former and was impressed by the special attention he received from the doorman, a man almost as tall as Lloyd's six feet four. One day the doorman, drawing himself to full height, said to him, "We Warners would all be from the South of Ireland, wouldn't we?" If the Irish like you, they want to identify with you and, especially, place you geographically in Ireland. Lloyd later discovered that this man, and the doorman at the Gresham, each owned the hotel he served.

Before going to work Lloyd visited American friends who were renting Leixlip castle, a stone structure on the River Liffey, spacious, of course, well staffed, but not overendowed with simple creature comforts. At a large party given for Lloyd he met many of the "county" people, gay, friendly, usually horsey. When a near neighbor, a charming and gracious lady in the old tradition, learned that Lloyd's room was in the tower, she warned him of the ghost he would surely encounter during his visit. At the same time she spoke scornfully of Irish folk beliefs in leprechauns, little people, and fairies—"but of course there are banshees."

Lloyd had a very satisfactory interview with the Irish political leader Eamon De Valera in which he obtained not only his approval of the proposed research but many suggestions for areas of study, people who might be helpful, situations to avoid. The Irish are a puritanical people basically, and the research had anticipated possible difficulties in obtaining approval for physical anthropology. Archaeology—the disturbance of things past—could also have presented insurmountable obstacles and social anthropology might be viewed as offensive prying into private lives. De Valera also arranged an interview with the cardinal, whose "blessing" was essential to the work. Lloyd was received in a beautiful garden with peacocks strolling about. The cardinal presented his hand for the ring to be kissed—Lloyd conformed easily to custom—and the interview concluded with a grant of approval. The cardinal rose as Lloyd was leaving, put his arm around his shoulders, and said, "You'd be a tall lad, wouldn't you?" His height was not always this well received. He had attained it early, passing most of his peers, which sometimes made him the target of their aggression in spite of his being so thin. One might say also that it often made him noticeable, not always to his advantage.

In selecting a county to be studied by the social anthropologists, he went first to the census records to determine the distribution of certain attributes that he had selected as important criteria. This task was made easier by the country-wide census by the Free State government in 1926 in which the category, occupation, for example, gave essential information on this distribution in the population. Next, his search was for a county having these characteristics in distribution approximating that of the country as a whole: English and Irish (Gaelic) speakers, for example, since some counties had no Irish speakers; townspeople and farmers in order to avoid a county like Limerick or Cork dominated by one city; and Catholics and Protestants. He selected Clare, on the West Coast, whose county seat of Ennis was large enough to have two inns, mostly patronized by county people, either of which could serve as headquarters for the social research. The county had medium-sized towns, small villages and hamlets, a port town, Kilrush, and resort towns on the sea. Clare, a blend of Gaelic and modern British influences, was agrarian, its few mills abandoned, with a mixture of small holdings, especially along the coast, and scattered large estates.

Satisfied that he had accomplished all he could during this preliminary phase, Lloyd returned to Harvard to resume teaching and the direction of the work in Newburyport, and to continue consulting on the Western Electric research.

Radcliffe-Brown had accepted an appointment to the anthropology faculty at the University of Chicago. His five years at Sydney had been highly productive in advancing and recording knowledge of the aborigines, and he was ready to move on. After leaving Australia he attended the centenary meeting of the British Association for the Advancement of Science in London as president of the Anthropology Section. His address on "The Present Position of Anthropological Studies" presented his ideas of "the newer anthropology," raising important theoretical issues under the designation Comparative Sociology.

After meeting Lloyd, I became interested in anthropology and took courses in the evening at Columbia, including an especially memorable one with Ruth Benedict, who came through to me as a special person, and in the summer of 1931 I had a course in South African tribes given by Radcliffe-Brown, on his way to the University of Chicago.

I had met Lloyd in 1929 in Paris. I had gone there to take a temporary job at the Rockefeller Foundation with Charles Merriam, chairman of the Political Science Department at the University of Chicago, where I had been studying and working. In Paris I met the assistant fellowship secretary, Mary Charles Cole, who very kindly helped me get a room with her French family. When she returned to New York in the fall I decided to return with her. Administration of the fellowship program had been transferred to the Social Science Research Council (SSRC), which Merriam and Beardsley Ruml had helped to found, so Mary Charles's work would be there; and she helped me get a job with Robert S. Lynd, the executive director. The SSRC, wanting its staff to continue studies in the social sciences, let me have time to take courses at Columbia and attend Radcliffe-Brown's lectures. Frances Farmer Stevens came with me. There I met Margaret Mead and her husband, Reo Fortune, for the first time. The Columbia experience made me feel that I was wasting time working in New York and that I should return to the University of Chicago for my degree. With the help of the SSRC I obtained a tuition scholarship; and I also began to work for Merriam, editing his report for Recent Social Trends, the project sponsored by President Hoover. I was taking courses from Radcliffe-Brown and others in anthropology. I had to begin at the beginning since I had changed my major from economics.

I saw Lloyd when he came out for research sessions at Western Electric. One visit was at holiday time when I had to remain on campus though the dorm was unheated, because I had taken a second job. Lloyd and Rex and I went downtown to a hotel to celebrate New Year's Eve. We enjoyed being together, though New Year's Eve, with all the forced gaiety of a public place, was not in general a pleasant occasion. Someone at a table adjoining decided in a loud voice that Radcliffe-Brown looked like John Barrymore and Lloyd like Lawrence Tibbett, a well-known baritone who was singing in Chicago at the time. This became increasingly offensive, and we left.

About a week later when Lloyd was due to return to Cambridge he became ill with a heavy cold. He was staying at the Stevens, a large commercial hotel downtown, and commuting to Cicero. I visited him and—perhaps he was so ill that he had no defenses—he proposed to me. My plans obviously had not included marriage, nor had his. But, without realizing it, we had been falling in love, and suddenly it was there. Ever practical, I thought we should wait and consider. Lloyd would be returning to Ireland the next summer and by fall I would have my degree, so I suggested that we wait until his return. But he said no, that inevitably events we could not anticipate nor control would interfere, and we would probably never marry. Through our thirty-eight years together I learned that his decisions and judgments were usually right.

My sister and Hal Wright from Western Electric attended us at a civil ceremony before a judge, and Rex joined us later for a festive little supper at an Italian restaurant where we could have wine served in coffee cups. Two days later Lloyd had to return to Cambridge.

It was difficult for me to settle down to studies. Donald Slesinger and his wife, with whom we had had cocktails New Year's Eve, reminded me that I now had a handsome husband who was being pursued, undoubtedly, by every woman in Boston. Donald had been brought to the university by Hutchins in the fall of 1929 and became the secretary of the University of Chicago branch of the SSRC. My professor of statistics looked at me sternly and said, "Young woman, what are you doing here? You are now a married woman and your place is with your husband." They did not have to try very hard to be persuasive. I phoned Lloyd that I had decided to come East. He was comfortably settled at the Faculty Club, so this change in plans meant finding a place to live. Dorothea Mayo helped, and I arrived to a comfortable little furnished apartment, filled with stephanotis, a symbol of Dorothea's thoughtfulness and kindness, a flower whose scent will have lovely associations forever.

Carleton Coon's wife, Mary, wrote to me after Lloyd's death recalling my arrival in Cambridge and being looked over critically by the anthropologists. Would they accept me? I was aware of this and Lloyd's concern that I try to "fit in." Midge had found Cambridge terribly parochial, on her short visit, and could not accept the way of life possible there on an instructor's salary. Frances and Kitch Jordan, Helen and Talcott Parsons, the Hootons, the Mayos, Carl and Mary Coon, and many others gave me a warm welcome. I was called upon by more distantly connected faculty wives, each leaving the conventional card for herself and two for her husband. Most of these were calls that I was not expected to return.

I had not given up on the degree and started classes at Radcliffe, including a memorable course from the philosopher Alfred North Whitehead and a course in anthropology from Alfred Tozzer. I did not realize that Lloyd was a bit nervous about what my academic performance might be. Liddy Davis and I went to Tozzer's course and became close friends. Her husband, Allison, with an A. B. from Williams, had come to Harvard as a graduate student in English, been attracted to Lloyd's work, and changed fields. Through them we met many of the interesting and able Negro students, including Sterling Brown, the poet, and Ralph Bunche.

Tozzer lectured from a card file in which he inserted excerpts from current reading; whenever he had to make a reference to sex he twisted his feet around the legs of the chair, looked up into the corner of the room, and said it, Sex—which seemed very funny, a welcome bit of levity in what seemed like a cut-and-dried course. So close did Liddy and I become that she even dreamed our baby before I was sure I might be pregnant. When Lloyd and I married we knew we wanted a family and, since he was thirty-four, wanted to start having children as soon as we were quite sure we had a good marriage.

We often had students in for tea, which gave me the opportunity to meet the young men working on the Newburyport research. I well remember one day when Dorothea Mayo introduced me to the Gardner Museum; I returned at tea time filled with Dorothea's complaints about the museum as well as her appreciations, and when I talked about the offense of placing quattrocento beside cinquecento and more of Dorothea's observations—which I of course was mouthing, with little understanding—Lloyd howled. He had no use for phony performances, false representations, or rationalizations.

Through the years Lloyd and I realized that in some ways we were not a good influence on each other; we were both achievers—I with a strong work ethic in which each day had to be productive and Lloyd highly motivated to push on with an urgency to accomplish what he had set out to do. It perhaps would have been better if one of us had been a little lazy. But Lloyd was also a project worker and knew the pleasure of taking time to relax. He had for a long time played golf with the Hootons, and we spent many evenings with them as well, Mary and I having personal, domestic conversations while she worked on a jigsaw puzzle she usually had around and I knitted—Lloyd and Earnest involved in professional matters or politics. Both Mary and Earnest were addicted to mystery and detective stories, as was Lloyd. A bookstore near Harvard Square had an excellent rental library with all the best sellers and supplied Mary's puzzles. It was also a favorite of Elton's—near the Brattle Inn where he so often stayed and across the street from his favorite place for tea. He always said that tea was the only mental stimulant.

Soon we were preparing to leave for Ireland. The Rockefeller Foundation, with its concern for vanishing races and disappearing cultures, asked Lloyd through Elton Mayo to stop in Paris to consult with Marcel Mauss, Durkheim's nephew, and other sociologists and anthropologists of the French school about a program that could be carried on worldwide to include the study of peoples whose cultures were most threatened. Foundation personnel had conferred with Radcliffe-Brown during his summer in New York, regarding his opinion of the work being done in the fields of anthropology and sociology in various countries and the ability of scientists working in each field. Radcliffe-Brown ranked sociology in France very high, still running on the momentum imparted by Durkheim, with Mauss first-rate though not well known because he had not published. Radcliffe-Brown approved the union of social anthropology and sociology in France and was glad to observe that resistance to the separation of the fields in the United States was being felt among the younger students. In his opinion the Institute d'Ethnologie de Paris was well organized for anthropological and sociological research but lacked effective leadership.

Lloyd interviewed the key anthropologists and sociologists in Paris and made a verbal report to Elton Mayo and Edmund Day at the Rockefeller Foundation toward the end of the year. After studying the total project and its ramifications, he made a detailed report with recommendations regarding areas of study, leadership by country and personnel, administration, and financing.

The week in Paris was, in a way, a delayed honeymoon and a nostalgic return to the place where we had met. Dinners at our favorite restaurants, especially the Pre Catelan in the Bois, where they had a good orchestra—Lloyd danced beautifully—so well, in fact, that others would stop to watch us. Frances Stevens had recommended the Hotel du Quai Voltaire, across the river from the Louvre. We loved the views, the traffic on the river, watching goings on around the bookstalls, and crossing the river in the morning to walk through the Tuileries to the Café de la Paix for croissants and coffee. Not until Krak wrote her book about her life with Kroeber did I learn that they had also stayed there, liking it enough to return as we did. We were there for Bastille Day, July 14, and joined in the street fairs, dancing in the streets, and big and little celebrations including great fireworks displays among the fountains at Versailles.

We joined the Mayos in London, staying in a pleasant but rather stuffy hotel they had selected in the West End. Elton was not only brilliant and highly perceptive, but a charming, witty, gay companion. Not very tall and completely bald, one might think he would not appear as an impressive figure. On the contrary, every place we went he was recognized as someone who should receive special attention from the maitre d' on down. He was knowledgeable about food and wines and knew the best restaurants. I learned more about wines from him than in all the time I lived in Paris—a knowledge that both Lloyd and I had the opportunity to enjoy when prohibition was lifted in this country. Even in our stuffy hotel where only a great array of condiments made the food edible, meals were better when Elton was present. It was essentially a residential hotel, and two of the permanent guests—their table adjoining ours—were Radclyffe Hall and her current companion, Lady somebody. *The Well of Loneliness*, the first book, I believe, that treated Lesbianism, had recently been published. A sensation, she dressed to an extreme degree in heavy tweed suits, mannish hats and shoes, in the general manner of the English countrywoman but with a clear statement of her sexual orientation.

We were invited to the DeChairs' country place. They were obviously fond of Lloyd, happy to see him so well, and delighted with our expected child. Lady DeChair gave us a wedding gift of an antique Roman pitcher and a gift of Venetian glass for the baby. We were pleased at the time but not when we encountered U.S. customs.

One Sunday evening we were walking down Haymarket to Piccadilly Circus, feeling a bit out of it because the crowd was very gay though all of the pubs were closed and we were wondering where they were getting drinks. Suddenly we thought of Frances and Steve's farewell gift as we left New York. We had visited a number of Steve's favorite speakeasies and found them recently raided, smashed, closed—all but one. And there Steve bought us a bottle of Kentucky bourbon as a sailing present—ridiculous since we were taking a Cunard ship. We had to smuggle it past British customs, feeling that the wiser thing would have been to toss it overboard, but what an ungrateful act. So here we were in London, drinking a toast to Frances and Steve with our American bourbon.

Lloyd had dinner with Julian Huxley and J.B.S. Haldane—fascinating conversation but an uncomfortable social situation. Huxley was a light, rather fussy eater whereas Haldane was something of a gourmandizer who could not bear to see the food on Huxley's plate being carried off. "I say, old man, if you are not going to eat that would you mind? — " and he would eat what remained, to Huxley's discomfort and embarrassment.

We visited Aletta Lewis and her new husband, Denis Dunlop, a sculptor of recognized talent. They had a little flat decorated in Aletta's favorite color combination of raspberry red and pink. Aletta, a direct, no-nonsense sort of person and Denis, gentle, a bit dreamy, beautifully complemented each other. Lloyd, very fond of Aletta, was pleased she had married such a nice person and a gifted sculptor.

Lloyd went on to Ireland for several weeks to regenerate his contacts of the previous year, to meet Conrad Arensberg, who had been part of the Newburyport research and would remain in Ireland during the coming year, and to select a hotel. He wanted to be sure that the hotel would serve a proper diet for me with citrus fruit and other essentials.

While he was away Elton had surgery for glaucoma. His anxiety had been very high; he looked forward to relief from pain, but the thought of an eye lying out on his cheek really troubled him, indeed troubled all of us. Poor Dorothea. She was rather an intense, involved person, sensitive, inclined to what she called nervy, and this was a difficult period. She had to think of their two young daughters who were in school in England — Patty, the elder, in Beadales in Kent, a modern co-educational school, and Ruth in a conventional English grammar school. The Mayos had tried having the children with them in the states but could not adjust to American ways; like colonials, they wanted for their children the standards represented by the motherland. So, although it meant long periods of separation when Dorothea would be in England and Elton in Cambridge at the Brattle Inn, they had reached the decision that the children could not remain in the United States.

Dorothea and I also had lovely distractions — a trip up the Thames to Hampton Court, where she especially wanted me to see the herbaceous border, a tour of famous London homes and gardens, and visits to the National Gallery and the Tate. Her interest in art and architecture was very keen.

Shortly after Lloyd's return we took off for Ireland, staying at the Shelburne in Dublin a few days before leaving for the West Coast.

As soon as we landed in Ireland Lloyd's speech took on the cadence of the Irish inflection, and he never failed to cross himself when passing a church. But he had learned during his first trip that, if we were to be accepted, we had to make it clear from the beginning that we were not Irish Americans. Their return was often an unfortunate experience. They came back filled with good Irish sentimentality to see the old family place and their relatives, totally unprepared for the poverty they often found, the earthen floors, the animals in and out of the cottages, the seeming lack of ability to cope. Often their accumulated security and new way of life made them lord it over their relatives; their shock they ill concealed as well as their impatience with what appeared to them lack of ambition and a willingness to accept what seemed a rural slum way of life. They could not realize that what they found had not changed. The symbol of the returned Irish American was a new pearl-gray fedora. It was culture shock on both sides, and one had to feel compassion for both—difficult because the Irish Americans seemed so arrogant and lacking in understanding. We had to remind ourselves of the trauma when they found reality, not their dreams.

On our way from Dublin to Ennis we went through the fertile fields of Meath, the horse and cattle breeding country, and stopped in West Meath to visit Hallam Movius and Hugh Hencken at their archaeological site. The archaeological fieldwork, begun in 1932, continued until 1936 under the general direction of Hugh Hencken with Hallam, a Ph. D. candidate at Harvard, in charge of Stone Age periods and Hencken, the later periods. The work was financed in part by the governments of Eire and Northern Ireland, where five of the six Stone Age sites were excavated. The American Council of Learned Societies, the American Philosophical Society, the Milton Fund, and the Division of Anthropology of Harvard (with funds from the Rockefeller Foundation), as well as some individuals, contributed financial support. Results of the research were published as *The Irish Stone Age*[2] by Hallam L. Movius, Jr., in 1942, based on his Ph. D. thesis.

Hallam had at this time become assistant curator of palaeolithic archaeology at Harvard. A number of articles in professional journals in this country and Ireland were written by Hugh O'Neill Hencken or by Hugh in collaboration with Hallam, in the period from 1933 to 1935. Assisting in fieldwork were Amory Goddard and F. L. W. Richardson, Jr., both of Harvard, and later, in 1935, Hallam's bride. Materials excavated were given to museums in northern and southern Ireland.

The site we visited was the excavation of a crannog, a semisubmerged structure built in the middle of a lake. Ireland has a kind of bowl shape, edged with low mountains that cause the rain to fall on the lowlands beyond. The lowland areas, if not too wet, are fertile grazing and cropland now. In ancient days, where lakes were formed or could be dug out, crannogs were built on artificial or natural islands, using the surrounding water for protection. Sometimes access was achieved through a guarded tunnel. Usually they were dwellings for single families. Like the ringforts they were built of wood, with wood or thatched roofs.

Hallam had just returned from a dig in Palestine in dry, hot, hard desert rock. Here the project was in complete contrast. The watery site had to be pumped regularly. Walls dividing rooms had been exposed; on their slithery tops we could walk within the site. Timbers disintegrated soon after exposure to air, though they had remained in fair condition under water through many years, and had to be treated with special preservatives. Their most exciting find was an ancient bronze lamp. Another expedition had found a burial chamber in Meath 4000 years old. Ireland was rich in copper and gold but had no iron ore, a serious deficiency in the Iron Age.

The warmth of the Gulf Stream encountering arctic air (Ireland is the same latitude as Labrador) causes almost constant precipitation. But as we moved west, the lush green fields gave way to bog and rocky country that made cultivation difficult, though when the rocks were cleared the limestone soil produced good grass, fine grazing country.

Our headquarters were in the Queens Hotel where Lloyd had engaged rooms for Conrad (Connie) Arensberg and for us, with an extra room to serve as an office. Since the Queens was a favorite of the county people we expected that the food would be quite good. Lloyd usually had three boiled eggs for breakfast, which always set the waitress into giggles—*three* boiled eggs!—she was such a darling we wanted to keep her with us. Midday dinner was usually oxtail soup, often served with flies, boiled beef, ham, or chicken, cabbage or vegetable marrow, potatoes, and some kind of sweet. Supper was usually a cold meal of whatever we had had for lunch. Sometimes the headwaiter would tell Lloyd that the butcher down the street had slaughtered a sheep so he could have a mutton chop, but often it was already spoiled because there was no refrigeration. The meat market had louvered iron doors which were opened during the day. When an animal was slaughtered it would hang at the front of the shop for several days; as it was dressed and sold the head would be thrown toward the rear, and the remains of the carcass disposed of. The weekly market was held in the center of town, the animals being driven in. Droppings, mixed with the mud, made a lively breeding place for flies; there were no screens, so sleep was impossible after daylight. One day I made the mistake of pursuing a kitten into the kitchen and saw the scones prepared for tea, laid out for baking, black with flies. Lloyd told me that I should have had better sense than to go into the kitchen.

Most fruit was imported, expensive, and sold in the confectioner's shops—a little paper plate with three plums making part of the window display. Because of the inadequacy of the diet, we both developed a craving for chocolate; that with the whole milk and crackers which were sent up to me at bedtime when it was learned I was pregnant made a very fattening diet. My pregnancy was soon quite obvious, which rather endeared me to the townspeople—I was one of them—the function of the ubiquitous black shawl was apparent.

Lloyd had overheard a street-corner conversation in which the participants wondered why the birth rate of the Irish dropped when they went to the United States. Was it diet, climate, something incompatible in the way of life? Birth rate is reduced in Ireland by late marriage. In spite of long courtships there are few births outside of marriage.

Connie studied the market, and I did the simple statistical work on his reports. Butter, hand-churned by the woman of the household, was sold in small wooden tubs called firkins. Eggs were the source of the farm wife's spending money. There were a number of varieties of potatoes, each with its own special quality, cabbages, vegetable marrow with hard skins that would protect them through the winter—like the English, they grew everything to its maximum. A good researcher, Connie joined in the customs of the country and had drinks with the men, beginning when they arrived at market and carrying on from there, which made it difficult to be a participant observer. He often treated and learned, almost too late, that it was the custom for the person buying the first drink to buy the last. He had unwittingly been prolonging sessions at the bar.

The parish priest was a big man, young, jovial, much loved by his congregation. He took Lloyd around the parish, introducing him, and making for us most effective contacts. He also took us to the mother superior of the local convent, who invited us to morning tea, took us to a classroom to observe the teaching, and then dismissed school in our honor. As we moved through the convent buildings and inner court we were struck by the work hierarchy among the nuns, some doing only the hardest physical chores, their habits to match, and others the office work and teaching. Lloyd was sufficiently knowledgeable of church ritual to be at ease in this and similar contexts.

Misty weather made the countryside brilliantly green. We often took walks in the evening, when the light was soft, for a long time past the dinner hour. It was easy to understand the belief in little folk, leprechauns, banshees—in the misty halflight one could see almost anything—and think what a day of nipping would do for the imagination! One evening a young ass was standing at the wooden gate of a field watching us pass. Enormous eyes and a soft heavy tuft of fur between his long ears, bent toward us in curiosity, made him a most engaging creature—we walked over to talk to him and rub his furry thatch; as we left he followed us on his side of the fence until it turned. He was straight out of James Stephens' *Pot of Gold*.

Folk beliefs in fairies and little folk are powerful in the daily lives of the country people. Butter is an important staple; it is the medium by which dairy products are marketed. A witch caused a herd's milk to turn bad. One farm wife could not make the butter come in the churn because someone had stolen the dead hand she customarily dipped into the milk. Throwing dishwater across the fairy path around the house could bring a series of disasters. Like the Australian aborigines, the Irish country people had supernatural explanations for all untoward occurrences.

The previous summer Lloyd had made contact with Patrick Meghen, of the Irish Civil Service, assigned to Ennis as special administrator to supervise fiscal affairs, which the local politicians had put in a somewhat chaotic state. Paddy was not only a delightful companion but an able politician and first-rate informant. Through him we made a great variety of contacts. A nurse at the county mental institution invited us to visit it with her. Ireland had a low crime rate and a high rate of mental illness. The shocker was that this particular institution made no effort at therapy—the patients were clothed, housed, and fed. Great quantities of cabbage and potatoes were being prepared as we toured the kitchen. In these respects the patients were kept alive. Most of those we saw were in a large room, in wooden chairs along the wall; some more ill were seated around a table in the center of the room, each chained by the ankle to the floor. Many were hallucinating and in almost every instance the theme was religious, some fantasying that they were Christ. The violent cases, and epilepsy was so defined, were in individual rooms. Those we saw were in bed, where some were secured. Lloyd alone saw the more severe cases.

The nurse lived on the grounds, which were spacious and well cared for. The superintendent and his family also had their home within the walls. The nurse was tough, in the sense of being able to take almost anything, and very competent. It was a family tradition. Her brothers had all fought in the Trouble that followed the Easter Rebellion and were all members of the Irish Republican Army. She recounted events that had occurred in the time of the Trouble—shoot-outs with the Black and Tans, torture often used to try to wring information from a Loyalist: fingernails pulled out, nails driven under fingernails, and worse. We met some who could show us the evidence.

The Irish love a fight and seem never to lose their sense of humor. St. John's Castle near the River Shannon was a Republican stronghold. They were expecting an armored car and had sent three of their men to bring it in. As they awaited the return, rifles at the ready to protect its arrival, they saw the car approach, but it opened fire on them. As they began to return the fire—it could only be that the enemy had captured the car—they heard the cry, "Don't fire, we're yours, it's a bloody joke."

In doing research in Ireland one learns the country's history. It has been overrun, invaded, occupied, the people disenfranchised, torn by civil war. The Spanish were followed by Gaelic Celts around 350 B.C. Christianity began with St. Patrick in 432, marking the beginning of intellectual development and ecclesiastical learning, since the monasteries were the centers that attracted students from the continent and from which teachers traveled with illuminated manuscripts, spreading learning. This,

Hugh Hencken, Mildred Warner, W. Lloyd Warner,
and Hallam Movius in Ireland, 1932

*Elton Mayo and Fritz Roethlisberger at the
Harvard Business School, ca. 1940*

the Golden Age, is the period the Irish like to recall. Repeatedly we heard, "Why can't Ireland reclaim this as its traditional role in the world? Why can't we once again be the center of learning rather than continue the futile, frustrating attempts to compete industrially, meanwhile serving as the breadbasket for England?" De Valera tried to recapture this spirit in the program to return to Gaelic—Gaeltacht—as the national language. But it is spoken in only a few counties: Galway, Mayo, Roscommon, Sligo, and Leitrim, which compose the province of Connaught. Schoolteachers staying at the hotel in Ennis were learning Gaelic to meet the government requirement. It was an emotional focus for unity but otherwise regressive.

The Norse invaded at the height of development of art and literature. They came to raid, not settle, except in the coastal towns that they named Dublin, Wexford, Waterford, Limerick, Galway.

The Anglo-Norman invasion of 1170 marked the beginning of occupation and subjugation, which many Irish feel has not yet ended. Hatred of the English in the southern twenty-six counties, it seems, will never end. It was the Norman King Henry II, having been granted permission to move into "irreligious" Ireland, who divided the landholdings among his land-hungry earls and knights and among a few of the Irish provincial kings who agreed to pay tribute to England. Intermarriage with the Irish was interdicted. But with Henry VIII, the religious war erupted, and in 1649 Cromwell, the stern Protestant leader, brought an army that killed and ravaged, sending 20,000 Irish soldiers into exile in France and Spain and shipping several thousand men, women, and children to the West Indies as slaves. The Irish landowners and tenants remaining east and south of the Shannon, the area of fertile plains, were forced west to the rocky land along the coast. "To Hell or Connaught" is still a classic expression of desperation.

Under William of Orange came the second forced exodus of Irish soldiers—"The Flight of the Wild Geese." In effect every Catholic was treated as an enemy outlaw, his possessions confiscated, and barred from holding civil office, teaching, or practicing law. The Catholic Irish responded to the penal laws with violence, guerilla warfare, lynching, killing sheep and cattle, raping, and kidnapping. In the northern counties the Scotch-Irish Presbyterians, resisting restrictions on industry and tithes, escaped to America; this eighteenth-century migration was the first to America.

The English statesman Edmund Burke described the Penal Law as "a machine . . . as well fitted for the oppression, impoverishment and degradation of a people and debasement in them of human nature itself, as ever proceeded from the perverted ingenuity of man." Daniel O'Connell, the Irish hero, won the fight for his people's legislative emancipation, standing for the House of Commons in County Clare in defiance of the laws. He could not take the seat he won, but the strength of the vote forced Britain to grant almost complete recognition of Catholic rights a year later.

Home Rule, proposed by the British Parliament for a unified Ireland with a representative parliament, was opposed in the north because of fear of domination by the twenty-six counties of the south (Home Rule = Rome Rule) where the Irish Republican Brotherhood and the Sinn Fein (Ourselves Alone) were organized for an uprising to gain independence. In the famous Easter Rebellion of 1916, suppressed by the British, De Valera was one of the leaders. The new government that ultimately emerged failed to win over the six Ulster provinces and also failed to win the support of Sinn Fein or the Irish Republican Army, which went underground and is illegal to this day in both north and south Ireland. De Valera became president. "No longer will it be taken for granted that Ireland's children, like her cattle, should be raised for export."

Meanwhile in Ulster there was savage violence, Protestants beating Catholics and attacking their neighborhoods, forcing thousands to flee south. Had they all left there still would be no peace because of the deep desire of so many southern Irish for a united Ireland.

The Irish are avid historians. Many are more familiar with the history of the United States than most Americans. A lively interest is shown in the heroes of Irish history from Brian Boru to Michael Collins, whose picture is found in most cottages along with a small shrine to the Blessed Virgin.

At the time of the Harvard research the country was still going through a social revolution. In the movement of small landholders and tenants to the west, under Cromwell, each had been given a limited holding of poor land. But none of the holdings could support a family under customary methods of agriculture. Potatoes were the most productive crop and could be used to nourish the family and a pig or two, supplemented by the produce from a garden patch, eggs from a few hens, milk from one or two cows, and some grain, the straw from which was used to thatch roofs. Number of cows was a very important consideration in the size of the dowry. A farm was known as a place of so many cows, a reckoning going back to the old Law of Status or Franchise, which distinguished no less than six grades of cow-lord in determining a farmer's wealth. It is sometimes said that the potato blight that struck first in 1846 was probably caused by overplanting, with no rotation or fallow years. The famine of 1846 to 1851 killed 1.5 million people and forced another million to migrate. The large landowners had trouble collecting rents from impoverished tenants, forced to sell their wheat and oats or be evicted. During this time enough food was raised in Ireland to feed everyone, but the large landowners exported beef, pork, lamb, and grain for income. The British, it seemed, really did not know how to cope with the emergency;

very late they bought American grain to distribute and started soup kitchens and food dispensing centers. But the Irish felt that Britain had not helped earlier because they were exploiting the famine to continue the system that Cromwell had started.

Under De Valera large landholdings were divided and distributed among the peasants according to the number of sons in the family. In the social system preceding Cromwell, a farm was divided among the sons whose marriages would then be the source of dowries for their sisters. In Clare and other counties along the coast the holdings had become so small, only one son—not necessarily the eldest—inherited a farm, another might go into the priesthood, one take training to become an accountant or even a barrister, and another migrate. Some of the daughters who did not marry went into the church as nuns, some migrated, and some became teachers. The redistribution of the land was accomplished in an orderly fashion by the Irish Land Commission: the government obtained three appraisals and paid the owner the averaged price, allowing him to keep his home and some acreage. After the land was divided it was often sold to the former tenants.

Daniel Coglan, the land commissioner for the district, lived at the Queens and was most cooperative in disclosing information on general procedures and specific cases, how appraisals of fair market value were reached, negotiations conducted with the owner, determinations made of which would be the best qualified family to have a chance to make a purchase and in what amount. It was a complex process involving emotional as well as economic factors; it seemed to us that the government was at least trying to proceed in an orderly, fair, and expeditious manner.

Experts say that to prosper an Irish farmer needs at least forty-five acres of good land; but 150,000 of the country's 235,000 farms had less than thirty acres each. Twenty-five acres was considered an economic holding in the redistribution, with smaller holdings along the coast where fishing could supplement crops. There harvesting was done by sickle, each handful of wheat or oats carefully laid on the ground to dry. The small acreage was divided by stone walls into separate fields, hardly larger than the house. There were usually a few pigs, some geese and chickens, and a cow or two. Each family customarily had a right to cut peat at the common bog. It was usually a man's job, but we saw women in the peat bogs in the Connemara country north of Galway, one with long fair hair in dramatic contrast to the black of the peat. This area was settled at one time by Norse.

Probably no other island exploits the sea to a lesser degree than Ireland. The coastal dwellers and those who live on Aran Island have fragile fishing boats, curraghs, made of a light wood frame covered with hides that they can launch from the rocky shore and, returning, lift over the barrier and up to safety. The fleet off the west coast takes its catch to Dublin, whence it is distributed to towns like Ennis. In fact, the Irish do not enjoy fish. They are good Catholics and observed the Friday ban on meat, then still enforced, which perhaps is the reason for their resistance to fish. During the famine the fish from inland lakes would have been eaten, but the large landowners who controlled the lakes would not permit the tenants access. While we were in Ennis the government declared Hake Friday and made quite a thing of it. The hake was caught off the west coast and brought directly to Ennis. But this was less than successful and not repeated.

The Aran Islanders live a precarious existence on land and sea. Topsoil is brought from the mainland to improve the meager cover of native earth in order to make some crops possible. As to the sea, it is said that the designs of the Aran sweaters, often knitted by men, are family designs to make it easier to identify the bodies of the drowned. We often saw men from Aran in the town of Galway, come for supplies, dressed in their traditional wool knee-length skirts and sheepskin boots, skin side out, the wool hand-loomed, everything made by hand.

The large landowners were not only forcibly bought out; they were also shot out. We met Colonel O'Callaghan Westrupp, a lovely old gentleman who lived with his grown children in what had been a beautiful country Georgian home. Wallpaper was hanging in strips, the house had not been painted in years, all was in sad disrepair, yet a certain graciousness was maintained. The colonel agreed to share with Lloyd information he had collected through many years, so we went to his home with some frequency. He sent his son to drive us over. The roads were narrow, bordered closely with hedgerows, which are deceptive since the flowers and vines cover solid stone walls, and quite heavily trafficked with jaunting cars and side carts, pulled by a pony or small ass and moving slowly, and by pedestrians of course. The son, a student at Oxford and quite arrogant, showed his superiority to this rural population by driving fast and blowing the horn, which we found not only offensive but at times dangerous. We had to tell his father that we could not continue to come, which would be a deprivation, unless he could control his son's driving.

Our visits with the Colonel were always informative and enjoyable. As he talked I recorded the conversations in shorthand. He had a map of the county with a cross marking the home of each owner who had been shot out or burned out or who had left to avoid such an event. We visited what was left of the home of a cousin. The house had been designed by an Italian architect who had had glass imported from Italy for the conservatory and marble for the steps leading to an artificial lake. The colonel told us stories of dining there after a hunt, the refectory table so laden that a boy had to kneel under each end to help support the weight with his back.

Food was not only plentiful but in great variety, much of it imported from England and the continent—while many of the tenants were hungry. When the Trouble came the cousin was shot out, the house set afire, and a heavy object dragged down the marble steps to shatter them. Later the marble was cracked and incorporated with stone to build a new county road, a symbolic act, charged with the drama that the Irish love.

The Colonel had two daughters, both of whom had turned Catholic, which almost broke his heart. They were not married and lived at home. The old man enjoyed good food; he went to a bay on the coast for crabs, made his own liqueurs, had table vegetables other than cabbage, turnips, potatoes, and marrow planted in the garden. The daughters were scornful of these interests and reproached him for raising only store cattle while buying milk. They knew that he was losing money on the farm and enjoyed telling him that his tenants, if the farm were divided among them, would use it wisely and make a profit.

Language can be an issue as emotional as religion. For most in the Irish Free State Gaelic was almost a foreign language, so the official movement to use it was slowed to the pace of the population's capacity to absorb the change. While we were there, however, the adoption of Gaelic became a driving force, in itself, of the expression of freedom from England: no more English absentee landlords exploiting Irish land and people, riding over the peasants' fields on their fox hunts, no more Ireland bread-basket for England, producing beef, bacon, butter, and eggs—but never industrial products—for the English market. Connie Arensberg had facility with languages and quickly learned enough Gaelic to make it an important tool in the research.

In Ennis were several abandoned mills along the river. Efforts were made to start them up again and to develop new industries. We visited a cannery in Limerick that was processing fruit imported from Australia. And another that was canning the portions of hogs that were not smoked. This was quite a modern operation in some respects—the hogs were electrocuted, a method more humane and a lot neater than slitting their throats as in the Chicago stockyards. Bristles were removed electrically. Shoulders and hams were smoked, and the bellies were salted down to make "American bacon." Salt pork was the only pork product imported from the United States, and it seemed not to be known that we smoke our bacon too. Salt pork was used as side meat in cooking cabbage, the meat most frequently eaten in country households, just as it is among the poorer families of our South. Scraps of the pork were then put into cans to make a kind of head cheese—face meat, tongue, brains, etc., in what appeared a most haphazard fashion, and then processed.

As Lloyd went around the county with Father O'Malley and Paddy Meghen he learned something of how the peasants lived. The cottages had one story with a loft under the roof where the children slept. The roof was often thatched or slate, but corrugated metal was rapidly replacing this. In most areas the exterior walls were whitewashed; but in the towns rows of houses, with party walls, were of pastel colors, yellow, pink, pale blue. The central room in the house was the general living room with a fireplace where all of the cooking was done, a pot of tea kept warm at the side. Colonel O'Callaghan Westrupp was certain that the high rate of insanity was due to excessive tea drinking and had statistics to prove the correlation between the increase in importation of tea and the incidence of mental illness, which he claimed was due to the effect of tannic acid. This kitchen— living room had a table for eating, chairs that could be pulled up around the hearth, sometimes a settee, usually a dresser or sideboard for the best china, and a shrine. The West Room adjoining was, if possible, used as the parlor where all of the family treasures, photographs, and best furniture were kept; it was also the bedroom for the older couple. At the opposite side of the kitchen was another bedroom, possibly two, for the parents and older children.

The kitchen opened directly to the haggard, or farmyard, in the rear, an area enclosed by a stone wall, with sheds for farm equipment, chickens, geese, pigs, and a pony, or, for the more affluent, a horse. Turf was stacked near the kitchen door, and in the center was the hayrick. The floors of the farmhouses we saw were compacted earth; chickens often moved freely in and out.

A plot near the house was cultivated for vegetables: cabbage, the only green and non-root vegetable in the diet, turnips, and potatoes. Cutting, drying, and stacking of hay were often accomplished by the joint efforts of neighboring families because, in a climate so wet, time was critical. Potatoes were dug as needed.

Milking the cows, separating the milk in large shallow vessels, and churning the butter were the housewife's chores. Butter was basic in the diet and was also the only way the milk could be marketed. The farm wife also fed the chickens and pigs and gathered the eggs. Cows were pastured. Sheep were raised usually in rocky hilly country.

The marketing was the responsibility of the head of the house. The weekly market day in Ennis, as in most Irish market towns, was for the sale of butter and eggs, vegetables, poultry, and small animals — calves, pigs, kids, lambs. Market day was lively, the opportunity for socializing with one's neighbors, especially at the pubs, exchanging news, settling problems. Each farmer hoped to return home feeling that he had outwitted his buyers and made the best bargains. As the sons grew old enough they would accompany the father, but he was in charge and they learned by observation. Market day in Ennis was a busy time for the research as it offered excellent learning opportunities.

In Ennis lived various types of professionals, merchants and small shopkeepers, craftsmen, builders, railway and road workers, the more affluent having two-story homes usually on the edge of town. The front gardens were often filled with flowers that maintained their blooms for a long time because of the cool, damp air. These gardens were reminiscent of the typical English garden, joyful, their colors intensified by the green of the countryside and the gray air and skies.

The "county people" also used Ennis as a market center and might even have a barrister there. Often they stayed at the Queens Hotel. Larger, widely known cattle and horse markets were the source of the beef or store cattle, raised on grazing land, and hunting and show horses. Like the peasant, the county people used the jaunting cart, or side cart, and the trap, usually drawn by a horse.

We attended horse shows and large fairs—always gay and fun. One especially memorable one had a children's equestrian event where the smallest entry, a little boy on a pony, literally climbed the stone wall obstacle and scrambled up and away. The crowd roared with delight.

We also went to the coast to a famous watering place, Lahinch, to play golf. It was on a stretch of coast famous for its rugged beauty, the Cliffs of Mohr. The course was laid out on the bluffs, the waves crashing on the rocky coast below, the water hazards the sea itself as it came into inlets.

Sheep were used on all of the golf courses to crop the fairways; I distinguished myself that day by hitting one in the rump with what otherwise would have been one of my better shots. The poor beast charged off, but briefly. We had looked forward to this trip knowing that Lahinch was a place of spectacular beauty and the course exciting—we also hoped for a good meal. Instead of the usual boiled ham and chicken of the Queens, we had baked ham and roast chicken. Lack of refrigeration exerted a strong restraining influence on the flowering of culinary arts. This was all to change before our return many years later.

When we left Ireland in September, Connie Arensberg remained to carry on the research. He was joined the following spring by another Harvard graduate student, Solon Kimball, who remained until May 1934. Both had worked on the Newburyport research. Connie's first year in Ennis was financed by Harvard College with funds received from the Rockefeller Foundation under a program in which the foundation aided a group of universities in the United States that showed promising beginnings in work with vanishing cultures—not that Irish culture was so defined, but that was the goal of the program, which in a few years ceased to receive foundation support in that form. The Society of Fellows of Harvard financed the second year of Connie's fieldwork and also the period in which he and Sol collaborated in writing *Family and Community in Ireland*,[3] of which

Connie was the primary author. Sol was working on material on town and country relationships that he intended to publish as a companion volume. But his rapidly developing career interfered and then the war, so this work was included in the 1968 revised edition of the *Family and Community* book. Meanwhile, Connie's academic ability and achievements were recognized by an invitation in 1936 to become a junior fellow in the Society of Fellows and to give the A. Lawrence Lowell Lectures at Harvard, published as *The Irish Countryman*.[4]

Both volumes present the scope of their research, the helpful cooperation of the Irish farmers, townspeople, clergy (both Protestant and Catholic), and government people, especially Paddy Meghan. Through their intimate contacts with the people of Clare—often a lonely and austere life for two young students—they performed a research that produced unique insights into the family and social organization of Ireland beyond other studies and was a pioneer study of its type in Europe.

Sol had come in contact with Lloyd through a research seminar led by Hooton and Lloyd in which the students measured various ethnic groups in the Boston area for physical typing and also studied their social communities. Sol and Burleigh Gardner worked with the Greeks, and Sol then went on to an Italian settlement. Lloyd was much interested in Sol's recording his interviews in dialect and asked if he would like to join the Newburyport research. He describes his world up to this time as bleak; Lloyd was the first person at Harvard to take an interest in him: "This is one of the plights of the graduate student—if you don't have someone interested in you you are done for." So he was pleased to spend his extra time going to Newburyport, working first with the Italians and later with the Irish—which led to Ireland.

But no funds were available for Sol's expenses and stipend. Alfred Tozzer at this point became very helpful. He told Sol that every once in a while it was anthropology's turn to get a Sheldon Fund Traveling Fellowship, and he felt that that time had indeed arrived. So Sol was selected to receive one of the dozen or so fellowships awarded that year. The total stipend of $1,500 had to cover transportation and living expenses for thirteen months from April 1933 to May 1934.

The physical anthropology phase of the research was carried out by Wesley Dupertuis and an assistant under Hooton's direction. They collected measurements and observations of 10,000 adult males and 2,000 females from areas representing the entire island.

We were sad to leave. We sailed from Cobh after a pleasant visit with the United States vice-consul, who brought forth in our honor some Irish whiskey of liqueur quality, made in the private distillery of a local family and especially aged for them. As we were taken to the ship in a small lugger, we had the most enchanting view of this small harbor city, the houses climbing up the steep cliffside to a chapel. That was the last happy moment for me. As soon as we entered open sea we were hit by a storm that sent us reeling, the ship rising on immense waves, then crashing into the troughs. We had a beautiful stateroom on the foredeck and I enjoyed my first and last dinner. Lloyd—a hero—insisted upon taking his dinners with me; often for other meals he was the only person in the dining room. One reason I think was that the storm was upon us before anyone had his sea legs. When I could stand the room no longer I clung to a deck chair and enjoyed the relief of salt spray in my face and marveled at the small size of the fishing boats against that relentless sea.

As we approached New York we had a cable from Frances' husband, Bill Stevens, that he would meet us on board, that Frances was in Reno for a divorce. He was in despair, and there was little we could do to comfort him. Frances was a strong-willed person, and we had been aware that trouble was brewing because Steve really did not understand the independent spirit that was finally breaking free.

When we reached the pier a number of reporters were waiting to interview Lloyd, which left me to deal with customs, pulling out drawers of steamer trunks, trying to satisfy questions about the age of the antique copper pitcher that had been given us by the DeChairs and wishing that Lloyd were available to help me. The pitcher was at last allowed to come in as an antique, but it had provoked an exhaustive search of our luggage and probing questions about trivialities. I never liked that pitcher.

Notes to Chapter V

Historical sources: Timothy Patrick Coogan, *Ireland Since the Rising* (London: The Pall Mall Press, 1966); Liam de Paor, *Early Christian Ireland* (New York: Fredrick A. Praeger, 1958); Joe McCarthy, *Ireland* (New York: Time Life Books, new ed. 1970); Conor Cruise O'Brien, *States of Ireland* (New York: Pantheon Books, 1972); Patricia Bunning Stevens, *God Save Ireland, The Irish Conflict in the Twentieth Century* (New York: Macmillan, 1974); Leon and Jill Uris, *Ireland, A Terrible Beauty* (New York: Doubleday, 1975).

1. *Harvard Alumni Bulletin* 13:2 (1939).
2. Hallam L. Movius, Jr., *The Irish Stone Age* (Cambridge: Harvard University Press, 1942).
3. Conrad M. Arensberg and Solon T. Kimball, *Family and Community in Ireland* (Cambridge: Harvard University Press, 1940).
4. Conrad Arensberg, *The Irish Countryman* (New York: Macmillan Co., 1937).

Hale House, Old Newbury, ca. 1933

BEFORE LEAVING for Ireland Lloyd had looked for a house in New-buryport in anticipation of living there for a year upon our return in the fall. The house he most wanted was known as the Noyes House, built in 1646 for the parish minister of Old Newbury shortly after the town was settled. Its owner, Albert Hale, was in the direct line of descent from the original owner, had a home in Dedham, and lived in Newbury, adjoining Newburyport on the south and an integral part of the community, during the summers. He had half promised that we could have the house for a year. While in Ireland we received a letter confirming this and were de-lighted, then a cable came saying disregard the letter. Negotiations of this order continued through the summer, unresolved.

Upon our return to Cambridge we stayed with the Hootons while searching for a house in Newburyport. We looked at the High Street home of Sarah Mulliken, the aunt of Robert Mulliken, who was later to become a distinguished professor of physics at the University of Chicago and was a Nobel Prize winner in physics. It was a beautiful old foursquare house where Sarah had been taken as a bride at the turn of the century. Her husband had discarded all of the family antiques and refurnished the home in the Victorian style for his bride—birds and flowers under bell jars, horsehair sofa and chairs, a zinc bathtub, all depressing. We looked at the home of John Marquand's aunt and visited him at Curzon's Mill to discuss renting it. We were in the midst of negotiations when the Hales relented and offered us their house.

It was the traditional saltbox in design, with a small front entry from which narrow stairs reached the second floor. To the right was the dining room, windows on three sides, with a large fireplace opening. This room had originally been the kitchen–dining room. The fireplace was immense—people would come just to see the masonry as it was exposed in the basement area. The chimney originally had been four yards square. This structure formed the central core of the house, serving as the fireplace in the original kitchen, used for all types of cooking and baking, and the fireplaces in the living room and in the two bedrooms on the second floor. It was said that the siding was original; certainly the floorboards were: wide pine planks, random width, with large crevices between. A wing had been added in 1715, also two stories, and later a one-story kitchen in the L formed by the wing, and a barn out back. Most of the furniture was an-tique, of various periods, and there was quite a beautiful collection of an-tique pewter.

Mrs. Hale was president of the Newburyport Garden Club; this interest was expressed in the garden, which had a large bed at either side of a gazebo surrounded by bergamot and there was planting around the house. Unfortunately, they had decided only that year to mow the grass in the pear orchard, the sort of thing done now in the days of riding mowers. Mrs. Hale said that she would like to return later in the fall to "put my garden" to bed. She had a plat showing the location of each perennial and asked that in spring we replace those that had been winter killed with plants of the same variety. The Hales had one son, born rather late in life; she was thrilled at the prospect of a child's being born in their house and was kind and thoughtful in every way.

It was not until we moved in that we became aware that a furnace man and chore boy came with the house, in a way. We welcomed the help but worried about the expense. The chore boy was the first to go, but not until he had brought us a Manx kitten. Before we married we discovered that each of us liked cats, so I knew that Lloyd would be pleased with the kitten. But he had always delighted in the way cats carry their tails at times, straight up, and I wondered how he would like this charming tail-less wonder. Of course he adored her. Later when she came in heat and we had all of the neighboring Toms courting, he threw light bulbs at them or anything handy to run them off, to the amusement of our friends who wanted to know how he would act if he had a female offspring? She was a little cat who, even near the end of her pregnancy, had not learned *not* to climb trees, so Lloyd was often called to rescue her—he was the only one tall enough to do it—because it seemed that she would surely break a leg or go squash if she were to jump to the ground.

We were quite a distance from the center of town, but Lloyd enjoyed walking to the train. Eliot and Marnie Chapple had been in Newburyport a year—Eliot as field director of the research—and were well settled in a pleasant house across from the green in Newburyport. Marnie often came for me in their car to shop or I would walk to town on a path that paralleled High Street along the backs of the houses, the cemetery, and the church. I would gather all of my parcels at one store and call a taxi to go home. The driver usually brought Lloyd from the train at night and, as the birth date approached, said to Lloyd, "A woman has to go into the valley of death to bring forth life."

In a short time we had met a variety of people. The research had obviously engaged the interest of many, especially in relation to the kinds of information sought. Often three or four ladies would come together to call—in those days one always had tea—life, even in a research situation, was relaxed. This meant that I had three or four calls to return, and it was important that I do so with some promptness. Marnie often went with me; as we approached a house we found ourselves hoping that no one would be home so that we could leave our cards and go on, not the attitude of an effective participant observer. We began to make friends who warmed our social contacts. I still feel close to Amelia Little. She lived with her aunt, Miss Eliza, and her cousin Agnes in the home built for the family in 1649 at the end of Little's Lane. It was a tradition in the family that one female remain unmarried in each generation to look after the house and in general be responsible. Miss Eliza's brother, Henry Bailey Little, was president of a local bank, a leading figure in the community, and one of the people helpful in sponsoring Lloyd's project. He remained active in the bank until he was 102. Amelia and I enjoyed walks—their farm was not far from our house so we were quickly in the country. Amelia still tells me that she could never decide whether in her relationship with Lloyd, who became very fond of her and Miss Eliza too, she was a friend or a specimen. This was undoubtedly true of others as well.

Lloyd became friends with Paul Lunt, whose family were longtime Newburyporters. He and his brother inherited the family home, a traditional foursquare house on High Street, but Paul lived nearby in Rowley and Dan near Boston where he worked. Paul became interested in the research, then involved, and was of great help in making contacts for Lloyd throughout the community. We liked to kid him about his clamdigger relatives—the family had been there long enough to have Lunts up and down the line. We met his friends the Parrys, the widow of a founder of one of the shoe factories and her two sons, both married, with children. Norman and Marion did interior decorating, had an antique shop in the center of town that they ran in a somewhat cavalier fashion, and had a small house, beautifully furnished. Don and Lois had a large home, colonial in design but not old. Both Marion and Lois were excellent cooks, among the sources of my growing knowledge of cooking, for which Lloyd was grateful. Marnie Chapple helped me too.

Since I typed all of Lloyd's field notes, I had to have help in the house. Lois Parry's maid brought a friend from Boston who lived in and went to Boston every other week for two days. One night as we were dressing to go to the Parrys for dinner, Bernice started to laugh—in fact, she was convulsed—but would not tell us why. At dinner we discovered the answer: the main course was baked haddock, which was selling for about five cents a pound at that time. It was delicious, beautifully prepared, the service very formal. Lois had silver service for eighteen and liked to entertain at large dinners or at dinners on successive evenings so that she could use the same flowers and candles.

Norman and Marion were amusing and gay. For Norman's birthday, Lloyd, Paul, and I went on a special shopping trip, not to antique shops obviously, but to secondhand shops down along the waterfront. Because Norman liked to play our old piano, we bought him a pump organ for $2.50, sprayed it with cheap perfume, and then bought a statue of a diving bathing beauty to stand on it. We arranged with Marion to have the organ delivered, the statue placed on top. It was fun, but not for Mother Parry, who was sure the organ was full of mice, at the least, and asked that they get rid of it. Norman went along with the joke and made real music come out of that thing, I don't know how.

Ann was born at Anna Jacques Hospital in January, Paul helping to sustain Lloyd. The hospital had agreed that our doctor could come up from Cambridge, and the whole process was long and tiring—I was glad that Paul could keep Lloyd company. We were thrilled with Ann, she was so beautiful, quite incredible, really. Every time I thought of a small child running around the house I could hardly believe it. We had a wonderful nurse who was so impressed with my ignorance of babies that she developed a routine for me to follow rigidly, and this almost led to my undoing because I was afraid to depart from it. One morning when I was not feeling well I discovered that I could bathe the baby before lunch instead of before breakfast. Of course for the nurse baby care was a profession and a full-time job, and this was what she created for me.

With spring I had the garden too. Far too many perennials did not survive the winter, but petunias reseeded themselves in the two large beds and were beautiful—large blossoms, long heavy stems. Lloyd made lovely arrangements, but he preferred tall flowers like phlox and delphinium, which fortunately were flourishing. When Mrs. Hale visited she was appalled by the petunias, but I was grateful to have less weeding. I don't think she understood.

I had invited her to lunch. It was a pleasant visit except that Bernice, in her eagerness to have everything as nice as possible, had lighted an enormous fire in the ancient living room fireplace. From the dining room we could hear the roar and rushed in, Mrs. Hale calling for salt and bringing the fire under control. It seemed inevitable that such a near catastrophe would occur when Mrs. Hale was there. We had really worked to take care of that house, which was not always easy, and had an awesome love and respect for its antiquity.

I believe that in any marriage responsibilities are assumed by each person as the relationship develops—quite unconsciously, without explicit agreement. I took care of the house and garden, the general maintenance, accounts and other financial affairs. I had always felt that a woman could make the greatest contribution by making it possible for a man, if he had the ability and his work was of value, to be relieved of routine chores. This is the relationship Lloyd and I developed through the years. I think we were happiest when we were working together on a project, research or a book. He was very proud of me when I did something special in the house, or sewed, or entertained well. He was a marvelous host.

Before Ann was born we invited a number of friends from Cambridge and Boston for the New Year's holiday. Lloyd and Paul had found a bootlegger, of course, and we made our own gin—alcohol, glycerine, and, instead of juniper, the thin rind of lemon. What we did not realize was that while we were entertaining our friends in the front of the house, Bernice was entertaining her friends from Boston in the back. It must have been a hilarious party altogether. Paul's aunt lived across the street and undoubtedly had much to report. I had been in the dining room one day and had a feeling of being observed, as indeed I was, with a spyglass. We passed the word to Paul, who communicated it quite effectively. During the party, I leaned on the back of one of a pair of loveseats that flanked the fireplace in the living room, and down it went. Since Ann's birth was imminent, everyone had great concern, but my concern was for the furniture. When we removed the slipcover we found torn horsehair and the leg that had broken had been mended so many times it would not hold another nail. Lloyd's indignation was immense. We then examined the other loveseat and of course found the same. Actually there was not a comfortable piece of furniture; the beds were beautiful, four posters in the guest room and sleigh beds in our room with single springs and mattresses two inches thick. Many afternoons I went to the Chapples for the bliss of sitting in a comfortable chair.

The Hales had modernized the kitchen by replacing the cookstove with gas thereby removing a source of heat; the icebox leaked, leaving a pool of ice on the floor to greet us each winter morning, and the hot water heater had no controls; it had to be turned on and off as hot water was needed. One day we were in Cambridge when I remembered I had not turned off the heater and had to call the furnace man to take care of it before it blew up. We were spending the night with friends in Cambridge because we were to chaperone, for the first time, a dance at Kirkland House. It was an important dance so the dates were not "Cliffies" from Radcliffe but were from New York and more distance places. The faculty were given various hours to be on duty, and I had difficulty staying awake until the time assigned us. This really troubled me and made me even more uncomfortable when I realized that the people I was helping to chaperone were hardly younger than I, now a settled matron. The headmaster of Kirkland House and his wife, the Whitneys, were quite sophisticated and certainly not stuffy. They served drinks and a buffet at the master's lodging so that the faculty could have a pleasant retreat between stints at the dance; chaperoning thus became a pleasant social occasion with friends.

We had to let the furnace man go because of the cost. But one late night, returning from a dinner party in Cambridge, we found a cold house.

I went down to the basement through the trapdoors on the outside since the inside steps were treacherous and found the basement standing in water, which had put out the fire in both furnaces. So back came the furnace man who assured us that the basement flooded every spring—he had standby planks to prove it. We had to remember that the Hales did not use the house year round; for them it was a vacation house for summer use and would have been quite comfortable.

When the Hales decided to let us rent the house they asked that we let visitors come, most of whom would be direct or collateral descendants of the original Noyes family. Through the years they had kept a visitors' book. There were so many things of interest—the fireplace, a little window about a foot square in an upstairs bedroom which, it was said, was an opening for a musket to defend against Indians (there must be thousands of these reputed musket windows in this country), the gently sloping roof of the kitchen addition which had to be swept clean of snow or it would cave in, and the handmade, original H and L hinges.

In 1978, when I visited on a sentimental journey, primarily to see Amelia, I approached Old Newbury on Parker Street, passing the Noyes house—in our family lexicon, "Ann's house." It was painted and in good repair. I stopped and introduced myself to the new owners, who had been told about us and seemed pleased to meet me and show me what they had done. They had even discovered a fireplace in a wall they had stripped in a room adjoining the kitchen to turn that room into a kitchen and the kitchen into a playroom for their children and a laundry. The experience lifted my spirits. Actually the house should belong to a historical society, Newburyport, Massachusetts, or New England. Since Amelia can no longer drive we had a good time doing a grand tour visiting the renovated market area, which satisfies even Amelia's high standards, Curzon's Mill, the old Marquard house now owned by a cousin of John's, and Plum Island, which is now a national bird sanctuary.

The Caleb Cushing House on High Street, a fine example of the foursquare, three-story house of the Federal period, was bequeathed to the Newburyport Historical Society by Miss Margaret Cushing, its last resident, and is used as its headquarters. Most of these Federalist homes had been built during the period of fine architectural development, when Newburyport excelled in shipbuilding; the wealth was available as were the craftsmen and the architectural skill to design and create homes consistent with the rather elegant lifestyle of the period. Miss Margaret Cushing will long be remembered for her walk down High Street each Saturday night, bath towel over her arm, to the home of a friend who had a bathtub. Perhaps anyone else in town who had a home without indoor plumbing would have had to bring it into conformance with town ordinances, but not Miss Margaret. Moreover, she had reached the age where people are often abstracted from the social mores of their peers, of their society.

Homes on the high side of High Street have sites at the crest of a rise, with broad sloping lawns and extensive gardens. All had wine cellars and every indication of gracious living; all required large staffs. It was one of these homes that Mayor (Bossy) Gillis started to tear down to erect a gas station but was stopped. So he then festooned it with chamber pots and other deliberately offensive gadgetry, as Lloyd recounts in *The Living and the Dead*, the fifth and final volume of the Yankee City Series, in which he deals with symbol systems.

Few people have the money or the need, in our present world, for thirty rooms. However, most of the homes are in repair; many have been converted into apartments and, as such, are being maintained, the architectural amenities retained insofar as possible. Amelia knew exactly what had happened to each and whether the conversion had been well done. Many new owners and residents are from Boston, not a bad commute by car (the train no longer runs); many over an extended period and through investment of time, muscle, and money have been able to restore some of the homes to their original beauty. Although they do not have staffs to maintain them they are excited to live in such grandeur. And one can always close off a dozen or so rooms and still have space to wander.

Our house became the headquarters for the research, giving me the opportunity to know the students as they came to do their fieldwork. Each was given an area in which he or she seemed to have special ability, and some worked across a wider spectrum. I felt rather motherly towards them in spite of the fact that I was not much older than they, except Budd (Buford) Junker, the only undergraduate. His special area was the schools because the high school students could identify with him and speak more freely, and he became skilled in interviewing administrative people as well.

The object of the research was not only to obtain a functional study of an American community but also to train social anthropologists and sociologists in field method to enable them to have something more than a theoretical understanding of how to do self-directed field research. In anticipation of working in Newburyport, the researchers, almost all of whom were Harvard and Radcliffe graduate students, were given a course in reading the theoretical works of functional anthropologists—Radcliffe-Brown, Malinowski, Durkheim, Granet, Simmel, and others—to become thoroughly acquainted with the concepts on which the methods of the Newburyport research were based. It was hoped they would be innovative and evolve ideas about the work they were doing.

Furthermore, it had been decided that individuals working on the project would be carefully trained in interviewing techniques in order to obtain the more intimate type of information necessary to the study. This procedure would preclude the kind of information frequently obtained by questionnnaires, such as tables of statistics that can be used to prove almost anything but not reaching the underlying realities in a social situation. The interviewing techniques were those used by psychoanalysts, or the free association type, in order to get at the intimate thinking of the person interviewed. Training was done by Fritz Roethlisberger and Bill Dickson of the Western Electric research, using the procedures developed there.[1]

An original survey was made followed by two more, using all of the geographic, political, economic, historical, and social records available. These surveys furnished the background for the approach to the community's leaders to enlist for their cooperation and support. In Australia Lloyd had said that he had been sent by the old men of his people (the Rockefeller Foundation) to give validity to his work there, a reason that the Murngin could accept since their old men made the important decisions and were most respected. In Newburyport the research needed approval by the leaders of the community, whose opinions were respected and whose approval would open doors to organizations and individuals. Sometimes questions were raised as to why this research was going on and just what was expected from it. The information was used in cross-checking for validity of all information gathered. For example, one informant had said that there were no concentrations of particular ethnic groups, but the survey material showed that this was probably not true and led to the work that revealed where each ethnic group was located, how it was organized, the importance to it of the church, political participation, and educational and mobility patterns.

The research began with Lloyd as the director, whose salary came from his position on the Harvard faculty, the field director, Eliot Chapple, who was paid a modest salary from research funds, and two others, but that number quickly grew to ten or twelve, all part-time, of course, and all working without compensation but with expenses paid. Areas of research activity were assigned according to aptitude and in relation to the avenues of approach available or to be developed. For example, contacts were made with the superintendent of schools by a member of the research team familiar with the New England "school teaching mind" who continued working with the entire system, high school and grades. A young man with a special aptitude for languages was interested in the ethnic groups and assigned there. Ethnic groups were divided among four researchers — French Canadians, Greeks, Poles, and Russians in one segment; Italians in another; Jews; Negroes. An economics major was put in charge of the study of stores and banks. A student who had made excellent contacts in the assessor's office continued working there, collecting all the records for both real and personal property. He was trained to pick up political gossip that could be followed up in checking political movements, an especially important activity at the time because many of the city's underlying antagonisms centered around the mayor, the rather famous "Bossy" Gillis. From the assessor's records were collected name and address of persons owning property, location, value of machinery and stock in trade, value and description of livestock, description of real estate, assessed valuation, and aggregate value of all assessed property. This information was then organized according to geographical distribution.

Several forays were made outside the specific boundaries of the town. The little community of South Seabrook nearby in New Hampshire was studied because of its reputation as a broken-down Yankee community with reputed asocial behavior such as incest and homosexuality, in contrast to the fairly well-balanced and well-adjusted community of Newburyport, and because a number of Seabrookers worked in Newburyport's shoe factories. It was thought that it could furnish a check on the work being done in Newburyport, but the study was abandoned when it was realized that the lower stratum of Newburyporters were the same kind of people, organized in approximately the same way.

Negotiations were completed with the warden of the new state prison at Norfolk for a special investigation of the Newburyport inmates to learn what place they occupied in Newburyport and to discover, if possible, what elements in the individuals and in the community contributed to their incarceration and to their adaptation to prison life. One researcher spent a summer there. An added goal was to follow the inmates upon parole to observe the kind of adaptation they would make and their successes or failures.

Toward the end of the fieldwork a decision was made to interview a broad spectrum of individuals for information on budgets and family expenditures. Without the general support of the community leaders, gathering such confidential material would probably not have been possible. Even so, objection was made by some of the researchers that this kind of information would not be disclosed, certainly not in New England. But Lloyd was confident that the project would be successful, provided the fieldworkers used appropriate interviewing techniques, and this is the way the project turned out. Checks on information had to be devised for validity; because of the careful preparation of the fieldworker, there were built-in checks in interview procedures as well. Also, many residents felt a responsibility to the research and to the town. Access was gained to individuals considered unapproachable for this reason — they were motivated to disclose information to help the research develop an accurate account of their community. The usual verification techniques were followed.

More than two hundred associations of all types were found — among them secret societies, clubs, and fraternities — a large number for a community of 15,000. They required the attention of everyone in attending meetings and ceremonies and clipping notices. Data were gathered and analyzed on crime and court cases, delinquency, health, the family, family and group consumption, the relationship between the community and the surrounding rural area, the relation of the welfare organization to the community and its economic structure, and the role of the church. Each aspect of the community was studied in detail to avoid a biased view and to prevent superficial generalizations. For the functional method of research to operate in describing a community and placing each segment in its correct place in the general configuration, a general understanding must be achieved of attitudes, antagonisms, and solidarities of all of the people.

Dividing this variety of work among a number of people required an exchange of information for coordination of effort. This was one of the functions performed by Lloyd as director, primarily through general weekly conferences and other material. Criticism and comment were of benefit to all involved. An appraisal was made of work accomplished, and new tasks were delegated. The conferences served as a clearinghouse of information but also stimulated each participant to make his best effort, to keep his records organized and presentable. Lloyd had weekly or more frequent sessions with each member of the research team, analyzing his work or discussing a report about to be given to the general conference to be sure of its merit. In order to sustain the morale of the entire research group and maintain its confidence and interest in its work, the reports had to be of high quality.

Those with whom I still have contact from that period often talk about the excitement of participating in the discovery of knowledge through observation and participation, teamwork, recognition of work well done, and recognition of self as well. Many, when they learn who I am, want to talk about working with Lloyd, studying with him, how it turned their lives around and set them on a new course of achievement. Many feel that he recognized and nurtured abilities that had until then not been disclosed to them.

To organize the vast amount of data collected and not lose any of its significance, a device was developed of entering all information obtained on each individual on a "personality card" which ultimately would show all of his reciprocal relations. These cards were classified on a pragmatic and empirical basis; within the generalized study of the community, the personality cards would show the place of the different types of social personalities within the sociological structure. The goal was to have a personality card for every individual showing address, kin, activities and place within social groupings, occupation, amount earned, movements around the city, health statistics, and other relevant information. The purpose was to use these cards in working out the generalized study of the Newburyport community and the sociological structure and at the same time understanding the place of different types of social personality within the structure and, thereby, understanding the dynamics in the social behavior of Newburyport.

As the research progressed it was possible—and helpful in the thinking of the staff about analysis and work to be done—to develop summary reports of phases of the research as they were completed. It was Lloyd's feeling that in all of the structural and functional studies that had been made of various cultures by social anthropologists, there was always some fundamental substructure on which the rest of the society was constructed and elaborated. For example, in his study of the Triobriand Islanders of Melanesia, Malinowski found that the *kula,* a ritualized economic system, formed the backbone of the society. A. R. Radcliffe-Brown found among the Andaman Islanders that the local group, organized on an age-grade basis, was the underlying structure on which the society created its elaborate ritual and myth. Marcel Granet demonstrated that the Chinese patrilineal kinship groupings created the basic pattern of behavior upon which the complexities of Chinese civilization developed. In his own work among the Murngin in North Australia, Lloyd found that a knowledge of the kinship system was essential.

As the study of Newburyport began it appeared that economic factors were the prime determinants of social behavior. But as the mass of material was collected and analyzed the basic pattern that began to emerge was social stratification, with three main divisions of the society, upper, middle, and lower, each with subdivisions. The primary nature of stratification is subordination, superordination, and coordination, with all of the attendant mechanisms by which a group dominates, or is dominated by, another group, including the larger group. It was then possible to identify the characteristics which differentiated each class from another and later to identify each individual and organization in the community by class according to these characteristics. Furthermore, it was found that each of the three classes could be divided into two groupings identified as upper-upper, lower-upper, upper-middle, lower-middle, upper-lower, and lower-lower. For example, the lower class is divided into old Yankee stock and ethnic groups—Poles, Russians, Greeks, French Canadians, Italians, Jews, and Negroes. The Yankees, often called Seabrookers, were thought of as incestuous, homosexual, degraded, and asocial—attributes that were used by members of the lower-middle class to segregate those considered below them. The lower-lowers were laborers and clam diggers; upper-lowers were usually small store owners, particularly among the ethnic groups, and the higher paid laborers. There was considerable interest in kinship among the lower class in contrast to the middle class, probably because of the interest in social mobility among the latter whereas the lower class had no interest in climbing. Lloyd often said that the people in the lower-lower and upper-upper have this in common: neither is interested in social mobility because the former have no desire to climb and the latter have no place to go.

Another unexpected finding was the large number of associations for the size of the population. Social anthropologists have often used Melanesia and West Africa as outstanding examples of societies with heavy proliferation of associational structures, but no society studied up to the time of the Newburyport research had such a large number. Because of the emphasis, the research was interested in the functions performed by this type of social structure, to understand and interpret its functions and general principles of behavior in order to reveal, if possible, some of the underlying mechanisms and principles that generally control our social behavior. A general survey of the anthropological and sociological literature disclosed that W. H. R. Rivers, a pioneer in the field, said that in Melanesian society associations exist for the sake of existing;[2] R. Thurnwald, the German sociologist, observed "the building up of the social organization, particularly through a general recognized system of classes and the emergency of chieftains and kings, seems on the whole to bring about the decay of secret societies"; and, in contradiction to Thurnwald, George Simmel states[3] "as a general proposition, the secret society emerges everywhere as a correlate of despotism and of police control. It acts as a protection against the violent pressure of the central powers." Actually the contradiction can be explained by the fact that each had examined only a circumscribed area, had evolved a general theory from inadequate sampling. H. Webster, in *Primitive Secret Societies*,[4] attempts historical and psychological interpretations: "they arouse the universal sentiments of curiosity, fear and awe," and appeal to those seeking prestige.

To Lloyd, an attempt to interpret the function of a social structure in terms of the individual is fallacious since it is bringing in generalizations outside the social sciences to interpret material and is very like earlier attempts to apply findings of physicists and astronomers to social behavior. H. Schurtz, the distinguished German anthropologist working with primitive societies, declares that man is a social being and woman unsocial, centering her interest in the kin group that based its behavior upon sexual relations and reproduction, and that innate "masculine gregariousness" created the associations. He also added a theory of antagonism of older and younger generations creating age grading, a theory Lloyd accepted as one of the first real indications of a sociological interpretation of sociological facts. Camilla Wedgwood and Radcliffe-Brown both defined the association's function as an extension of the circle of social relations of the individual, which Lloyd felt was obviously true but true as well of all other social groupings.

None of these seemed to apply adequately to the Newburyport findings. In the research team's analysis of the function of the associations for the community, the hypothesis was developed that the function of an association is to integrate the larger inner structures of the society to the total community; that each larger structure, in its attempt to integrate itself to the total community, creates antagonisms for itself which must be organized; that the association helps resolve these antagonisms not only in the community for the larger structure (church, school, and so forth) but also in the structure for the community—it organizes and integrates them.

Some associations have membership from only one class, some crosscut the entire community (American Legion); and the latter thereby integrate all classes in their meetings and ceremonies and integrate the society with the spiritual community, the dead.

As a matter of good organization and in order to keep lines of commitment clear between the research and its sponsors and among the research people themselves, Lloyd felt that an agreement should be prepared and submitted, to be signed by himself as director, Eliot Chapple as field director, and Paul Lunt, who had been assuming increasing responsibilities. The number of proposed volumes reporting the research was reduced from eight to six, the final one to be a data book, which was later eliminated. The Natchez research was included since it would be current with the Newburyport work. Mary Gardner's name does not appear since she did not participate in the research until her marriage to Burleigh just before leaving for the South. Lloyd was careful to avoid emphasizing the contribution of one individual over another or to credit individuals with certain portions of the research. Not everyone was happy with this last point, but Lloyd felt strongly that the research was a team effort.

Surely only lack of experience with a publishing project of this magnitude could have led anyone to propose the original publication schedule. Of the five volumes published, the first four appeared between 1941 and 1947 and the last in 1959, the interval due to involvement with other researches and reports and to the development and maturation of concepts in symbolism with which the final volume was concerned.

Processing of data was begun, of course, while fieldwork was still being carried on. Two dictaphones were purchased for use in the Harvard office in reporting fieldwork by members of the research, and a secretary and stenographer were hired. Dorothy Moulton, Lloyd's very able secretary, was recruited part-time and is listed by George Lombard among personnel paid from funds of the Harvard Business School. It was very close to the depth of the depression when WPA and FERA had their inception, and the research was fortunate in qualifying for the use of personnel from these sources for the analysis, recording, organization, and collating of the vast amount of written material and punch cards generated in the fieldwork.

This work was carried on at Harvard and, later, at the University of Chicago when Lloyd joined the faculty there in 1935.

Fortunately, Professor George F. Lombard, of the Graduate School of Business Administration at Harvard (now retired), in 1975 was able to make contact with the person who had been comptroller at the Business School during the period of the Newburyport research and writing. She very kindly offered to look up the files and gave Professor Lombard a detailed record that he sent to me together with the following summary of total expenditures:

1930–31	$4,400
1931–32	6,900
1932–33	8,150
1933–34	10,200
1934–35	11,550
1935–36	6,500
1936–37	3,100
1937–38	2,200

The detailed report includes the names of all persons in both Newburyport and Deep South research and the years in which they were active either at Harvard during Lloyd's tenure there or later at the University of Chicago. WPA and FERA grants were administered by the Business School.

Notes to Chapter VI

1. William J. Dickson and F. J. Roethlisberger, *Management and the Worker* (Cambridge: Harvard University Press, 1939); F. J. Roethlisberger, *The Elusive Phenomena,* ed. George F. F. Lombard (Boston: Division of Research, Graduate School of Business Administration, Harvard University, 1977).
2. W. H. R. Rivers, *Kinship and Social Organization* (London: Constable Co., 1914).
3. Georg Simmel, *The Sociology of Georg Simmel (1858–1918),* ed. and trans. Kurt Wolff (Glencoe: Free Press, 1950).
4. Hutton Webster, *Primitive Secret Societies; a Study in Early Politics and Religion* (New York: Macmillan, 1908).

ONE OF THE GOALS of the Committees on Industrial Physiology was to use the techniques of the Newburyport research in studying communities in other parts of the country, and the decision was reached to have Lloyd select a community in the Deep South in much the same way he had selected Newburyport, design the research, and direct it, the fieldwork to be done by students who had worked with him in formal studies and in the Newburyport research. The Deep South was defined roughly as South Carolina, Georgia, Florida, Alabama, Mississippi, and Louisiana, with some overlapping into contiguous states.

Lloyd and Paul Lunt drove south together in the summer of 1933 to select a site. It was hoped that a community could be found that would yield data comparable to those of Newburyport, a community that would more or less parallel Newburyport in size, age, background, old families, and stability. When they reached Mississippi Lloyd wanted to visit Meridian, where his mother's family had lived, and there he found in an old cemetery part of the headstone from his great-grandmother Carter's grave. They moved on to Natchez and felt that it had many of the characteristics Lloyd was seeking. So they settled in for the preliminary work to test the suitability of the community and proceeded to make the contacts necessary to gain a receptive attitude toward the research and the researchers.

Through friends in Jackson, Lloyd met the mayor of Natchez, a graduate of Yale Law School and head of the local Democratic organization, a person whom Lloyd found compatible and sympathetic with his research interests. The mayor wondered if, in terms of gaining insights into the real Deep South, the research should be based originally in Woodville, a little town south of Natchez. He made contact with the editor of the newspaper in Woodville, and this is where Burleigh and Mary Gardner settled for several months in 1933. Mary had been a student of anthropology at Radcliffe. The newspaper editor introduced them to the leading families in Woodville, where several old plantations were still being operated. They were given access to records, including rough drafts of a census of 1830 showing such data as number of acres in each plantation and number of slaves.

But the town was very small, only several hundred people, and Lloyd decided that it would not yield the kind of research data required and that clear definitions of social structure were lacking. So the research base was moved to Natchez, a community comparable in size to Newburyport. Moreover, Liddy and Allison Davis were about to arrive; problems that as Negroes they hoped to handle in a larger community would be insurmountable in a small one. The Gardners' experience in Woodville yielded effective results in information about the operation of the plantation system, and the interest of the newspaper editor, who had connections in Natchez, especially a woman who was an historian and reporter, led them to other newspaper people. The mayor introduced Burleigh to the sheriff and chief of police, very important contacts.

The Gardners had been working in Natchez about a month when the Davises arrived. Allison had been at the London School of Economics for a year and returned to take part in the Natchez study. Burleigh took Allison to meet the mayor, who passed the word to the sheriff and chief of police that Allison was working for Burleigh—the proper relationship between white and Negro and one that would have credibility. They were studying the social history of Natchez. That powerful word, history— everyone was overflowing with history and would talk about historical events by the hour and about family events and geneaology. The Gardners did not mind listening because it was beautiful background for following the current period—it was the whole social system of the community. So they referred to their work as a social history of Natchez, avoiding the term social structure. Often they improved their cover by examining old documents—as passionate historians.

The Gardners found a small house on a side street which had enough room for Allison to work too. The Davises found rooms with a Negro doctor, upper-status. Allison and Burleigh had their first meeting one rainy Saturday afternoon, working several hours on research material and procedures. Then the Davises took off for Baton Rouge for the rest of the weekend. When they returned, the maid in their doctor's home said, "I heard you were in that house and sat in the front room with the curtains drawn all afternoon." The grapevine was working; they could not meet there again. One would telephone the other and make an appointment. Allison would wait on a certain corner, Burleigh would pick him up, and they would drive out to the country, to a back road, and sit and talk for a couple of hours. When the whole social situation got too much for the Davises they would clear out for a holiday with friends in New Orleans or Baton Rouge. The Gardners promptly sent a copy of all discussions, interviews, and field observations to Lloyd in case they had to leave quickly.

Newspapers were clipped as in Newburyport. Clippings were organized by groups of events and people, in clusters, which became the basis for two excellent chapters in Deep South, one on social class and one on the way different age groups cross class lines.[1] Who interacts with whom? The Davises had to follow events and people's activities by word of mouth, observation, attending functions, filling endless notebooks.

The concept and conduct of the research are well expressed in "A Comparative Study of American Caste," a chapter written by Allison and

Lloyd, for Edgar T. Thomson's 1939 book, *Race Relations and the Race Problem.*[2]

A white fieldworker and his wife, and a Negro fieldworker and his wife lived in the society for a little over one and one-half years. All of the fieldworkers except the white woman had been born and reared in the South or in the border states, living there continuously except during their college or university training. In Old City they conformed to the behavioral modes of their respective castes; they participated chiefly with the upper and upper-middle classes. After about six months of residence, they appeared to be accepted as full-fledged members of their caste and class groups, and dropped their initial roles of researchers. Their observations of group behavior were therefore made in the actual societal context, in situations where they participated as members of the community, within the limits of their caste and class roles. The interviews also were obtained in this normal context, and except where matters of fact, such as factory or plantation management were concerned, few questions were asked. Every effort was made to adapt the principles of "free associative" interviewing to intimate social situations, so that the talk of the individual or group would not be guided by the fieldworker, but would follow the normal course of talk in that part of the society.

In this manner, both overt behavior and verbalization with regard to all the societal institutions were recorded for all color, class, age, and sex groups, down to the small, intimate cliques. The white and colored fieldworkers continually checked with each other all of their observations and interviews pertaining to Negro-white relations, in order to bring into the field of discussion their own initial caste dogmas, and to learn to see both sides of this behavioral relation. The methodological aim from the beginning was to see every Negro-white relationship from both sides of the society, so as to avoid a limited "white view" or a limited "Negro view." The same type of objective approach was brought to the study of class behavior; all interviewers participated in both formal and informal affairs, with all classes in their caste.

In addition to records of overt behavior and verbalizations, which cover more than five thousand pages, statistical data on both the rural and urban societies, as well as newspaper records of social gatherings, were collected.

Earlier Lloyd had written on caste and class structures in the society of the Deep South: "Formal Education and the Social Structure," and "American Caste and Class."[3]

In his introduction to *Deep South*, the report written by the Gardners and Allison, Lloyd called the research a social anthropological study of caste and class. "The social anthropologist looks at all the societies of the world, where he observes the similarities and differences in the social institutions, beliefs, and customs of the people he is studying. The present-day social anthropologist has added his own society to the others as part of his comparative scheme. We feel justified in being just as much interested in the life of our modern American communities as some of our colleagues are in the peculiar practices of the polyandrous Toda."[4] He used Kroeber's definition of caste—"an endogamous and hereditary sub-division of an ethnic unit occupying a position of superior or inferior rank or social esteem in comparison with other sub-divisions"[5]—feeling that the social system of Natchez, other parts of the South, and some sections of the North fit this definition.

He adapted this definition to the social organization of the Deep South, where there was a caste system but also a class hierarchy. "'Caste', as used here, describes a theoretical arrangement of the people of a given group in order in which the privileges, duties, obligations, opportunities, etc., are unequally distributed between the groups which are considered to be higher and lower. There are social sanctions which tend to maintain this unequal distribution. This much of the definition also describes 'class.'

"A caste organization, however, must be further defined as one where marriage between the two groups is not sanctioned and where there is no opportunity for members of the lower group to rise into the upper group or for the members of the upper to fall into the lower one.

"In 'class,' on the other hand, there is a certain proportion of inter-class marriage between lower and higher groups; and there are, in the very nature of class organization, mechanisms established by which people move up and down the vertical extensions of the society."[6]

Lloyd described what was happening to the caste and class systems in the Deep South.

> The gradual elaboration of the economic, educational, and general social activities of the Negro caste since slavery (and to some extent even before) has created few groups which have been vertically arranged by the society until certain fairly well-marked class groups have developed within the Negro caste. As the vertical distance of the Negro group has been extended during the years, the top Negro layer has been pushed higher and higher. This has swung the caste line on its axis (c) so that the top Negro group is higher in class traits than the lower white groups and is so recognized. . . . . This tendency to bring the two groups out of the vertical opposition and organization into a horizontal arrangement is being reflected at the present time in such movements as 'parallelism,' a 'solution to the race problem' expounded by many Negro and white leaders.[7]

The authors of *Deep South* comment on the fact that the members of the superordinate white caste are only vaguely aware of the existence of social distinctions within the subordinate colored caste, but the awareness has caused modifications in caste behavior. However, few of the whites are aware of the subtleties of these distinctions within the Negro groups or of the systematic nature of class controls there. See the chapter "Class System of Colored Caste" in *Deep South* and also *Color and Human Nature*, a study of the Chicago Negro community's distinctions among color gradations by Lloyd, Buford Junker, of the Newburyport research, and Walter Adams, a Negro psychoanalyst.[8]

Lloyd and Paul drove to Natchez at Christmastime the first year of the research. Lloyd had been receiving regular reports and was in close touch with the progress of the work but wanted to make contact with the Gardners and Davises and with the Natchez people he had met earlier. By this time the research people were fairly well settled in, the Gardners having come to know a very social group of upper-middle and upper-class people, their acceptance facilitated by the fact that they were Harvard people studying history. They were receiving commiserations from their new friends about having the wonderful, gay party-time of the holidays spoiled by having to entertain a poor old professor, which delighted Lloyd when he heard it. Of course he and Paul joined in the parties and were probably enjoyed as much as they enjoyed. Because the upper class was small, parties contained a mixture of upper and upper-middle people.

The Gardners developed various ways to interact with members of other classes. Burleigh feels that they did the poorest job with the lower-middle people, not making as many contacts with them or spending as much time as with others, though they met with them and obtained several types of interviews. The poor whites, the lower-lowers, were reached especially by Mary, who volunteered to serve as a social worker with the government welfare program. The paid social workers had to be selected from people in need and were usually lower-middle and often poorly educated. She was especially welcome when she asked to be given a white case load, the poorest. Middle-class social workers did not like the poor whites because they were "uppity," a term often encountered. When her cases learned that she was in Natchez studying social history, she elicited the usual response, "Well, I want to tell you about it," and thus learned their view of the upper and upper-middle classes. Burleigh would often go with her when she was working at the lowest social level, people living in houseboats or "down under the hill." Little as they had, these people would always invite them to sit down for a cup of coffee and talk.

These were the people Burleigh encountered most often when he visited the courtroom where he spent a great deal of time watching the system at work, the jury selection process, the interpersonal relationships of lawyers, jurors, and criminals—or, in a civil case, who was suing whom and why. The roots of some animosities went back perhaps two generations or more. Burleigh covered all of the court work because it would have been dangerous for Allison to appear. In two cases, a Negro was being tried for the murder of another Negro. Juries, of course, were white—judge, juries, attorneys all white; in one case the defense attorney was the best lawyer in town. In both cases the verdict was to hang, and the defense attorneys and the people around the courthouse said the reason they hung was "The damned Niggers are getting uppity. We got to put them in their place." While the case was still at trial the defense attorney told Burleigh that his client would hang. "I haven't got a chance. They're going to hang him. Hanging is in the air." It was said that every sheriff (who served a four-year term) hangs a man. The cycle of the Negro pushing against social barriers builds, and the whites say they are getting uppity, have to put them in their place, cool them down. They thought the system worked, and there was no one who could effectively deny it.

When the research was under way, St. Clair Drake joined the team, his work financed by the Julius Rosenwald Fund. St. Clair had been a student of Allison's at Dillard University in New Orleans, where Allison taught before going to the University of Chicago. He studied Negro cliques especially and later helped edit the manuscript down to publishable size.

John Dollard came from Yale to look in on the research and reported to Lloyd that he thought his people were doing an excellent job. He became interested in the caste-class aspect of the research and later wrote *Caste and Class in a Southern Town,*[9] and then he and Allison collaborated on *Children of Bondage.*[10]

At the writing stage, funds were received from WPA as well as Rosenwald. *Deep South* was published by the University of Chicago Press in 1941. Its dedication to Edwin R. Embree, director of the Julius Rosenwald Fund, expresses his important role in the social sciences—"Social engineer with a faith in the sciences of human behavior." He had gone to Rosenwald from the Rockefeller Foundation, where he was director of the division of studies. It was in that capacity that he, with Clark Wissler and with some input by Steffanson, had prepared the report on the feasibility of the foundation's financing anthropological work in the Pacific—the report that led to the foundation's role in the organization of the Australian National Research Council.

Within an hour of Lloyd's departure with Paul for Natchez in June our neighbors, the Holtons, made their first call. They were retired missionaries who had lived for many years in India and still maintained a routine similar to their life there—up at five, cold shower, curry every day. We were not even well into a conversation when it was clear that they had observed most of the activities at our house; this did not disturb me because they were so dear, no malicious inquisitiveness. Most of all they wanted to hold the baby, whom they promptly called Rosy Ann. From that day on, during the period of Lloyd's absence, they watched for the lights to come on in our house, signaling that Ann and I had come in from the garden, where I worked almost every afternoon for the pleasure of its beauty but also wanting to please Mrs. Hale. Then they would come over with freshly cooked asparagus, strawberry shortcake, and other delicacies from their garden for my supper. When they learned that I was considering taking Ann to meet Lloyd in New York, as he returned, they asked if they could keep her in my absence. I was pleased because it would give them pleasure, give Ann pleasure—she had become very fond of them—and allow me a holiday, confident that Ann would have tender care.

When we returned we were invited to the Holtons for lunch and learned about their pleasure in their little house—especially the thermostat, which they considered a great luxury since it allowed them to have heat any time of year. Would that we had had the heating in the Hale house under that control the previous winter.

From the mayor of Natchez Lloyd brought a gift of real corn liquor which the mayor aged in his attic in charred oak kegs. With mint from our garden, Lloyd demonstrated how to make an authentic mint julep. He was delighted with the results of the trip; in a way, he had gone home.

Notes to Chapter VII

1. Allison Davis, Burleigh B. Gardner, and Mary R. Gardner, *Deep South* (Chicago: University of Chicago Press, 1941).
2. Edgar T. Thomson, *Race Relations and the Race Problem* (Durham, North Carolina: Duke University Press, 1939).
3. *Journal of Educational Sociology*, May 1936.
4. Davis and Gardner, *Deep South*, p. 8.
5. A. L. Kroeber, "Caste," in *Encyclopedia of the Social Sciences* (New York: Macmillan Co.), pp. 254–57.
6. Davis and Gardner, *Deep South*.
7. Davis and Gardner, *Deep South*, pp. 9–11.
8. Walter Adams, Buford Junker, and W. Lloyd Warner, *Color and Human Nature* (Washington, D.C.: American Council on Education, 1941).
9. John Dollard, *Caste and Class in a Southern Town* (New Haven: Yale University Press, 1937).
10. Allison Davis and John Dollard, *Children of Bondage* (Washington, D.C., American Council on Education, 1940).

SOON WE FOUND IT NECESSARY to start looking for a place to live in Cambridge. We decided to consider Boston's Back Bay, but found only townhouses with two rooms to a floor and four or five floors, so we concentrated on the Harvard area. We were fortunate in finding a charming apartment only a block from the Hootons. The building was on the side of a hill, sloping down from Concord Avenue, and our apartment was in the back, on the lower floor, quiet, with a pleasant grassy plot where Ann could sun and we could have a flower garden beneath our windows.

Poor Lloyd. He had never wanted to be burdened by possessions, yet he knew that family life would change these and other entrenched attitudes. We discovered what the mover already knew, that we had collected more than we realized, including a lovely 1715 cherry blanket chest from the Parrys' antique shop, for which we paid $15.00.

Lloyd drove with Paul in his open convertible, taking Hortense and her three kittens in the rear seat in an orange crate Lloyd had secured with rope and wire. When they reached Cambridge, they discovered Hortense and two of the kittens had disappeared, probably so frantic that they were able to get through the narrow slits. Lloyd and Paul undoubtedly were deep in discussion, a pattern of driving often commented upon by Newburyporters held up in a line of traffic behind Paul's slow car, which they called Paul's Bride since he had not married. The car was beautiful, received much tender care, and seemed to be the love of his life. Lloyd and Paul retraced their route, looking, calling, asking, stopping to place ads in local papers, but returned exhausted and frustrated. The kitten remaining was the tailless wonder and upon him we concentrated our affection.

We were fortunate that Harvard faculty could buy furniture, drapes, and rugs at wholesale through the dealers who had supplied the houses built under the new Harvard plan. Paul had put his share of family furniture into storage when he and his brother sold their Newburyport home and said he would be pleased to have us use it and save him storage charges. Frances gave us beautiful rugs that she and Steve had had made in China. Mary Hooton used the occasion to replace Earnest's favorite davenport with a new one she had long wanted. Soon we had an attractive, really delightful apartment, close to friends and near the Peabody Museum.

In its periodic progress report, the Division of Research of the Harvard Business School summarized the studies in social anthropology in charge of W. Lloyd Warner, assistant professor of anthropology in the university—studies conducted by graduate students under Warner's direction: Newburyport, County Clare, Natchez. The Newburyport research fieldwork was almost completed, Dr. Arensberg (elected a Junior Fellow on the basis of his work in County Clare) had returned to Ireland, and Natchez fieldwork was to be completed by the end of 1934.

Earnest Hooton, in a later report to the Rockefeller Foundation on the use of grants to the Department of Anthropology, also referred to the five-year study of Ireland which, of course, included archaeology and physical anthropology as well as social anthropology. It is interesting that this latter work was included in the programs of both the Business School and the Anthropology Department, especially since the Rockefeller Foundation (as distinguished from the General Education Board and Spelman Fund) did not have an active program in the social sciences.

Lloyd's monograph on the Australian research was still in rough draft waiting for time taken from the Newburyport research, the Natchez study, and teaching. The following articles were published in 1933: "Kinship Morphology of Forty-One North Australian Tribes";[1] "A Methodology for the Study of the Development of Family Attitudes";[2] and "Methodology and Field Research in Africa."[3]

One of Lloyd's early visits to the offices of the Rockefeller Foundation was related to the Newburyport research, to the Harvard industrial research program, but especially to the study of vanishing races, the reason for our earlier stop in Paris. Flora Rhind remembered meeting him in 1933 in the office of Edmund Day, director of social sciences of the foundation and also director of social sciences of the General Education Board. Flora was Day's assistant. She had joined the staff of the foundation in 1927 and experienced the reorganization that occurred when the program of the Laura Spelman Rockefeller Memorial first expanded into the social sciences and was then reorganized as the Spelman Fund with much of its program taken over by the Rockefeller Foundation and the General Education Board. She recalls the impression Lloyd made on Day and herself — "a tall good-looking young man with an eager, rapid speech, pleasant smile, and quick laughter. He and Rufus Day responded well to each other because they had much in common. Basic honesty, high intellectual standards, and a keen sense of humor were the basis of their congeniality. Day began to interest Lloyd in the General Education Board program.

"I remember becoming aware of Lloyd's capacity for friendship. Awareness of it started in many ways. When you talked with him you felt he was listening. When he talked of his own interests it was with pleasure without any insistence that his interests and points of view be adopted by his listeners. All through his life, as I knew him, Lloyd was an eager man, and somehow in the progress of learning he was also a remarkably fine teacher — a teacher whose contagious enthusiasm went hand in hand with an insistent prodding and digging for new knowledge, for reexaminations and interpretations, and for new approaches to facts long taken for granted.

So often the listener learns without awareness that he is being taught. Time and time again I have been struck by the influence Lloyd exerted on research of brilliant men and women who absorbed and took for their own the insights that Lloyd had given them. I have been struck by the generosity with which Lloyd shared his insights.

"As a lecturer and teacher he seemed at ease and happy in the classroom; but I have always thought that his deepest satisfaction came in research and writing. In those, I think, he had a sense of fulfillment that is rarely given to any man. All through his life, as I knew him, there was an eager, magical quality about his approach to knowledge, people, and nature. At the Hanover Conference I remember his running after a squirrel to watch his antics in outwitting a jaybird and his pointing out the jauntiness of the catbird's figure. He was very tall and walked loosely. His eyes were clear, and he looked at you directly and sharply, but he laughed readily. One's general impression was of a good-looking, good natured, very intelligent man. His brilliance was something that one became aware of more slowly because he was a modest and gentle person."

Lloyd had almost uncanny insights into people and sensitivity to situations. He seemed to know what someone was thinking before that person was aware of his own thoughts. I was often asked how I could live with Lloyd, with whom there was no possibility of dissembling. It was easy—candor and honesty to myself and to him. He had the ability to analyze social situations, large or small, intimate or international. This led at times to problems between us because so many people came to him for advice and counseling, so much of his time was given in an already overloaded schedule, that I felt the need to make it clear that the children and I were there too, wanting attention.

In the Vanishing Races Project, he prepared two memoranda for Day dated September 1933 in which he proposed plans for administration and organization that would achieve effective collaboration among the many types of people in contact with aboriginal cultures. Such collaboration, to be achieved through a central body that would settle the conflicts and obtain cooperation, could overcome, he felt, the open or covert mutual antagonisms among these people—missionaries, government officials, traders, and scientific men. Since the members of the scientific group would undoubtedly participate most fully in the direction of the work, they could be used to obtain mutual aid among most of the social science groups. The director and board, however, should function to make each group feel important.

He used examples of "under-cover battles" within the American school of anthropology to demonstrate the point that antagonisms are always expressed between two men or two groups and never spread over a number of conflicting groups. In obtaining support for a project through a central organization, expressed hostilities between individual scientists would be avoided as they worked for a common project. Along this same line of reasoning he proposed dividing geographical areas of investigation into "natural divisions" to be allocated to those groups who feel a proprietary interest and suggest various scientific groups that could be involved in North America, South America, Australia, New Guinea, Melanesia, Polynesia, Africa, Siberia, Malaysia, India, Arabia, and Asia Minor. Each of these areas would have a committee subsidiary to a larger central committee so that all groups would have a feeling of participation which would hopefully preclude jealousy. He suggested individuals to serve on the central committee and substantiated his recommendations in detail. For example, Radcliffe-Brown should be on the central committee because in many respects "the plan for the study of vanishing races was his idea initially, he sees the whole scheme as a unity, and views social anthropology as a comparative science. The primary hope of a science of sociology and anthropology at the present moment is dependent on a greater objectivity which can come only from comparisons of *whole societies* with other *whole societies.*"[4]

Radcliffe-Brown had long been concerned with the urgent need to study threatened cultures before they disappeared. He thought of the 1930s and 1940s as the period when most effort would have to be made; by the end of that time the science of comparative sociology would have become so important and have had such recognition that there would be little difficulty in finding appointments for good people. He was concentrating on winning recognition for comparative sociology as the basic science for all of the other social sciences and was confident that this effort would ultimately succeed. He felt that in this respect Lloyd's work at Harvard was being helpful. But even if comparative sociology would not develop as he hoped, he felt that plans should be made for an organized effort to study disappearing cultures.[5]

Because of the enormity of the project there had to be concern that the amount of financing would preclude its ever being started. Therefore, Lloyd proposed a modest beginning with a half-time director and full-time secretary, building to a well-organized nucleus around which the larger organization would develop. He urged avoiding spending major sums on organization to the neglect of research. The director would travel enough to coordinate the efforts of the many types of people working in numerous fields. He had devised a budget reflecting initial activities. Important as it was to send people into critical areas, he felt that this procedure should be delayed perhaps two years. Most emphasis was placed on organizing the entire project in a way that would enlist the interest and support of the groups involved, create a collaborative working situation, and avoid conflict and hostilities. The project should stimulate research in the universities and preclude overlapping of projects as happens when some areas become "research fads." He wanted the research to be "rationalized" in order to cover as many areas as possible by preventing duplication. Radcliffe-Brown's idea of people ultimately working on research for a long period of time and moving from one area to another seemed attractive.

Lloyd stressed urgency because of the number of critical areas, known to many anthropologists, where valuable information was about to be lost forever with the death of the old men. Specific research concepts were not developed since they had been so well covered by many scientists. The greatest effort should be made to enlist the interest of universities in coordinating their researches, to contribute to the general project funds that were being used in duplicating work of other institutions.

Mayo commented to Day that he had read Lloyd's proposal and thought it excellent but felt that the proposed budget was too low and that, if the project were to be activated, it would replace some other projects in anthropology and free their funds—that it would result in a redistribution of expenditures if unnecessary duplication were avoided. "I believe one of your most persuasive officials would need to visit foreign centres. . . . I hope that those in charge of the plan will not forget altogether the need for, and the value of, investigation of our contemporary culture situation. . . . If you accept the scheme and it can be made to work as Warner sees it, then it would be valuable as a beginning in a small way of that international collaboration upon a clearly defined piece of work which Sir Matthew Salter (for example) so greatly desires but which he and the League of Nations have not succeeded in beginning—principally because their thinking has necessarily been confined mainly to urgent political or economic problems. Collaboration—international—begins more easily in the relatively simple questions and not in the most complex."[6]

This comment of Mayo's reveals the extent of his involvement in anthropology, especially of course the study of contemporary cultures; it reveals why he and Lloyd could collaborate so effectively and why he was so sensitive to Lloyd's interests and goals.

Lloyd's proposal had a positive reception at the foundation, where the project continued within their thinking but had slipped somewhat to the background.

Meanwhile, Lloyd had been appointed to the Committee on Personality and Culture of the Social Science Research Council, possibly because of Day's interest that Lloyd's ideas should be represented in the committee's work. Lloyd reported to Day that the SSRC had favorably accepted the committee's report and acted upon it by discharging the old group and appointing a research committee to follow up the proposals. "The final report to the committee indicates that I had at least some small influence on the successful termination of the committee's activities and the development of the work into a new area. I was pleased to see that Bott and Judd in their final report to the Council stressed the Newburyport work as the kind of thing they would like to see done elsewhere." However, no member of the exploratory committee was appointed to the newly created committee, which was confusing since if a Newburyport-type study was to be emphasized it would seem that Lloyd would have to have a hand in it or at least be represented—if for no reason other than avoiding errors which had been made in the Newburyport research and to take advantage of the methods and ideas which that research had developed.

At the SSRC Lloyd met E.B. Wilson, the statistician from Harvard, who became interested in the analysis of the Newburyport research data and, as a result, became involved in consulting on statistical techniques. He helped to design the multivariate analyses used in the Newburyport work and developed to a higher degree in later researches when computers became available. This was another of those fortuitous situations in which eminent scientists became interested in Lloyd's research principles and procedures and involved with his work. I had known E.B. Wilson as a member of the SSRC, where he tended to intimidate by brilliance, tenaciousness, and his capacity to become embroiled in open battles with other statisticians, as in the famous incident with Raymond Pearl over population statistics.

In 1933 the Progressive Education Association, with funds from the General Education Board, had set up a commission for human relations under the chairmanship of Dr. Alice B. Kelleher. Lawrence K. Frank, a very active member of the board's staff, had worked closely with the commission; in 1934 he and Day sponsored a month-long summer conference at Dartmouth College for the purpose of discovering how a body of teaching material could be developed for working with secondary schools and freshman and sophomore students. Frank, in a memorandum preceding the conference, stated eight fields of value in the study of the synthesis on human behavior and relations: "Ideally the task of orienting and illuminating the all-pervading problem of human adjustment should be shared by all the disciplines through a conscious effort to make explicit the implications of their materials for understanding man in relation to society and the universe."[7] At Day's suggestion Lloyd was invited to the conference.

The group was an extraordinarily interesting one: Mark May and John Dollard, of the Institute of Human Relations at Yale; Dr. James Plant, a psychiatrist; Lura Beam, student and writer in the field of sexual behavior with special reference to adolescence; Margaret Mead, anthropologist; Mary Fisher and her husband, both professors of literature at Sarah Lawrence College; as well as artists, philosophers, and others. Helen and Robert Lynd were there (through her association with Sarah Lawrence College), the staff of the General Education Board, including Robert

Havighurst (who later was closely associated with Lloyd at the University of Chicago), Frank Stubbs (Flora Rhind's brother-in-law), who was with the Laura Spelman Memorial, Hugh Hartshorne of Yale, Carl Engle, of Columbia, and V.T. Thayer, of the Ethical Culture School in New York. Day, Frank, Havighurst, and Flora were there as helpers and observers from the staff of the General Education Board. Flora: "The Progressive Education Association was opening up new ground for teaching, the subject was unlimited, and there was a touch of the prima donna in each of the conference members. So discussions were intensive and hard to control. Quantities of materials were read and written, and in the process the conferees learned from each other, changed in the process of confrontation with almost unsolvable problems, and made friendships that were to last through the years and possibly effect a change in teaching procedures that would be difficult to trace. This was not an annual affair but a unique event." Repeat conferences were supported by the Laura Spelman Rockefeller Memorial to bring together individuals of one discipline or of one set of associated disciplines. In 1928 annual conferences were begun for the Social Science Research Council, first in Hanover, then Nantucket. The whole thing was started by Frank Stubbs, really quite skilled in bringing people together in a conference setting.

Lloyd had wanted me to come to the conference for at least a few days' visit, and I did arrange to go for a weekend, borrowing a car and taking Ann with me. Many of the people there I had met at the SSRC; the Lynds, of course, others from the board and various committees. The Franks were friends of Mary Charles Cole, with whom I had shared quarters in Paris and New York. She had lived for a while in an apartment in the Franks' house at 72 Perry Street, in the village—a marvelously expansive welcoming house with which so many of the social scientists had contact. Through her I had met Edmund Day, Flora, and many others.

Lloyd's invitation to the Hanover Conference was to be as a participant observer—Day wanted him to analyze the meetings as they proceeded, the roles of the participants, and the results. He prepared a written report. I think the conference was important for Lloyd in putting him in touch with a great variety of professional people working on a common, complex problem; important too in having explicitly acknowledged the function of social anthropology in understanding group behavior in our society, even the group behavior of intellectuals.

At this time Lloyd became aware of fundamental changes in progress in the social sciences at Harvard. Edwin F. Gay, the economist and one of Lloyd's mentors, Mayo, Dean Donham, and others were stressing the importance of working out a comparative sociology that would allow various social sciences to collaborate effectively and pool their knowledge and problems. This very type of thinking had been discussed at the

Hanover conference as the solution for some of the difficulties in the study of anthropology and other social sciences. Gay was interested in having a research done near Harvard that would include the Departments of Economics, Government, Sociology, Anthropology, and possibly the Business School and others. A place nearby would bring closer collaboration among the directors from various departments and bring in more graduate students.

Lloyd was also interested in a semiprimitive place, perhaps in one of the Central American republics. He worked out a research scheme similar to one that he and Margaret Mead had discussed with Day at the conference—arranging for anthropologists to go into the field for a year or two to work out the general organization of the modern and primitive peoples and become acquainted with the language, to be followed by economists, political scientists, and others. In attempting to get the departments together emphasis would be on research rather than courses, though they would be part of the general scheme. His hope was that forced interdependence would bring collaboration. He had not approached the Department of Anthropology with these ideas, feeling that they would have an unsympathetic reception. Rolan Dixon was about to retire as department chairman because of illness, but Lloyd did not feel that the resulting faculty changes would alter the department's thinking.

Meanwhile, he was working on a course which he would give with Mayo the following semester.

Social life in Cambridge was busy and pleasant. We had many friends nearby, a few in the suburbs, most on the faculty but some from the town. We especially enjoyed our close relationship with the Hootons, and Lloyd continued to play golf with them, although he did not take the game as seriously as they. We had dinner or supper with them almost every Sunday, always a lovely rib roast that was served cold in the evening as sandwiches, except that Mary streamlined hers and ate buttered beef. She was so direct in her approach to life, impatient with irrelevancies, highly organized. Earnest worked in his study at home when he was not lecturing, always had lunch at home, usually followed by a nap, and then more work at his desk. After this was tea, over which ritual he enjoyed presiding.

One always dressed for dinner parties in those days, but dinners with friends were usually gay and informal. Often some of the guests would drop by the next morning, if it were a weekend as it usually was, and pick up where the evening had ended. One memorable morning Frances and Kitch Jordan dropped by and Frances happened to go to the kitchen with me. There she saw the calf's head used in making mock turtle soup for the dinner. She was horrified. She had always considered the soup a delicacy until she saw the essential ingredient. I continued making the soup until calves' heads were no longer available during the war.

The end of prohibition was certainly a cause for celebration. We had resented not being able to buy wine. S.S. Pierce was well prepared for the time when it could be sold, and an important amenity returned to our life.

A totally new person was added to our group of friends when Josiah Orme Low arrived in Cambridge. He had received his A.B. from Harvard many years earlier, gone into the securities business, where he was very succesful, and had had the foresight to sell his seat on the New York Stock Exchange before the crash. Feeling that this was a time for total reassessment of his life, he decided that he had frittered away his college days and would return to Harvard as a serious scholar to attempt to study his society and find a few answers and more significance in living. He had just remarried, having divorced his first wife, the mother of his four children, now adults. The Lows took a large house near Harvard Square, and Joe began his search for the academic niche that he hoped would bring him what he was, without guidance, seeking. Hearing of the Newburyport research, he came to see Lloyd and, after a long discussion, asked if he could study under him and work with him. Lloyd, impressed by Joe's seriousness and obvious intelligence, agreed, so Joe joined the Newburyport team; here he worked very effectively and later collaborated with Lloyd in writing Volume IV, *The Social System of the Modern Factory*.[8] They were a delightful addition to our social group. Joe's family had lived in Salem but their identification was really with Brooklyn Heights in the old days. His uncle, Seth Low, was the reform mayor of New York City; an aunt was Juliette Low, founder of the Girl Scouts. In the Salem days the family had owned one of the famous clipper ships, and Joe had a love of the sea, was an accomplished sailor, and had been commodore of the New York Yacht Club.

We had friends in Boston. Hallam Movius, then a student in archaeology, lived in Back Bay, his mother a West and a Saltonstall. Dinners there could be very formal or—if Hallam had had some successful shooting—wild duck, served bloody rare, according to his and Lloyd's principles. There was a formal reception one night, very exciting, for the first ambassador from the Soviet Union, Troyanovsky. We were there for dinner preceding and amused by the concern of Hallam's mother and aunt as to the propriety of white gloves—elbow length or higher? For the Communist ambassador? But of course.

Hallam had a beautiful sister Rose who became engaged to a student of Lloyd's, young Potter Palmer from Chicago. Having lived most of my life in Chicago, where the Potter Palmers were considered one of the first families and, indeed, had been a strong moving force in the development of the city and its culture and since Potter's grandmother had been the reigning social queen in Chicago, I had difficulty in accepting Mrs. Movius' feeling that Rose would definitely be marrying beneath her. To many east-erners, even then, anything west of the Hudson was outland; most had never even considered visiting there. But her attitude was similar to that of many upper-class Newburyporters who felt that old Bostonians were up-starts who had barely arrived.

We spent some interesting weekends with the Dollards in New Ha-ven. Lloyd and John had become close friends and had great interest in each other's research. The Institute of Human Relations had recently been established at Yale with Mark May as director and John and his sometime collaborator, Neal Miller, and many other able people as members. Mar-garet Mead would sometimes come up from New York to join us. Fre-quently the evening became a party with anthropologists, including Wil-lard and Susan Park, sociologists, psychologists, and psychoanalysts having a wonderful time. Paul sometimes went with us. Victorine Dollard was a special person, a beautiful, lovely personality, intelligent, able, and a won-derful mother. We really loved her. She and John had definite ideas of child rearing that were very permissive and fascinated me, a product of the schedule/training current school, I regret to say. Lloyd would say, "Now you are on the firing line, and it is easy for me to talk when I am not acting"—and then he would explain what I was doing and its effect. He believed in immediate discipline, if that were necessary—never lecture and never promise discipline in the future when it would no longer be related to the act. I don't know if the Dollards ever disciplined their chil-dren. I do know that they were all beautiful and, I believe, all developed into good adults. However, as we observed, all of the attention and clean-ing up exacted a toll from Victorine. John had a set of precepts that she was expected to follow, and this was not always easy.

We had many overnight guests. They had to be special because the apartment was not sufficiently spacious to stretch out for anyone not spe-cial. Frances came whenever she could. Though she had worked only as a tutor to a family in China at the time she divorced Steve, she got a job in New York with a courier service just beginning and soon folding, and then went to Rockefeller Center as director of their guided tours. Radcliffe-Brown visited but not as a house guest; I cannot now quite see Rex in a household of babies. Many of Lloyd's students could not picture Lloyd in this situation either, could not imagine his working in the garden or per-forming a menial task. He continued to appear as a formal, well-groomed, pleasant, but not intimate sort of person.

We had made plans to visit my parents and Lloyd's parents during the summer of 1934 when word came that Lloyd's father was ill of per-nicious anemia, and he left at once. It was a difficult journey—his plane developed engine trouble and had to make an emergency landing in the Wasatch Mountains of Wyoming where only a skilled pilot could set a plane down. He found his father terminally ill; being there to confer with the doctor was a comfort to him and to his mother and sisters. His father died soon after Lloyd returned to Cambridge. It was our great loss that we had not had the opportunity to go to him during his life so that I could meet him and he could know his only grandchild.

Our daughter Caroline was born on Feb. 22, 1935. Our own doctor was out of town when I experienced miserable morning sickness and went to Dr. Huntington, who assured me that he would modify his usual bills for us, that he liked to deliver anthropologists' babies—wearing a dinner jacket! Only part of this came true. Under his care I gained very little weight, but the experience with Ann had left me with a vulnerable back, and the orthopedist told me I could wear a steel brace and steel arch supports (in what looked like men's shoes) or stay in bed. I had been so determined not to look so awful with this pregnancy. Lloyd was sympathetic and brought me gifts that would brighten my appearance and my spirits. I had started taking courses in Harvard Extension, having learned that I could get a degree there in short order, given my many credits, that would allow me to get a masters degree at Radcliffe in the same time as an A.B. should I transfer there as an undergraduate. I wanted to continue those courses so I wore the brace—anything, moreover, than be confined to bed. They were lovely courses, financed by the Lowell Institute: one in Renaissance Art by Dean Edgell, in Romanesque and Gothic Cathedral Architecture by Kenneth Conant, in Physical Geography, and in History, given at the Old North Church. My companion in the art courses was Marion Wild, wife of a young professor of international relations whose course, in the evening, we also attended. Since Marion and I had Edgell's course that afternoon, we met Payson in the Square for dinner before his class. Soon after our going to Chicago, Payson accepted an appointment at Northwestern and later became its vice president. As with the Parks when Willard went to Northwestern, Evanston seemed far away. We saw more of the Parks when they were at Yale and we at Harvard.

Dr. Huntington insisted that I stay in the hospital for three weeks although I was fine—it was his minimum. I longed so to see Ann; Lloyd brought her over to the hospital garden along the river so that I could see her, though she could not see me, and this was almost harder than not seeing her at all since I could not touch her. At last the day arrived when I was dismissed, and the baby nurse engaged by Dr. Huntington appeared. I had been reading a collection of Dorothy Parker, including the story "Horse Face." And here was Horse Face. At home while we were involved with Ann's acceptance of the newcomer, Horse Face was busy not finding things or, if she did find, promptly breaking them or otherwise being certain they would not work. I was still to remain in bed, so Lloyd was forced to have dinner with her. At meals she took advantage of her captive audience by expounding her philosophy of socialism-communism—she was proselytizing for the local group which met in the astronomy building across the street. This gave us the excuse we needed to ask Dr. Huntington to release us, to dismiss her, to let *us* have our baby.

Shortly after Caroline was born Lloyd told me of a conversation with Robert Redfield, dean of social sciences at the University of Chicago, about the possibility of going there. He was obviously much attracted so we had a lot to talk about. Since I had been at the university both before Hutchins's arrival as president and during the early period of his incumbency when his new plan was already being put into effect, I had some definite notions about what it might be like. Things were going well at Harvard; Lloyd's students were bright and able, contributing at a high level to the Newburyport research and the research in Natchez; many exciting projects were planned. Yet comparative sociology was far down on the list of current interests.

The University of Chicago had strong appeal, especially the prospect of working in both the Departments of Anthropology and of Sociology, each a strong department. Fay-Cooper Cole, chairman of anthropology, had that rare capacity to create an intellectual working environment compatible with the needs and demands of eminent scientists, often as hard to please as prima donnas. Never was he competitive with members of his department; the welfare of the department came first. He was a brilliant lecturer, could make a discussion of the cranium as exciting as a suspense novel; he was a superior fund-raiser and indeed had commitments sufficient to build a new anthropology building when the stock market crashed. He assured Lloyd of supportive interest in community research and in comparative anthropology. The presence of Radcliffe-Brown and Robert Redfield in the department fortified this assurance.

Ellsworth Faris, chairman of sociology, was not an asset as far as Lloyd was concerned. But the Department of Sociology, founded in 1892, the first in the country, was based on the teachings of W.I. Thomas, John Dewey, Thorstein Veblen, Robert E. Park, and George Herbert Mead, all of whom Lloyd respected and admired. Park, chairman of the department before Lloyd arrived, and Ernest Burgess were responsible for the community studies of Chicago.

A formal proposal from Bob Redfield on February 28 made a quick decision necessary.

Dear Warner:
The matter raised in this letter is something I had hoped to talk over with you here in Chicago before I left for Central America. But as your visit to us had to be deferred until May, I am presenting it in this letter.

Are you in a position to consider an offer of an appointment to our faculty? If you should be interested, I would propose a joint appointment to the departments of Anthropology and Sociology. I have talked this suggestion over with members of both departments and find it strongly supported in both quarters. Professor Faris and his associates welcome the idea as warmly as do Dr. Cole and Dr. Radcliffe-Brown.

The suggestion is made upon the supposition that you would continue the kind of research work upon which you are now engaged. I do not know whether funds now available to you for that purpose would remain available to you should you join us. We have, as you know, some funds for social science research. My view is that the community studies we have been making would be strengthened and vitalized if brought into more direct relation with your own. I think we could develop here a group of students of culture, studied in the field and treated comparatively, that would be second to none.

I am thinking of an appointment which would enable you to devote about half time to research and half to teaching. If you look with favor upon my principal suggestion, will you please in replying indicate what contribution to our teaching you conceive of yourself as perhaps making?

This proposal is based much upon the regard we have for you, and also upon the great regard of our group for Mayo's research interests and viewpoint, in which, in some manner, we would hope to profit by having here one of his associates, yourself.

I should appreciate an immediate reply to this letter. The suggestion must be either laid aside or pushed within the few days that remain before I go away.

Sincerely,

Of course the presence of Radcliffe-Brown in anthropology drew Lloyd strongly. But most of all was the attraction of a university preeminent in the social sciences, striving at the time to reduce, at least, the barriers between departments, which made possible the offer of a dual appointment. This was the hope at Harvard of Henderson and Mayo, but they did not even want to broach the subject with sociology.

We made the decision to go to Chicago. Lloyd had discussed each step of the proceedings with Earnest Hooton, who was torn between wanting Lloyd to stay at Harvard and feeling that he would have at Chicago the environment that would advance his interests, his research, his career. Clyde Kluckholm had joined the department so they were not without a social anthropologist.

Lloyd went to Chicago in April to discuss details of the appointment and to see Radcliffe-Brown, who would have left for Yenching University by the time of our arrival in the fall.

My dear Redfield:

I heard recently you were back from Yucatan and on the chance that you are I am writing directly to Chicago to tell you my family and I are coming through Chicago in all likelihood on the 11th of June when we shall stop over a day or two before going on to California, where I am going to teach summer school. I shall call you when I get in Chicago, but I should like also to tell you now how much I enjoyed being in Chicago when I was out there last month. Everything about it made me realize I was in a milieu which was comfortable and right for me mentally. Cole was so direct and open about everything, I knew more about, and felt more a part of, the department of anthropology after two days than I have the whole time here — and this is not an expression of animosity to my present location. I hope the course on the family and the course in modern communities meet with your approval.

I understand that it has been the custom, if not all the time at least part of the time, to pay the moving expenses of the incoming professors. Since we are absolutely broke and will have to go into debt to get to Chicago I am writing to ask you if it would be possible for the University to help me in this matter? Had I known this was possible when I talked with you in New York I should have brought it to your attention at that time.

Do you mind telling Donald Slesinger and R-B about our arrival? I think it is possible that my wife has already informed Slesinger.

With my kindest regards to you,

The announcement of our going to the University of Chicago caused much consternation. One did not leave Harvard. No one seemed to understand that we were not leaving Harvard so much as we were going to the University of Chicago. It was hard to think of parting from our friends.

The research would go with Lloyd and the financing. The Committee on Industrial Physiology, Henderson especially, wanted to spread the study of behavioral sciences. Lloyd had been considered for a position at Columbia upon Boas' retirement, and Henderson wanted him to accept it even though it would mean a Department of Anthropology entrenched in the notion that its concern should be primarily the American Indian or at least other primitive cultures. Lloyd could not consider it.

He agreed to return to Harvard for the spring and summer terms to complete work with certain students in a seminar and to wind up research work with students who remained there. Paul Lunt, Joe Low, and Buford Junker made plans to go to Chicago when we did. Burleigh received his Ph.D. degree at Harvard and Allison at Chicago.

Shortly after Lloyd's acceptance, I received a letter from Donald Slesinger, dean of students in the Social Science Division, asking me to be assistant dean, a post which would soon be vacated by Patricia Rosten, Margaret Mead's sister. After much correspondence in which I expressed our concern about flexibility in relation to the needs of our children and much reassurance from Slesinger on all the points I raised, I accepted. Slesinger agreed that it would be a two-thirds' time position so that I could take courses and finally finish my degree; at Chicago I had more than enough credits and only needed to fill residence requirements.

Lloyd had to arrange office space for staff. Failing to see Donald Slesinger, he wrote from Berkeley on June 26, 1935 what his requirements would be.

June 26, 1935

I attempted to see you while in Chicago for some sort of living (i.e. office) quarters to house my researchers when we arrive on September first. It seemed wise to Redfield and, I believe, Cole, that I should be placed in between sociology and anthropology.

I shall have the following people to take care of:

1. Eliot Chapple, who has been my chief assistant and help; in Chicago, from September 1 to February 1.
2. Leo Srole, who has been in charge of the ethnic studies and will be with me permanently.
3. My secretary.
4. Mr. Paul Lunt, who has been associated with me for the last two years.
5. Mr. J.O. Low, who has been with me for the last year and a half. These last two men will be with me for at least the coming year. All of these men will be working on the Newburyport material.

Mr. Burleigh Gardner will most likely be with me all next year. He has been doing the work in the Natchez study, and will not necessarily have to be near the others.

My Newburyport material is so arranged that it is important that at least Chapple and I shall be near to each other, and, it is almost necessary to say, all of us.

I should like my Secretary's place so arranged that she could keep people out.

I am sorry that I did not see more of you while I was in Chicago, but I presume we can remedy this matter next year.

Sincerely yours

Lloyd had accepted an invitation from the Department of Anthropology to teach at Berkeley during the summer while Kroeber was doing field work in Peru. We would put our furniture in storage to be sent to Chicago in the fall. Going to California meant meeting Lloyd's mother and sister Marjorie and especially bringing our children into his mother's life. We were to stop in Chicago on the way to be with my family and to look for a place to live the following fall. We loved our apartment in Cambridge, especially after the management built a dining room, beyond the kitchen, reached by a glassed-in passage on the exterior. Many had exclaimed over its charm, the large open living room and garden. But no one wanted to rent it. The mover suggested that he get our furniture over the state line at night so that it could not be attached for rent. We declined his offer. Though the management promised to make very effort to sublet for us, we paid rent until the following October. This together with the expense of our trip to California, of moving, and of settling in Chicago was to affect our finances for some time to come.

All negotiations about our going to Chicago had been conducted with Bob Redfield, who regretfully told us when we reached Chicago that—had he been more alert to fiscal matters at the university—he could have offered us moving expenses at least. It would have helped. Harvard's system allowed us to liquidate our annuity upon departure, and this eased us through the transition period but left us with no resources. We agreed that in future our financial welfare would not be left to the considerations of two academics.

Lloyd and Paul and other friends had often had Saturday lunch at the old Parker House in Boston, and they wanted me to join them in one last sentimental lunch the day we left. With final packing, for the children especially, yet to be accomplished, I could not see that it was possible. This disappointed Lloyd very much; I am sure he felt that had I really wanted to go I could have managed. So the friends went off alone. As the hour for their return came and passed and train time grew ever closer, I became increasingly anxious. They had taken all of the luggage, except last-minute baby things, to check in at South Station. Their return left just enough time to catch the train at Back Bay—and there we discovered that a group of friends had waited at South Station for final farewells. When we did not appear they had had our luggage removed from the train. Lloyd felt abashed, but at least we had the baby bag for Caroline.

We were met in Chicago by my parents, who could not understand how anyone could manage so inefficiently as to arrive without luggage. It came the next day, requiring another trip to the city from their suburban home. Their delight in their grandchildren overcame their distress with the parents, and they urged us to let them care for the children while Lloyd made arrangements about courses and offices at the University and I apartment-hunted. We wanted to be near campus and felt that we should bc on the first floor with a garden for the children. The more apartments I saw, the more depressed I became—that lovely old house in Newburyport and our delightful apartment in Cambridge made it almost impossible to think of living in such dismal places. It was hard to leave for California facing a houseless return with our furniture still in Boston, but we had no choice. Our one hope was the offer of the secretary of the anthropology department to try to find a place that would fill our requirements.

Krak and her friend—and Lloyd's—Mary Ellen Washburn had found a house for us in Berkeley. Lloyd's sister Marj was a student at the university and would live with us, and his mother would come from Whittier and get to know her new daughter and her grandchildren, so we required a fair-sized house. It could not be an exciting house in the hills where all of Lloyd's friends lived because we would not have a car and had to be close to campus and shops. So it was a comfortable pedantic sort of house, no views of the bay, of course, but adequate for our needs, and we were most grateful to Krak and Mary Ellen for finding it for us.

What a pleasant summer! Mother Warner was a loving, able, caring person who was quite thrilled with her first grandchildren. Child-rearing methods of the time were very rigid, adhering to schedules and other regimens totally unrelated, I now feel, to the needs of a new reaching-out little human being. Mother Warner was determined not to interfere with my methods though they must have broken her heart. Had she taken over completely we would all have prospered. But in my insecurity as a mother I could not do other than follow the directions of the pediatrician, though often they set both Lloyd and me on a course that we found almost impossible to follow.

Lloyd enjoyed being back at the university, renewing old friendships with Lowie, the Kroebers, the Ralph Beals, the Washburns, and others. Although the Washburns were not anthropologists they were part of what Lowie had called the Hyperarboreans and their house was often the gathering place for the anthropology clan. No one had any money. Mary Ellen often served a huge dish of lima beans baked in a delicious sauce, salad, sourdough French bread, and wine. We had no place for a party so borrowed the Beals' house one night and brought the dinner. Life was simple and fun.

Notes to Chapter VIII

1. *American Anthropologist* 1:63–66.
2. *SSRC Bulletin* 18 (1933).
3. *Africa* 6, No. 1 (1933).

4. Rockefeller Foundation Archives.
5. Radcliffe-Brown to Day, Rockefeller Foundation Archives.
6. Mayo to Day, Rockefeller Foundation Archives.
7. Rockefeller Foundation Archives.
8. J.O. Low and W. Lloyd Warner, *The Social System of the Modern Factory*, Yankee City Series Vol. IV (New Haven: Yale University Press, 1947).

THE CHICAGO APARTMENT awaiting us met all of our specified requirements, and it was near the lake and two beautiful parks, yet we were dismayed. It was on the first floor as we had requested and therefore dark in every room except front and rear. It was a railroad apartment. An open porch looked usable, but was impossible to keep clean. All of the time we were there I house-hunted.

The warmth of our reception at the university, however, overcame any negative feelings. The Redfields invited us to their home in the country, on Bob's mother's estate, with a garden so beautiful it reminded us of Hampton Court. The Coles were darlings. Edwin and Kate Embree lived just a block from us and introduced us to many of their friends and to the Contributors' Club, a small informal group that met regularly to hear papers read by members. Since most of the members were pursuing interesting, highly varied careers, the meetings were lively and enlightening.

Lloyd was given a warm welcome by the faculties of both sociology and anthropology. The Robert E. Parks were most kind. The grand old man of sociology had been influential in inviting Lloyd to join that department as well as anthropology. (Park had met Lloyd in Cambridge through L.J. Henderson, whom he had known when they were both students in Strasbourg.) "Introduce me to that young man, Warner, who is doing the kind of research that ought to be done." His program of courses and the degree of interaction among faculty members pleased him. One course was on modern communities, using material from Newburyport, Natchez, and Ireland.

Leonard White and Charles Merriam, of the Political Science Department, had been influential in having a new building constructed for the Social Sciences. It had, on the second floor, an attractive social room where faculty and students could meet each afternoon for tea.

Someone, probably Donald Slesinger, in planning for us put Lloyd's office and mine side by side on the first floor, windows facing the inner court. This would not do—it was too much of a family affair and seemed to give me status equivalent to Lloyd's somehow. The problem was automatically solved by the insistence of the dean of students for the university that I be in his complex in the administration building, old Cobb Hall. He also insisted that I work full time, contrary to my agreement with Slesinger, who had unfortunately departed the university before we came so I had no one to front for me. We felt that my working full time was not possible, so I notified Dean Works that I could not continue. This put him in something of a dilemma since he had a new dean of students in the social sciences, Jerome Kerwin, who was unfamiliar with the regulations of the new plan, whereas I had spent part of the summer in California learning them. So we reached a compromise allowing me to stay on a part-time basis, take courses, and use time in the office to prepare for the courses should that time be available. A new dean of students in the Humanities Division, Clarence Faust, was also in our office, and his assistant, Ruth Thompson. Her mother was a friend of Mabel Cole's and a member of a little group to which Mabel was devoted, the Friends in Council, which I later joined.

However, there were problems, some anticipated, in moving the research from Harvard. Satisfactory arrangements had been made about the financing but not about the custody of the materials. This was solved by sending them in the care of the university's Social Science Research Committee, a kind of local branch of the Social Science Research Council. Some of the materials were retained in Cambridge, however, for the use of people still working there, including Eliot Chapple and Leo Srole.

The head of FERA for Massachusetts made it clear that he expected an interim report that Lloyd had not anticipated. Leo Srole, Lloyd, and Eliot Chapple prepared and submitted the report on adolescents in the depression, material which FERA wanted to use with their own people in their efforts to reorganize secondary school curricula to fit the needs of the adolescent in the environment of the depression. Lloyd was willing to help them in their contacts with laymen but felt that any solution for the adolescent group would really have to begin with the socially mature "who had gone through hell." Research material was used that had been intended for a report to the General Education Board, and then it was learned that FERA would also make a report to the GEB in relation to its study program. Lloyd later submitted a revised final report as he had originally planned. FERA then reported to Mayo that their expenditures on the project to date totaled $6,985.66, with an estimate of $2,000 to finish the precoding, ten weeks at $200 a week.

Lloyd had become dependent on Dorothy Moulton, his able secretary at Peabody, a most resourceful person in running his office and helping with the research. Now he felt that he should have someone who was a first-rate editor and was most fortunate in obtaining Sylva Beyer from Berkeley. She worked on the Newburyport monographs but first finished editing the manuscript for *Black Civilization* for publication by Harpers in 1937. Lloyd's first book was an exciting event and a cause for celebration.

In the late fall of 1935 Lloyd received an invitation from Columbia to teach there the following summer. Since he had agreed to return to Harvard for the spring and summer sessions, there was an obvious conflict, but he wanted the Columbia experience. His Harvard invitation was based on an arrangement for Eliot Chapple to come to Chicago and work with Lloyd in writing the first two volumes of the Yankee City research and for

Lloyd to go to Harvard to work with Eliot. The invitation from Columbia had come through MacIver of the sociology faculty, and it appealed to Mayo's and Henderson's interest in disseminating behavioral science concepts in key universities (as they would have tried to do at Harvard had it not appeared so difficult). Another complication was that Dean Redfield wanted Lloyd at the University of Chicago during the coming summer but agreed that spring term could be substituted. As Lloyd had anticipated, Mayo was pleased to have Lloyd "carry the word" of the behavioral sciences to Columbia and recalled his prediction that it would be the next university "to crack." Dean Donham agreed to an arrangement whereby Lloyd would spend as much time as possible during spring and summer terms at Harvard; he was most anxious that nothing delay the Newburyport work.

When Eliot received his Ph.D. he was appointed to the faculty of the Department of Anthropology and of the Graduate School of Business Administration.

Lloyd's going to the University of Chicago had left Earnest Hooton with some problems. The foundation attached importance to Lloyd's departure since he was one of a small number of anthropologists compiling and studying social data from the anthropological point of view. It was felt that his leaving could be interpreted as an indication that there was no great disposition at Harvard to experiment in the application of anthropological techniques to present-day American life. Hooton wrote a reassuring memo to the effect that the department had offset the loss by adding Eliot Chapple, Clyde Kluckhohn, and Conrad Arensberg who, as a junior fellow, could spend part of his time teaching.

In Chicago Lloyd was fortunate in finding an excellent secretary at that time, young and still working for her A.B. but fully qualified: Alice Chandler. She stayed with him and gave him full support until he left.

Analysis and writing were slowed by organizational difficulties. Eliot had been expected at Chicago to fulfill his commitment to this phase of the work, but he had developed a system of analysis inconsistent with that used in the research, indeed, inconsistent with the purposes for which the research material had been gathered, and he felt that he could not meet his commitment since his report would conflict with others. His primary interest had become a system of quantitative analysis on which he and Conrad Arensberg were working. Lloyd was troubled by Eliot's not living up to his part of the general research agreement to analyze interviews and write them up and to collaborate with Lloyd in the final report of the statistical study. On the other hand, he realized the impossibility of having reports using different systems of analysis and knew that Eliot's part of the work could be done at Chicago but would certainly add to the work of others. Paul Lunt was a welcome resource and helped in the preparation of both of the first two volumes to a degree that Lloyd felt warranted the status of co-authorship.

Lloyd had a keen sense of obligation to the Committee on Industrial Physiology to produce the research report he had promised. He and Eliot had spent considerable time systematizing the analysis of interviews, which was now Lloyd's responsibility along with the analysis of the 17,000 personality cards. By spring of 1938 this work had been completed, the clerical work being paid for in part by WPA.

Plans for the sequence of volumes changed as the writing proceeded. Talcott Parsons was asked to come in as a consultant on publication; he and Lloyd met to clarify Talcott's conception of the general series and of the place and function of each volume in the publication scheme. There was some confusion about the relation of the Natchez report to the one on Newburyport. Lloyd felt that the several volumes on Newburyport should be one detailed scientific study of an American community and the Natchez study another, each telling the story of how the two oldest parts of the United States had solved the problem of social adjustment — in New England with a class system and in the South with a caste system.

At this stage Lloyd and Talcott agreed that a general volume dealing with both societies would be a good way to proceed. It would be of a popular nature designed to introduce both studies by comparing and contrasting them in a way that would give the reader more understanding of each community. Lloyd wanted this volume to be not so much an introduction as a statement of methods and development of thought. Talcott felt that methods should probably be divided among the various volumes, but Lloyd was convinced that reports on field studies that do not clearly state the operations underlying the published conclusions do not give the reader an opportunity to test and compare results. Spreading the methods through several volumes would fail to bring attention to the development of the thought and operations the researchers used to test their ideas and the facts of the fieldwork. "The literature of sociology is loaded with . . . reports on field work," he wrote to Elton Mayo. "Sociology courses are filled with similar material. But few people have . . . attempted to tell systematically how the work was done. Until we can communicate this kind of information to our colleagues and students, the social sciences are still merely pretending to be sciences."[1]

In discussing plans for publication in the letter to Elton Mayo, he observed that the narrative in the methods volume was written to show how the researchers changed the ideas they started with and how they continued to change their ideas as they learned about the facts under observation. The same idea had been used by Elton in his volume on the Western Electric research. "I borrowed it," Lloyd wrote, "to demonstrate to social anthropologists that if they start with the ideas that they now have about social behavior they must consider modern society as part of their field and stop making the ruinous dichotomy they now have between modern and primitive social behavior. . . . In my opinion, only a book of the type I have written will do this. It takes them by the hand and leads them step by step to the conclusion that we can have a science of the comparative sociology of man and we can forget such departmentalizations of knowledge as anthropology and sociology."[2] But he found persuasive Talcott's argument that the reader did not want to work his way through a volume of methods before reaching the report on the community itself. Thus, he placed the methods volume third among the planned three volumes on the total community, a unit of the series that would start with a summary account of the general setting of the community and then describe the class system, followed by an account of the social institutions and their interconnections. In having the methods volume third, it was felt that it would answer the questions the reader would by this time have raised about how the preceding facts had been discovered.

At this point, the manuscripts of the report on ethnic groups, written by Leo Srole in collaboration with Lloyd, and the one on the modern factory, by Joe Low and Lloyd, were both far enough along to receive Talcott's review as well. Little revision was required in the first but, as Lloyd had already recognized, the factory volume had to be integrated into the study of the larger community. The preceding reports had not been written at the time of the work on the factory volume.

Lloyd made the comment to Elton that he had found Talcott's help extremely useful, that he appreciated Elton's wisdom in choosing him, and the he was about to see publishers. As analysis and writing had proceeded, the original number of volumes projected had been scaled down to six, including a data book. Even in the days before publication costs soared, this was no small undertaking. Moreover, Lloyd had many professional articles to his credit but only one book. The Committee on Industrial Physiology had anticipated the need for subsidy and planned to get funds.

At the University of Chicago we had made friends with Dr. Douglas Campbell and his wife, Berta Ochsner, daughter of a famous physician, and a professional dancer in the modern tradition. Douglas was a psychiatrist on the faculty of the medical school of the university and in charge of student health. He and Lloyd were interested in each other's work. Douglas was quite knowledgeable in anthropology and semantics, and as a student of Alfred Korzybski was vastly interested in his society. Lloyd, stimulated by working with Radcliffe-Brown and Elton Mayo, had read all of Piaget, Freud, and Jung, and was interested in symbols, including the symbol system of language. He often spent an hour or so, when relaxing, reading the dictionary. Douglas had a friend Cornelius Crane, a member of the old Chicago family who were among those comparatively few who had built the cultural institutions of the city through their efforts and financial support. Corney was an amateur anthropologist, lived for extended periods in Tahiti, supported research in New Guinea, where he studied the natives, and through Douglas had become interested in Lloyd's work. The Crane family had long been associated with Yale University and had established the Richard Teller Crane Memorial Fund there. Since the Yale University Press was one of the publishers most interested in the Yankee City Series and was certainly eminently qualified to publish it, Corney arranged to allow proceeds of the fund to be used, if necessary, in its publication. This interest and support are acknowledged in the dedication of each volume. Negotiations had been initiated for funds from other sources, but the Crane Fund support made these unnecessary since the sum required was not large.

As I considered the number of volumes the Yankee City research would require and the fact that Lloyd's life would undoubtedly involve much research and writing, I decided that my most important contribution to his work would be as an editor. I took courses in syntax, and the fundamentals, and was most fortunate in receiving expert training from my friend Kate Turabian, publications secretary of the university and an author of the *Chicago Manual of Style*. Kate had an office adjoining mine where all Ph. D. dissertations were submitted for approval of mechanics, including clarity, and all publications of the university were processed before printing. Whenever I had problems I could always turn to Kate. She was not the most popular person in the University because of her position, but she was my dear friend until she retired. I was able to do editing, rewriting, proofreading, and indexing and became sufficiently proficient to work for publishers and later for the Committee for Economic Development in its series on the transition in the economy from World War II to peace, under the direction of Theodore Yntema, professor of economics and business at the University of Chicago.

George Peter Murdock, professor of anthropology at Yale University, was asked by the press to serve as a consultant on the publication project. Jane Olson, editor on the staff of the press, was assigned as editor—a happy choice since she was first-rate and worked harmoniously with Lloyd throughout the many years of their association.

Volume I, *The Social Life of a Modern Community*,[3] with Paul Lunt as coauthor, was published in 1941. This volume, as Lloyd had planned, presented the concept of the research, the techniques and methods, and some of the findings—the class system and general cultural life of the community.

Volume II, *The Status System of a Modern Community*,[4] 1942, also coauthored by Paul, describes and analyzes the social institutions and relates them to the class system. Lloyd had developed a system, with eighty-nine possible interactive positions, that made it possible to show the relationship of every individual with other individuals and institutions. Carl Doering and E. B. Wilson, both eminent statisticians at Harvard, and Earnest Hooton had given their expert help in developing the statistical analysis and concepts, as did later Samuel Stouffer, professor of sociology and statistics at the University of Chicago. Lloyd considered this volume of fundamental importance in an understanding of his work.

Volume III, *The Social Systems of American Ethnic Groups*, coauthored by Leo Srole, 1945, describes the ethnic subsystems of the Yankee City social order and, through composite character sketches, attempts to give some insight into the lives of individuals of each ethnic group at various class levels. A portion of the manuscript was presented by Leo in satisfaction of the dissertation requirement for the Ph. D. degree at the University of Chicago. Contributions of all of the fieldworkers are represented and acknowledged in each volume, but this book in particular drew on the work of Burleigh Gardner, Allison Davis, Solon Kimball, and Conrad Arensberg in the ethnic group on which each concentrated.

Volume IV, *The Social System of the Modern Factory*, 1947, coauthored by J. O. Low, studies the social organization of the shoe industry in Yankee City, the interrelations of workers and management in the job situation and in the larger community.

Volume V, *The Living and The Dead*, 1959, is a study of symbolic behavior. The study of symbol systems had long involved Lloyd's interests as he studied psychoanalysis, art, religion, and language. He was especially intrigued with the comparative study of symbols, as perceived in the Yankee City social system and those of the Murngin and other primitive societies. Based on the Yankee City research, this volume departed from the strictures of a one-commmunity study to include Lloyd's thinking as it developed during the years intervening between the completion of the fieldwork and analysis through the writing of the first four volumes.

Writing began in the winter of 1941. Lloyd was teaching at UCLA, at the invitation of Ralph Beals, chairman of anthropology, and we were living near the Bealses in Santa Monica. I drove Lloyd to the campus in Westwood each morning and worked in his office on the final editing of Volume II. One afternoon he decided that he was far enough along in writing the fifth volume to start dictating. As he began from his longhand notes I had an almost overpowering feeling that this was to be a great book, that at last he was producing a book that represented knowledge accumulated through years of study and experience. Many have asked why there was such a long interval between the appearance of Volume IV in 1947 and the final volume in 1959. His publication record reveals part of the reason: he was working and writing in a continuing pattern of developing interests. More than that he was formulating his own concepts of symbolic analysis. He was thoroughly familiar with the work of others in the field—Piaget, Durkheim, Radcliffe-Brown, Malinowski, Mauss, Freud and Jung, John Dollard and Neal Miller, Clyde Kluckholn, George Mead, Ogden and Richards, Korzybski. He was assimilating this knowldge in his own critical way, comparing it with his experiences and perceptions, and from this process producing his own formulations. Before going to sleep and sometimes when waking in the morning, Lloyd liked to read either the Bible or a dictionary. When he was really involved in writing, however, he frequently would waken and go at once to his desk and begin—with not even a cup of coffee to get him started. Often when he was writing he would be so involved that he was abstracted from daily routines and responsibilities. He liked tough, well-written detectives, but there was only one other book that he read repeatedly, Wallace Smith's *The Captain Hates The Sea*, a story of the passengers on a cruise ship and its captain—outrageous, bawdy, even vulgar, and very funny. If I heard Lloyd laughing while alone I knew what he was doing. We lent our only copy to a friend who lost it, and Lloyd turned the bookshops of Chicago inside out until he found a copy, well used—as he felt, appreciated.

Increasingly he studied the symbols of the fine arts and religious symbols, especially those of the Catholic Church, where the use of oral and visual symbols in ritual and thought surpasses any other religion. This portion of Volume V was considered so important that the Yale press asked to publish it in a separate paperback edition. With two added chapters comprising Part I, this little book was published in 1959 as *The Family of God*. Professor Ong, S. J., of St. Louis University, wrote to Lloyd that his study was considered by Catholic scholars to be one of the most profound ever made of Catholic symbolism. He was asked to give a dedicatory address of the Pope Pius XII Library at St. Louis University.

An abridged one-volume edition of the other four Yankee City volumes was published by Yale in 1963. It required only three weeks of uninterrupted time one winter in the desert for Lloyd to pull that volume together. He had the capacity to deal with a great mass of material, organize it, and communicate it.

The completion of the Social Science Building in 1929 had been an explicit recognition of the movement within the University toward cross-departmental programs. Robert Maynard Hutchins, who became president of the university that same year, encouraged these programs. The Division of the Social Sciences had students working for the divisional master's degree. The Committee on Child Development was a cross-divisional research committee having faculty from psychology, education, and the biological sciences, which were emphasized. The committee was empowered to grant a master's degree and, later, the Ph. D., which had not previously been given as a social science divisional degree. Then the Committee on Social Thought, under the chairmanship of John U. Nef, the economic historian, close in his thinking and personal relations to both Hutchins and Redfield, was formed as a degree-granting group, followed by the Committee on Human Development, which grew out of the Committee on Child Development. Child-development committees—institutes really—had started in several universities about 1925, including at Berkeley, where Lloyd, in subsequent years, had close contact with Jean McFarlane, the director and a close friend of Theodora Kroeber, and Eric Ericson. He had the opportunity to observe the research and the techniques of observation, records, and data analyses. This was a continuing study, following the same subjects from preschool through adolescence to maturity. The Berkeley institute was supported by the General Educational Board. About twelve degree-granting committees were formed in the social sciences in the 1940s before a reversal to more conventional procedures occurred, with departments asserting their priority through department chairmen.

Lloyd had been invited to join the Committee on Child Development shortly after arriving at the university and continued with the Committee on Human Development. Robert Havighurst came to the university as professor of education in 1940 from the General Education Board, where he was director for general education (the position held by Edmund Day until he left in 1937 to become president of Cornell University). Bob felt, however, that his real assignment was to make the Committee on Human Development interdisciplinary. It meant that the orientation of the Committee on Human Development would be shifted from biological and neuropsychological to sociological. Bob feels that Lloyd was the crucial person in the committee's being able to expand. They collaborated on a course on Education in the Social Order and began to draw students from various departments; there was no dearth of students from that time onward. Ralph Tyler, chairman of the Department of Education and later dean of the social sciences, was responsible for bringing Bob to the university and very interested in seeing the work of the committee expanded. Bob Redfield, then dean of the social sciences, was in agreement. Bob Havighurst first met Lloyd at the Hanover conference where, he says, he began to learn from him. Lawrence K. Frank, a sociologist, and Margaret Mead were working at that time to bring social science, particularly cross-cultural material, to bear on child development. This was the field of study remaining in the Laura Spelman Rockefeller Memorial when its funds had been spent and its program taken over by the GEB and put under the direction of Larry Frank, who ran the Hanover Conference. When he left in 1937 to go with the Macy Foundation, Bob inherited the program.

Bob and Lloyd later agreed that the work they did best was going into communities to study them. Lloyd was the central person. Actually the precursor for these projects was the study of Dowagiac, Michigan, undertaken while Bob Havighurst was still at the GEB, which had become interested in an exploratory study by a sociologist and a social anthropologist of the relations of the school to other institutions in the community. Bob knew of Budd Junker's work on the staff of the American Youth Commission's Negro Youth Study, working under Lloyd's supervision, and of his study of Newburyport schools. Bob talked with Budd and with Burleigh Gardner, who was doing research at Western Electric, and became convinced that their viewpoint could well be brought to the attention of educators. He wrote to Lloyd about recommending Junker to be director of the Michigan Study of the Secondary School Curriculum. This Lloyd was happy to do, and he offered to consult with Budd on the research.

The research report, published as *Hometown*,[4] was seen by Flora Rhind as a possible basis for materials on social stratification for the use of teachers; she suggested to John Dollard that a short conference be held to include Lloyd and Allison Davis, who had both expressed interest. Leo Srole also agreed to attend. The conference, held in Chicago in May 1940, was called the Conference on the School and the Community. By this time Leo had competed researches under Lloyd's direction not only in Newburyport but in Ligonier, Indiana, and among the Winnebago, all touching on the problems of schooling. The Ligonier study had been instigated by James Senior, professor of theoretical chemistry at the University of Chicago and a friend of ours. As a Jew he had become interested in the special qualities of the Jewish community in Ligonier, and he helped to finance the research. His interest in this community, near his birthplace in Cleveland, was that it is an old settlement, going back to the mid-nineteenth century.

The work among the Winnebago was undertaken because Fay-Cooper Cole told Leo that he had to do a study of a preliterate primitive tribe to qualify as a candidate for the Ph. D. degree. Rachel Commons, daughter of the famous economist, had started the study but had to break it off, so the department funded Leo's work, with the expectation that his report would become his dissertation. But there was still the book to write on ethnic groups in Yankee City and this became his dissertation. The Winnebago study grew cold.

The first community studied by the Committee on Human Development was Morris, Illinois. Lloyd and Bob together set up the research, made the necessary contacts, and organized a research team. One of the books reporting this research was *Democracy in Jonesville*,[5] to which individual members of the research team contributed a chapter individually or in collaboration. The editor had to bring continuity and conformance to the writing, which for many was a first experience. In addition to Lloyd, who wrote four of the sixteen chapters, there were nine authors, all well on the way to successful academic careers.

A. B. Hollingshead, sociologist at Yale, had his Ph. D. and an SSRC fellowship. He had expressed an interest in getting into community research, so Lloyd told him about Morris, where the committee had been working for several years, and suggested that he go there. He wrote the chapter on schools. At the time *Democracy in Jonesville* was published, Hollingshead was studying the youth of the community, and he published his work later as *Elmtown's Youth*.[6] Lloyd was troubled because he seemed to take full credit for his part of the research rather than representing it in the context of the total research and giving proper acknowledgment to the fact that, although he worked independently, he could not have done what he did had he not been working within an ongoing community project. But he was a skilled researcher. Bob Havighurst wrote a book on the older people and another on the veterans. As he says, they really made use of that town. Many articles were published. The study is an excellent example of what can be accomplished by a continuing research in a community over a period of years—shifting the emphasis, mining other fields, developing new concepts and techniques.

A somewhat larger city was being considered as better suited to research—if possible a place not more than two hours from Chicago. South Bend, Racine, and Peoria were considered. Kansas City offered to cooperate with the committee through its Institute for Community Studies, an offer too generous to refuse. Martin Loeb, Eugene Friedman, Elaine Cumming, and David Riesman were all involved in the research, which first focused on social structure and then on adults and gerontology. The research continued until 1964. Bernice Neugarten and Richard Coleman wrote the definitive research report, *Social Status in the City*,[7] the culmination of the studies Lloyd had helped to start. Bob Havighurst considers it the best big-city study of social structure.

In addition to the community studies, the Committee on Human Development was also collaborating on the research project on the American Indian under the auspices of the U.S. Bureau of Indian Affairs when John Collier was director. John and Lloyd had always been friendly. The committee was given responsibility for the overall project, the psychological tests, and interpretation of results. Later Laura Thompson was appointed director of research by John Collier. The first planning seminar was held in Santa Fe in 1941 while we were living in Santa Monica and Lloyd was teaching at UCLA. Frances Stevens and I drove to Santa Fe toward the close of the seminar.

Lloyd and I returned to Santa Monica in a rather leisurely fashion, stopping to see the Grand Canyon for the first time, feeling awed and ashamed that we had not stopped sooner. We visited Sol and Hannah Kimball in Window Rock where Sol was working for the Soil Conservation Service, a program conducted in collaboration with the Bureau of Indian Affairs. Ephraim Shevky had consulted Lloyd at Harvard about able students for this project, and Lloyd recommended Sol and Burleigh Gardner, who went to Albuquerque with Mary. On the road to Window Rock the setting sun made visibility poor through our dusty windshield; indistinctly we saw something on the road ahead and, as we approached, discovered an old wagon drawn by a haggard, tired horse carrying two Navaho women, a small boy, and an old man. A sad and weary little group emerged from the dust into clearer vision. Their destination was a trading post, quite distant, and we agreed to take the two women and their bundle of goatskins, but the little boy had such a severe cold that we had to leave him behind with the old man. After the women departed the car we discovered that under the goatskins they had been carrying a puppy not yet house trained.

We stopped in Canyon de Chelly to visit the anthropologists working there and went up to the Hopi town Oraibi. There we saw for the first time how the Indians lived on the top of this narrow mesa where they could protect themselves from the Navaho, using a steep winding road to reach their fields below and to bring up everything necessary for survival living. We were weary travelers when we reached the Kimballs and had become homesick for our children. We enjoyed seeing Sol and Hannah and their children and meeting their friends—behind drawn curtains so that we could celebrate with a drink, because this was an Indian reservation.

The direction of the Indian Personality, Education, and Administration Project was finally turned over by John Collier to the Society for Applied Anthropology. Six monographs were published: *The Hopi Way* by Laura Thompson and Alice Joseph (1945); *Warriors Without Weapons*, a study of the Sioux by Gordon McGregor (1946); *The Navaho Individual and His Development* (1947) and *Children of the People* (1948) by Clyde Kluckhohn and Dorothea Leighton; Alice Joseph, Rosamund B. Spicer, and Jane Chesky, *The Desert People: A Study of the Papago Indians* (1949); and Robert Havighurst and Bernice Neugarten, *The American Indian and White Children* (1955). Laura Thompson also wrote *Culture in Crisis* (1950) and *Personality and Government* (1951).[8] Hopi and Papago day schools were studied, as were Navaho and Sioux boarding schools and Zia, a pueblo. Zia and Zuni were not published, but all of the research material is in the Smithsonian archives in Washington.

As one of the initial planners and directors, Lloyd participated in the Indian Personality, Education and Administration Project fairly extensively. (He certainly carried the brunt of Collier's invective about the progress of the research when Collier had come to place his full reliance in Laura Thompson. Furthermore, he was given no official credit because he did not publish. This did not trouble him. It had become almost a pattern that he would organize a research, plan and direct it, often secure the financing, staff it, but let the field people do the writing while he went on to other projects in which he had more immediate and continuing involvement and which he brought to fruition in book form, especially the Yankee City Series and subsequent work. In many ways he acted as a catalyst. For Bob the Indian research came at a time when he felt he was "kind of growing into things" and he coauthored many books. His interest was almost entirely in the study of the education of children.

Burleigh stayed about a year before returning to Chicago to the Western Electric study; Sol stayed until the spring of 1942 when he went with the War Relocation Authority after the start of the war.

Lloyd had gone out one time before our visit in 1941, at the request of M. L. Wilson, head of the Extension Service, U.S. Department of Agriculture, for the purpose of trying to get some feeling for the situation on the Navaho reservation because it was a period of great turmoil, with stock reduction and all of the government programs halted except schools and hospitals. Any kind of progressive program involving the Navahos had stopped because of their objection to the land-management program. Sol and Lloyd went deep into the Navaho country, the Black Mountain area north of the Hopi, with an interpreter, and Sol arranged for Lloyd to talk to a person who, in his opinion, had a very good view of what was going on, a pure Navaho who spoke no English but was progressive in outlook. Sol: "It was a very dramatic situation—our sitting there that evening, talking for two or three hours, Lloyd interviewing the old man—not directly about the government program but about how people were living, how they saw the future. And the old man told the story that he had had dreams at night of clouds coming down from the sky and surrounding everybody, suffocating them. Symbolically this was particularly interesting since in Navaho mythology a circle is never completed because that is death. Designs on pottery, baskets, or in sand paintings always leave a place that is an opening into and out of. His dream was telling us symbolically of the extinction of the Navaho by the pressure exerted by the white man. Government programs are not seen as efforts to help them but as oppressive action which would eventually result in death, would take their sheep and horses, would so limit their ability to live that they would be wiped out."

By the end of the 1940s, when the university began to abolish the committees, a report was required of all interdepartmental committees by a self-study committee of the Social Science Division. Most of the committees failed to defend themselves and were disbanded. Bob Havighurst left for New Zealand in 1953, to be gone a year; Lloyd as acting chairman had the responsibility of preparing the report. Bob feels that he did a remarkable job in proving that the Committee on Human Development was turning out Ph. D.s and good research—that he was the person who really organized the position of the Committee on Human Development and regularized it during the period he was acting chairman. He gained approval for some committee faculty appointments whereas previously every faculty appointment had to be in a department. Bernice Neugarten was the first appointment in Human Development. Ralph Tyler, the dean, was a major supporter of the committee. He was chairman when Bob Havighurst was executive secretary. Bob: "So it was really Lloyd Warner and Ralph Tyler who organized things and put the Committee into a fairly firm and secure position in the Division."

After retiring as head of the Center for Advanced Studies at Stanford, Ralph became head of the Foundation for Systems Analysis, a research organization in Santa Monica. He was a consultant for Science Research Associates, which Lyle Spencer sold to IBM, and became a director of the Center for the Study of Democratic Institutions, whose activities are divided between Chicago, where it had hoped to gain support from the community and an association with the university, and Santa Barbara. Santa Barbara did not supply sufficient support after funds from the Ford Foundation were discontinued. This organization succeeded the Fund for the Republic, started by the Ford Foundation with Hutchins head after his term as president of the Ford Foundation. Some say that he was the reason for starting the Fund for the Republic—to have a place for Hutchins so that they could get him out of the foundation where, apparently, his administration was not successful.

Notes to Chapter IX

1. W. Lloyd Warner to Elton Mayo, Jan. 12, 1939, Baker Library, Harvard.
2. *Ibid*.
3. All five volumes in the Yankee City Series, *The Family of God*, and the one-volume edition, *Yankee City*, were published by the Yale University Press.
4. Buford H. Junker (pseud. John Flint), *Hometown, A Study of Education and Social Stratification*, mss. 1940.
5. Warner and Associates, *Democracy in Jonesville* (New York: Harper and Bros., 1949).
6. A. B. Hollingshead, *Elmtown's Youth* (New York: J. Wiley, 1949).
7. Richard P. Coleman and Bernice L. Neugarten, *Social Status in the City* (San Francisco: Jossey-Bass, 1971).
8. Laura Thompson and Alice Joseph, *The Hopi Way* (Chicago: University of Chicago Press, 1945). Gordon Mae Gregor in collaboration with Royal B. Hassrich and William E. Henry, *Warriors Without Weapons*

(Chicago: University of Chicago Press, 1946). Clyde Kluckhohn and Dorothea Leighton, *Children of the People; The Navaho Individual and His Development* (Chicago: University of Chicago Press, 1947). Alice Joseph, Rosamond B. Spicer, and Jane Chesky, *The Desert People; A Study of the Papago Indians* (Chicago: University of Chicago Press, 1949). Laura Thompson, *Culture in Crisis; A Study of the Hopi Indians* (New York: Harper and Bros., 1950), and *Personality and Government* (Mexico, 1951). Robert Havighurst and Bernice Neugarten, *The American Indian and White Children* (Chicago: University of Chicago Press, 1955).

At Dune Acres with Ann, Mildred, and Caroline, 1939

MOTHER WARNER had gone home to California before we returned from New York after Lloyd's summer teaching at Columbia. We wanted to take the children off for a holiday. Earlier we had made friends with Paul and Emily Douglas. Paul, the eminent professor of labor and economics and later U.S. senator, felt that the solution to Lloyd's abhorrence of the flatness of the Chicago area was the community in the Indiana dunes where he and his wife spent summers and weekends. Lloyd and Paul Lunt visited the place, Dune Acres, fell in love with it, and found a house on the beach, where they could knock golf balls about and the children could play in lovely quiet pools left after a storm. It was the beginning of our love for this place, its great natural beauty and rare plants and birds, and we found Lake Michigan very exciting.

We spent a delightful month there. The children adored the water—we could spill off our porch onto the beach and into the lake. The Douglases had a house on the dune above us—an attractive, simple house designed by an artist in the studio of the sculptor Lorado Taft, Emily's father.

The return to the apartment for the last six months of our lease was difficult. We had no prospect of an attractive place to live. Toward spring, the real estate office phoned about a large old house for sale near the university; since the owner had not been able to sell it, he would consider renting. Liddy Davis and I went to see it that evening. The owner was Bertram Nelson, a professor of speech at the university who was ill with heart problems. He had been the voice of Samuel Insull on a radio program promoting Midwest Utilities, the company that Insull had pyramided into an empire before its collapse in the depression. When he was accused of unethical conduct that had impoverished millions of small stockholders he fled to Greece, then Turkey, and was extradited and charged in federal court. Harry Bigelow, dean of the University of Chicago Law School, who was to become a friend of ours, represented the stockholders in their effort to recover some assets. Guilt was impugned against Nelson for associating himself with Insull in promoting stock sales, whereas he had simply used a talent, his voice. A gentle man, he with the others was acquitted. But it was a damaging experience, personally and emotionally, from which he did not recover. His first wife had died several years before, and he had married her sister, who gave up a business career not realizing that her husband would soon be an invalid. Illness and hostility were so pervasive that, had Liddy not been with me, I think I would have left, which would have been a great loss since the Warners had eighteen happy years in that house.

The house, built in 1860, was country Georgian with four round pillars across the front porch, spacious central hall, library to the left, then a substitute dining room and kitchen beyond; on the right were the living room, the original dining room beyond, and a study with a fireplace and bath. The dining room—paneled, manorial—had yards of velour covering the windows and was used for storage. The living room was also closed off. The library was lined with narrow bookshelves suited to a classical library. All of the upstairs bedrooms were rented, one to a couple who in lieu of rent took care of the house.

I could see its possibilities and took home a report. Lloyd was delighted. He realized that it was the house he had been passing en route to his office that was the only one he had seen on his varied routes (always house hunting) where he would like to live. So I went to the real estate office in the morning, made our commitment, paid our deposit, and we all rejoiced. But many other people also wanted it, and Mrs. Nelson felt that I was too young to carry such a load, that the house was a woman killer and should go to a family with grown sons who could remove the storm sash and care for the garden! I went to see her, persuaded and cajoled; indeed I had been the first to see it as a rental, to say we wanted it, and to pay the deposit. Finally, blaming the real estate office for the problems of too many people wanting the house, she agreed that we could have it, but not until fall.

For the interim we found a lovely log house in Dune Acres, with natural red cedar logs built by a craftsman. It was a summer house, with the living room rising to a gable roof, a huge stone fireplace, and three bedrooms, one of which was under the roof and reached by steps from the end of the living room. The simple kitchen had open shelves, and the great screened porch overlooking the dunes to the south had views all the way to the terminal moraine country fifteen miles distant. No furnace. Not having a car, we sent out by an express company most of the things we would need and stored the rest. The Douglases happened to pass by when the express company arrived, signed for the shipment, and paid the bill. My family drove us. None of us had been realistic enough to know that a house closed for winter months would be dirty and inhabited by mice, especially if food and soap had been left about. We all cleaned; my mother, a resourceful lady, found a soup kettle in which she started a pot roast, and then we sat down for a drink. We had sent out some liquor and wine for our four months' stay. Everything had arrived at the house except the liquor.

It was a lovely summer in which we all thrived. Lloyd walked about two miles to the electric train that ran between South Bend and Chicago with a stop at Dune Acres and one quite near the university in the city. We had the phone removed because we wanted the feeling of isolation. It was an ideal place to write. In May we had almost no neighbors since most of the residents were summer people. Groceries were delivered from a little store in a nearby town twice a week, the order taken each time for the following delivery. The delivery men didn't seem to mind our thirty-five steps. It was a cold May. Each morning Lloyd was first up and built an enormous fire in the huge fireplace in the living room that heated the whole house.

He and Paul Douglas were both away a fair amount that summer, and Emily and I became close friends, taking turns with the children on the beach (they had a daughter Jean six months younger than our Ann), and always joining for a dinner cookout and a late swim. Since we both liked to swim some distance, we took turns watching the children.

I visited our Chicago house to take measurements and prepare for our fall move. When September came I met the movers, spreading our meager furniture as far as it would go. We would use the manorial dining room, of course, and convert the Nelson dining room into a playroom for which, with all of its cabinets and drawers, it was well suited. Apparently it had once been a private chapel, with a beamed ceiling and French doors opening to a porch that had been removed.

Our friends were so delighted with our house they all made contributions or loans to furnishing it—stair carpet, rugs, chairs that responded to the magic of slip covers. Paul's lovely antiques and beautiful family things from Joe Low's homes in Salem and Brooklyn Heights really suited the Georgian setting and made it quite elegant. It was a receptive house. However, we were restrained by not wanting to make the house so attractive that it would sell. The fact that the exterior had not been painted for twenty years and needed repair was a strong deterrent to any prospective purchaser.

John Drury included the house in his book *Old Chicago Houses*.[1] Often thereafter we would see a crowd outside listening to a lecture by a tour guide. Drury stated that the house was built in 1863 by Charles H. Botsford and had been occupied by an artist, Cornelia Fassett, and her husband, Samuel Montague Fassett, a photographer.

Mrs. Nelson told us that it had been built by a retired Norwegian sea captain named Nelson—no relation to her husband. My maternal grandfather had been a seaman in Norway, and I think she felt this gave her some kind of mandate to rent to us; it helped to overcome her resistance to my youth and inexperience. But for a long time I met strangers who knew me because I was the one who had "taken their house."

The property had included a famous rose garden. We all had gardens; the trees and shrubs attracted many varieties of birds, almost as many as we found in the dunes. It was parklike, and Lloyd planted many beautiful flowers and shrubs.

To the north and south were cooperative apartment buildings, one designed by Louis Sullivan. The Robert Parks lived nearby in the penthouse of a high-rise, quite an innovation in our little community, which seemed more small town than part of a metropolitan area. We had many pleasant evenings there, with good talk. Their daughter, Greta, was married to Bob Redfield and lived with their four children down the street from us. Thorstein Veblen had lived in the apartment building at the corner when it was a fine place, built for the Columbian Exposition, with large apartments now divided into small ones. The *Theory of the Leisure Class* and his work on conspicuous expenditure were landmarks in Lloyd's studies.

One great thing about Chicago: it is a way station for anyone traveling across the country, so one is always in touch with scholars in many fields.

We were caught up in a social life more intense than ever. We often gave a dinner party twice a week and dined out most other nights. Elinor and John Nef, who lived nearby, entertained beautifully. Elinor and her cousin, Mrs. Alfred Tozzer, were of the Honolulu Castle family, one of the five missionary families who made fortunes there. She was very beautiful and intelligent; she and John enjoyed having guests they had met on their travels, so we had most interesting dinners there. One memorable night Artur Schnabel and his wife were guests of honor and on another Jacques Maritain, who was lecturing for the Committee on Social Thought, of which John was chairman. Schnabel talked about the role of the musician in relation to the composer with all of the simplicity and insight that he displayed in concert. I had had John Nef as a professor in a course that covered the economic history of western Europe up to the industrial revolution in the low countries, all in three quarters. Later in a course on the economic history of the United States at Harvard, in which we learned about the development of railroads with no mention of the Civil War, I realized again the depth of cultural background John Nef brought to his courses. Required reading was 400 pages a week. Actually too much was covered in three quarters of ten weeks each, too much to assimilate.

The Contributors' Club had many members we enjoyed immensely: Lloyd had been associated with Edwin Embree in the programs of the Rosenwald Fund for Negro schools in the South and in the financing of *Deep South*. Frank Sulzberger, of the *New York Times* family, was a trustee of the university, of the Rosenwald Fund, and of many civic and charitable institutions in Chicago. Their daughter Kate later married Edward Levi, subsequently president of the University of Chicago, and another daughter was a professor of law there. Members who were business people, professors, lawyers, writers, architects, and artists took turns reading papers that were varied and interesting. At the close of each year we would have a party, usually at the country home of Sam Marx, the architect and art collector. Bob Pollack, a stockbroker and also music critic for the *Chicago Sun Times* but a composer and lyricist by avocation, would produce a skit, using the talent of members in song and story—and dance! all based on papers read during the year. Lloyd had read a paper on the Murngin, and Bob wrote a skit with an explorer, in pith helmet, prowling through the jungle, wearing an identification that read "Department of Public Relations." A close look—Department of Pubic Relations. Another year Bob Pollack produced a skit with this song:

THE MASSES AND THE CLASSES

Singer stands before a blackboard. A drape hides what's on the blackboard. He's in a cap and gown. He sings:

I have made a little survey of some people in a town
As a consequence, I'm working on a book.
He slyly pulls his gown open a little, exposing pages of mss.
If you'll stick around a minute
I'll explain to you what's in it.
It's all absurdly—complicated. Look:

He unveils the blackboard. On it is written:
"Yankee City Classes—Upper Upper, Lower Upper,
Upper Middle, Lower Middle, Upper Lower, Lower Lower."
I divided allllll the people into classes
According to their status
In the Social apparatus,
I gave them allllll positions in my system.
I divvied up the masses,
Took the blue bloods from the asses.
And it wasn't all as easy as you'd think.
'Cause often it's the blue-blood guys who. . . .
I hadn't aaaaaaany mercenary whims.
I merely took my data
And I built me up some strata.
I separaaaaaated out the fats from thins.
By examining my data
I could get my strata straighta.
It wasn't all as simple as it sounds
'Cause like divorce, we had to have our grounds. . .for. . .action. . . .
We took each case and scrutinized it well.
And then we tossed it in its proper cell—
Offstage klonk
According to the dough it had,
The prestige of its Mom and Dad.
We tested each one out on cups of tea.

To watch it lift its little finger, see.
And everything above an inch
We figured was a certain cinch
To toss up in the upper class
The very top of all the mass
Skips about, clapping hands on next two lines.
—The more the ass the higher the class,
Whoops! I'm a Russian!
Comes forward, leering at audience.
But all the interesting folks
Were down among the lower blokes
(In fact, the Lower-Lower gals
Were definitely better, pals)
Suddenly remembers self.

Through this he's pointing out each class with his stick on the blackboard, jumping from one to another. Sings:
Now the lower upper's lower than the upper upper class,
And the upper lower's upper than the lower lower mass,
And the lower lower's lowest, and the upper upper's top,
And the middle's in the middle, and that is where I stop.

Voice from audience:
Would you mind explaining that again, please? I was asleep.

He stalks to the front of stage. Snarls:
Oh, you were, were ya? Well, this is the New Plan. I'll explain it anyway. You see, the upper upper is higher than the lower upper. The lower upper is higher than the upper middle, which is lower than the lower upper. The lower middle, being lower than the lower upper, tho' higher than the lower lower, is just below the upper middle and higher than the upper lower, which is three below the lower upper. All this is dependent on the upper and lower middle being above the upper lower and below the lower upper, midway between the upper upper and the lower lower. If the upper up— (Hiccoughs)—pardon me. If the upper upp—(hiccough)—er—Since the lower lower is below the upper upp—(hiccough)—er—excuse me—is below the upper upp (hiccough)—

Voice from audience:
You better go back to your singing.

He seems relieved, and sings as he dances around:
With my handy positional system
I can take all the people and twist 'em
Right into my pattern
From any old slattern
To millionaire brethern and sistern.

The following is patter, with piano chords:

We found the upper upper men
Were much too tired to have the Yen.
While *women* in the upper crust
Were simply going wild with lus—longing.
Which led them to descend the scale
In search of fellows not so pale.
And when they found them, things were, well,
Soc'yalogical as hell.

Piano break.
The people in the middle were
In one way, more pe-cu-li-er
Than those below, or those above,
Because the middle folks had *love*.
The lower, and the upper lower
Both were animal, and slower.
While those on top, and this ain't funny,
Were much too busy making money.

He pulls out handkerchief. Coins drop out on stage.

Piano break.
But the fact that we found most amazin'
Was the following deep observation:
People in the lower, lower,
Though perhaps they're somewhat slower,
Often have a better lot
Than all the floozy ones on top.
Because they have no fear of falling
From their class. The thought's appalling.
Means that, for security,
The <u>bottom</u> is the place to be.

Starts offstage. Turns:
Except for me.

Goes off.

Bob Pollack usually did the skits for the annual party, the Revels, at the Quadrangle Club, a combined faculty and neighborhood club in a very pleasant building on campus. There was usually a chorus line that was remarkably good; it was always a pleasure to see how much talent and good looks were in our university community.

During our first year the faculty wives had a dinner on the night that the trustees held their annual dinner for the faculty. Some of the women had recently started a cooperative nursery school in which everyone with children in school, and others too, contributed services. I was amazed and delighted to see Mabel Cole, wife of the chairman of anthropology and a lovely, dignified lady, dressed in a romper suit for a spoof on the nursery school.

At Harvard, faculty wives had come together as a group for weekly teas at the faculty club. When James Bryant Conant became president, he and his wife joined in many social occasions, usually in an informal fashion, which gave us all great pleasure after so long a period with no Mrs. Lowell. So we were looking forward to being in a university where there would be a president's wife. Our first year we went to the New Year's Day reception at the Hutchinses; promptly at six the receiving line disappeared and so did the Hutchinses. Some of us went off to dinner agreeing that we felt tolerated rather than welcomed, and it was the last time Lloyd and I attended. The first faculty wives' dinner Mrs. Hutchins did not decline nor appear; but old Mrs. Harper, who was truly the dean of faculty wives, was there.

Mabel Cole became a warm friend. She was a member of Friends in Council, a small group, said to be the oldest club in Chicago. Meetings were held in members' homes; papers were read on the subject for the year. When she took me as a guest, the general subject was poetry and the paper was on Greek poetry. It was impressively erudite, and the essayist was dismayed because of her inability to find a citation to illustrate a certain meter, whereupon another member spoke up with the citation and quoted it in Greek. It was that kind of club. I was flattered to be asked to join and worked as hard at preparing my papers as ever I had for a college assignment. One of my papers was a comparison of Karl Marx and Spengler that Lloyd felt was good enough to read at a meeting of the Contributors' Club.

The Coles felt as we did about entertaining students in our home. Mabel especially felt that as products of the University of Chicago they should be equipped to go anywhere in the world, mingle with any kind of group, and feel comfortable and be a credit to the university. Realizing at dinner one evening that the student seated beside her was mystified by the arrival of the maid exactly when she was needed, she showed him the service bell at her foot and decided then that they would have students from time to time among their other guests to add to their social experience. No country bumpkins would represent the Department of Anthropology; they would be people at ease in any social stratum anywhere.

The Coles had a warm, intimate relationship—mutual confidence and trust—which in itself gave pleasure to their companions. They did field work together in the Phillipines. Mabel's own writing as well as her collaboration with Fay established her reputation as a professional recognized by an entry in *Who's Who in America*.

Lloyd had not felt well in the fall, especially lacking his usual energy. I should have taken a cue from the fact that quite a quantity of hair would lie on his pillow each morning. Fay-Cooper Cole decided that he had been working too hard and should take time off but felt that in order to take this position with the administration, he should have a medical opinion. After his examination and the recommendation to Fay that Lloyd "be put on ice for a while," the doctor followed me down the stairs and commented that having a baby was sometimes hard on fathers too. I was sufficiently troubled to feel that this was a comment I could well do without. And it sounded too much like the couvade.

Our son Bill was born in March 1939. Our friends had expected us to have another baby now that we had such a big house! It is true that we felt social space important to a developing little person, important that each child have a room of his own and play area within the house and outside as well.

William Taylor, named after Lloyd's father, was the first baby born to a member of the Friends in Council in many years, so his anticipated arrival caused quite a little excitement. I was overwhelmed with gifts. Flowers and flowers arrived at the hospital — an enormous bouquet of red roses from the Hutchinses, a very nice bit of attention given new arrivals.

During the quarter "on ice" Lloyd worked on a curtailed schedule, and we eliminated all social life. It was an important regenerative period and one in which we seriously assessed how we were living and how we wanted to live. We realized that we were actively involved in about three social groups, all of whom we enjoyed and with whom we wanted to continue, but on the fringe and not in the center. As Lloyd resumed teaching we began to go out again and found that many of our friends had been hurt by our absence; they had not realized that it was necessary and not due to lagging interest. One afternoon we were returning from a series of holiday parties — Hyde Park was another Lewisburg Square at Christmastime — and as we came up the walk we saw Ann and Caroline kneeling at the library window, waiting for our return. We asked them to join us at dinner, had a most delightful conversation, and realized that the best companionship we had had that day was right here. From then on the children had dinner with us. Lloyd set some ground rules — no subjects of conversation that would lead to arguments and each person would have the opportunity to talk about his experiences that day.

In 1940, as Professor Nelson's estate was increasingly anxious to sell the house, yet would make no improvements — preferring to reduce the price — we realized that it would soon be sold and knew that it meant so much to us that we could not give it up. So we bought it and had the great joy of doing all of the things that we had longed to do — siding repaired, pillars renewed, the exterior painted white, new roofs (there were eight!). And then Lloyd decided we should remodel the interior and create a small apartment across the back. We had an architect do the working drawings, removing the walls in the servants' rooms upstairs, making a study for Lloyd, with a fireplace, and glassing in the porch adjoining. His downstairs study became the living room of the apartment, half of the old kitchen became the bedroom, and there was space for a small kitchen. The other half of the kitchen became the children's playroom, and the former playroom the kitchen—easy, with all its cabinets. We found beautiful wallpaper for all of the rooms, and I sewed drapes, slipcovers, bedspreads, doing the handwork while watching Bill playing in the front yard. We had had it fenced to give the house a setting and to keep out blowing trash and dogs. We invested as much in improvements as we had paid in the initial purchase, using all of our resources and a big mortgage. It was well that Lloyd had started adjusting his attitudes toward possessions when the first baby arrived because we had possessions now in double decibels. It is hard to describe the joy we had in bringing that house back to the beauty it had lost. Our neighbors hung flags at their windows to express their pleasure and relief when we bought it. They had been fearful that it would be converted to apartments.

But the period of remodeling was one of the worst either of us had experienced in terms of physical discomfort and lack of good faith in relationships with workmen. Having baskets of plaster hauled down the steps made it impossible to clean. I don't know how we kept help. Lloyd could not work at home. Bill at two imitated the workmen by hammering wood into freshly finished walls, climbing ladders, and using anything as a toy, including the family silver, which neighbors helped retrieve. We had decorators for six weeks, after all of the carpentry had been completed—six weeks for interior work alone. They were Swedes, of great skill and integrity, and of course were working in the phase that brought the house to life. When we finally had to call a halt to further expenditure, they taught me tricks of the trade in painting mullions and beautifully carved door frames, came each night to prepare me for the next day, mixing white paint with such skill that one coat would cover the dark brown of the library woodwork, and I finished the project. My parents, who had helped us with a loan as they had helped my sisters acquire their homes, were delighted. In his explorations, my father found a newspaper, brown, brittle, dated 1912, stuffed into a cranny in the attic. There were manuscripts of Professor Nelson there, and furniture, some quite nice but of no interest to anyone in the Nelson family.

Mother was becoming distressed about our family silver—what had happened to it? The Hootons had started the set—Mary had taken Mary Coon and me to Shreve, Crump, and Low in Boston, and made a wedding gift of the pattern each selected, and my family had filled in. I could offer no excuse.

There were times when the children were little when we felt that

Chicago, Dorchester Avenue

Mildred and W. Lloyd Warner

we had too many guests; it was confusing and disruptive to the youngsters. But as they grew older and could appreciate good conversation and meeting distinguished visitors they were pleased and no longer minded sharing their parents' attention.

Margaret Mead was staying with us while having pregnancy tests at Lying In. She and Gregory Bateson so much wanted children, and when the report was negative she was upset—needlessly, as it turned out, for the test reports were in error and Catherine was really on the way. She watched me give Bill his bottle and gave me a lecture (as she had done with her sister Priscilla) about how all primitive women could breast-feed their infants and so could we if we really wanted to. She did not mention the fact that in most primitive societies there is always a breast available.

Gunnar Myrdal came for coffee one morning when he was traveling through the country interviewing social scientists for his *American Dilemma*. At the time Lloyd was involved with research on the Negro community in Chicago. Myrdal had a talent for gathering much knowledge in a field from others and putting it together in one work. We had just finished the remodeling of our house and were happy about owning a beautiful home, which we treasured. As he was leaving Myrdal expressed his disappointment that people in the academic profession were not appreciated in the United States as in China—or even in Sweden. He looked around our house and said, "For instance, this house in Sweden would be considered a slum."

In spite of Lloyd's close feelings and admiration for Bob Redfield, his closeness to Hutchins did not warm Lloyd's feelings for our chancellor. He admired him for his brilliant mind, his wit, yes, but deplored his arrogance and his effect on the university. Lloyd and Hutchins had respect for each other's ability but realized that they were incompatible spirits. We were not aware of Maude Hutchins' problems until the Christmas cards appeared with her line drawing of a nude figure of a young girl, her legs spread, an arm upraised holding a candle—or this is my recollection. The figure was generally identified as the Hutchinses' daughter Joanna; the story in the press caused reverberations throughout the country.

It was our understanding that Maude Hutchins had refused to come to Chicago; her interests were in the arts and she preferred to stay on the East Coast. Then she agreed upon the condition that the president's house be redecorated professionally. The university asked Louise Wright, the wife of Quincy Wright and a talented person in many fields, to undertake the task, which she did with great good will and excellent results. Charles Merriam, a member of the "search and seizure" committee for a new president, had felt that the choice of Hutchins was a mistake not only for the university but for Hutchins himself, that Hutchins was lacking in the maturity required for the presidency of such a large and complex institution in spite of his position as dean of the Law School at Yale; that it would hinder the development of his career, ultimately, for him to assume the post. He was only thirty years old.

His presidency began in the fall of 1929. By fall of 1930 he was reorganizing the university into four graduate divisions that would begin with the usual junior year. Students in the first two years would be in the College, which would take students at the junior level of preparatory school if they qualified in the entrance examinations. The four divisions were the Biological Sciences, the Physical Sciences, the Humanities, and the Social Sciences. History would be in both Humanities and Social Sciences. This plan was essentially first announced by President Harper in 1902 when he called for the designation of freshman and sophomore classes as a junior college, separated from higher work and assigned to an independent faculty.[2] At that time Harper also announced the four-quarter system with the summer term to be an organic part of the university year and stressed the importance of liberty, individualism, and flexibility. Hutchins' problems occurred not with curricula but with proposed new faculty appointments: Mortimer Adler, from the Philosophy Department at Columbia, Scott Buchanan, Richard McKeon, and V. J. McGill. Adler in his book *Philosopher at Large*,[3] in which he shows remarkable maturation as well as understanding and candor about his earlier years, says that Hutchins, when his new appointments encountered barriers, remarked that it had never occurred to him that academic appointments are not made by presidential fiat. Appointments to several departments were consistent with the cross-discipline theory being followed by the university—the "cross fertilization of ideas" theory that led to the Committee on Social Thought and the Committee on Human Development. The problem was that the Department of Philosophy felt that an appointment was being made to its faculty initiated not by the department but by the administration of the university, and there was resentment and hostility.

Stringfellow Barr and Scott Buchanan went on to take over St. John's College, which had been a kind of private naval college now defunct, where they would fulfill Hutchins' and Adler's dream of education based on readings in classics of western European literature.

At Chicago the curriculum in the College was based on survey courses that would introduce the students to all fields of knowledge through large lecture courses followed by small discussion groups. The lectures would give students exposure to all of the fields of study available at the university as presented by distinguished professors, thus not only giving them a sound general education in the four primary disciplines but helping them make a wise decision about their fields of concentration at the divisional level. This program, with some modifications, is still in effect. The university had problems for a while at least in getting students for the first two years from the preparatory schools that had fed students to them in the past, for the university was competing for the very students the schools wanted most to keep until graduation. There were also problems with the lack of social maturation of students, the equivalent of high school juniors, entering a large urban campus. Class attendance was not required, nor were attendance records kept at first. But when parents learned in a few instances that their children had disappeared and the university was not aware, they were outraged that the university was so unmindful of its trust. The program of the University High School was coordinated with that of the College.

When our daughter Ann graduated from the University High School at age sixteen, after completing what would have been conventionally the sophomore year, and entered the College, we were appalled at the students she would bring home. The lack of social graces was not apparent in the general society at that time, but it certainly was in the group of students who had done sufficiently well to enter the College but had done so without learning how to participate in the larger university community. Under the New Plan, a student could enter the College as a freshman, attend classes or not, as he wished, pass the comprehensive examinations in his field of concentration, and receive his master's degree in one and two-thirds years, thereby meeting his residence requirements. While I was assistant dean of students in the social sciences, two students did exactly that. In each case there was considerable pride in achievement and much praise; my own feelings were that what both needed most from the university they did not receive, social maturation and a little wisdom. They entered campus as serious scholars, precocious, able, to the exclusion of everything else that our society has to offer, and this is the way they left.

In his inaugural address Hutchins recommended a scheme of pass and honors work which would divide courses into large lectures and small discussion groups. Adler had mentioned to Hutchins the General Honors course at Columbia, and says that Hutchins wanted to follow it, read the books for his own enlightenment, and that out of this grew one of the main parts of the program of educational reforms associated with Hutchins. Adler proposed that Hutchins develop a new department of philosophical studies that would project philosophical thought into the Law and Medical schools, the Departments of Education, Psychology, the social sciences generally. The synthesis would be provided by a "Summa Theologica" or, as Adler and Buchanan put it, a "Summa Dialectica."

Adler had brought Arthur Rubin with him from Columbia to work closely with Hutchins. He harangued Adler on the scientific pretentions of the social studies "which had just begun to assume a certain prominence on the academic scene." Adler wrote some memos critical of the logic and method of the so-called "social sciences"—how they fall short of the precision of "exact sciences" (a hackneyed concept, to be sure)—and he showed them to Bob Lynd, who suggested that a paper be presented at the Dartmouth Conference. Lynd was executive secretary of the Social Science Research Council at the time. At his suggestion the title of the Memos— "Theses on the Distinction between the Exact and the Inexact Sciences"—was changed to "The Social Scientist's Misconception of Science," and, in Adler's absence, it was circulated at the conference.[4] Lynd was not known for perception or skill in handling people in relation to issues; he had a kind of head-on approach that made it difficult for him to have his ideas accepted. Adler should have known better than to follow Lynd's advice in presenting his ideas as an attack and in mimeographed form rather than in a discussion group with at least a few sponsors.

Donald Slesinger, now Dean of Students in the social sciences, who had worked with Hutchins at Yale on psychology as applied to the law of evidence, proposed that Adler read the paper before the fall meeting of the local SSRC, attended by all of the leading professors of sociology, economics, political science, and anthropology. "The distinction between exact sciences (the physical sciences) and in-exact sciences (the social sciences) is a distinction between good and bad science, not between two different kinds of science.

"Current research programmes in the social sciences are misdirected and methodologically ill-advised because of erroneous conceptions of the nature of science which comprise the 'raw empiricism' characteristic of contemporary social science. ... We can now enumerate the leading misconceptions which prevail among social scientists." Only theoretical and mathematical economics received a friendly nod as an approximation to exact science, and sociology was acknowledged the worst offender, the farthest from what a science should be. It was not long before Adler realized that he had now succeeded in alienating most of the social scientists at the university (and elsewhere) as well as members of the Department of Philosophy. If there were any doubt—and one wonders if it were possible that he had not deliberately set out to be offensive—this was resolved by Merriam's reprimanding him for having trodden so heavily and clumsily on people with whom he and Hutchins would have to work in effecting reforms, educational and intellectual, at the university.

The General Honors Course, given by Hutchins and Adler to twenty freshman students who qualified, emphasized the teachings of St. Thomas Aquinas. As a result, it was said generally that Adler and Hutchins had both become Catholic and were proseletyzing for the Catholic Church, which was most unfortunate, because it aroused the parents of young students entering the university who felt they were being betrayed, especially the Jewish parents. We heard of this first through Frank Sulzberger. Frank, for years treasurer of the board of trustees of the university and a member of the United Jewish Charities, was deeply troubled by the complaints about the growing Catholicism among their children at the university. The course with its reading list became the Great Books Foundation.

In 1933 Beardsley Ruml, from the directorship of the Laura Spelman Rockefeller Memorial, where he had done so much to advance the interests of the social sciences, came to the University of Chicago as dean of that division. Ruml's position, according to Adler, was that social science departments dealt with closely related aspects of the same subject matter. "Society, after all, was one thing and should be studied as one thing even though sociologists, economists, political scientists, and cultural anthropologists each approach it differently." He thought that differences in approach and jargon could be overcome to produce a unified social science. So with Adler he conducted a seminar in Systematic Social Science. Adler lectured to a distinguished group of graduate students and senior professors on pure and applied logic, philosophy, and psychology.

In spring quarter the floodgates burst, professors allowed their graduate students to unleash an attack on the very idea of a unified social science and on the total irrelevance of Adler's lectures.[5] Ruml left in 1934 to become vice president and treasurer of R.H. Macy—and developed the concept of the withholding tax. I had known him as a friend of Mary Charles Cole, as an able administrator, amusing, somewhat outrageous. Lloyd had known him as a most supportive person for his research ideas and as the brother of Frances Jordan who, with her husband, Kitch, was a friend of Lloyd's from early Harvard days.

During this period it seemed to us that the faculty spent more time fighting Hutchins than in teaching and research. With the war and increasing absences of faculty from campus as they went to Washington to work in advisory capacities, the administration of the university instituted the four-quarter system. Faculty salaries would be raised 25 percent to reflect the fourth quarter, which had always been free time and, in return, all outside earnings—lecture fees, salaries during residence in other universities, royalties from books written after the inception of the plan—were to be given to the university. Joining this plan was voluntary. We chose not to—not because we would not have welcomed the increase in salary that was certainly in excess of Lloyd's outside earnings, but, like many people throughout the country, we opposed it in principle. By extension, the university's claim to all of the output of a faculty member became ownership of that member's person. It was called slavery. Faculty meetings were held and an opinion study made by the faculty senate. I was asked to work up the results; a person was needed with some knowledge of statistics who could be relied upon not to disclose names of respondents. Of course the plan was voted down. After its demise it was difficult for the university to reduce salaries, so those who had chosen to be part of the four-quarter system had some financial benefit. We had anticipated this when we made our choice and were content with our decision.

With all of Hutchins' hostility to the social sciences, Lloyd's work proceeded pretty much as he wanted it to. Financing came from outside sources; he was always successful in securing research funds. In part this was because he completed the projects foundations financed and published his findings. All too often foundation grants have no visible results. I saw this first at the SSRC, where the wall behind my desk was lined with shelves of research reports in non-publishable form, and often a grant did not result in a written report of any kind. Lloyd was also successful in securing research funds for his students and in placing them in good positions. Often he was asked to recommend graduates by colleges and universities in excess of any number possibly available.

Lloyd and Hutchins, however, had a kind of respect for each other and enjoyed meeting; each was tall, quick-witted, amusing, intelligent, and committed to his own way of thinking. One could have predicted that Hutchins would belong to America First. He was joined by many distinguished citizens—General Robert Wood, of Sears Roebuck, the Charles Lindberghs, Bill Benton, who had left Benton and Bowles, the advertising company he helped to found, to become vice president of the university, and the Will Ogburns, among a host of others. But when the university was asked to take on the Manhattan Project, Hutchins accepted. We had many friends in this project who certainly did maintain secrecy; it brought delightful people to our campus—I think of the Enrico Fermis, quiet, lovely, rather shy people, both tremendously able though her ability was not apparent until after his death. And it involved many of the outstanding scientists on our faculty as well as laymen in the community.

Not long after Edmund Day became president of Cornell University he offered Lloyd a full professorship in both sociology and anthropology, unlimited tenure, and the assurance that his proposal had the endorsement of other members of the department. Lloyd's closeness to Day, his high regard for him, and his confidence that Day cared sufficiently about his career to feel that his interests would be advanced at Cornell made the offer very appealing. On the other hand, he was excited by the work being done at the University of Chicago and felt that he had not been there long enough to have a solid experience. We felt that we should accept the Days' invitation to spend a weekend with them in Ithaca. While Rufus took Lloyd around to meet people, Mrs. Day showed me living areas, the campus, and the shops. The president's house was most attractive, the guest suite beautifully arranged and appointed with every convenience. The house was meticulously clean yet we never saw anyone cleaning. Boys from the university cleaned the fireplaces each day and laid a fresh fire.

Guests were invited to meet us, dinner was formal, and the conversation was interesting. Mrs. Day had a hearing impairment that had troubled her for a long time; a member of the board had a device made which allowed her to hear perfectly, but it was too large to be mobile. Yet as she took me around to the women's dorms she spoke easily with the students, who were pleased with her interest.

Ithaca, in the Finger Lakes country, is beautiful with deep wooded ravines and many homes with magnificent views. But people who live there often complain of its isolation since it is difficult to reach by train or plane. Lloyd felt this in the intellectual life of the campus.

March 6, 1940

Dear Lloyd:

At long last we are in a position to talk business. I am sorry to have been so slow in getting to this point but budgetary complications have made it impossible before this to see just what we could do. Furthermore, I have thought it best to canvass rather thoroughly with Cottrell and other members of the Department the general ideas we have had under discussion before moving into any formal negotiations. The situation at this end is now thoroughly cleared and I am eager to go forward with an exchange of views looking toward an early decision.

The proposal which I am now able to present to you follows the lines which we talked over when you were here. It involves the headship of the Department of Anthropology and Sociology, with an appointment as full Professor on unlimited tenure at a salary of $7000. We operate under the customary arrangement regarding a pension on retirement at age 65, this arrangement calling for a contribution by the incumbent of 5% of salary, this contribution to be matched by an equivalent sum on the part of the University. Unless I am mistaken, these same arrangements are in effect at the University of Chicago.

This proposal has the approval of Professor Cottrell and the other members of the Department in the College of Arts and Sciences and has, as well, the endorsement of the members of the Department of Rural Sociology in the College of Agriculture. I think you can be assured of the enthusiastic support and cooperation of the several colleagues with whom you would be immediately associated, to say nothing of the larger company of the University Faculty. While the Department in the College of Arts and Sciences which you would be heading is a new one and is still in an early state of development, it is to be noted that there is a rapidly increasing interest in anthropology and sociology on this campus and a disposition on the part of the administration to promote more work in this field. We have already made arrangements to bring in an additional member of the Department next year to take care of the field of social statistics, which is not now adequately covered.

As you know, I earnestly hope that the opportunities here will seem as unusual to you as they do to me and that you will decide to cast your lot with us. If, when you have canvassed the matter thoroughly at that end, you conclude that you are favorably disposed toward our proposal, I suggest that you come in to see us again so that we may talk further details with the Department members and close a formal agreement. We shall be glad, of course, to cover the expenses of such a trip. In general, I am anxious for you to see the situation here in all its detail before you make your final commitment. You know already how much satisfaction I would take personally in having you as an associate in the work in the social science field here at Cornell. I have rather definite ideas regarding the developments which I should like to see come in this area over the next few years on this campus, and I am quite sure that we have an unusual chance to do things which would have large significance and which cannot be as readily effected elsewhere. While I realize fully that you are well situated where you are, I would not be suggesting that you come to Cornell did I not think that you might fare even better here. Will you not let me know as soon as you can how matters are now shaping in your own mind. Do not fail to let me know right away if there are any phases of the opening here with regard to which you do not have as much information as you need to reach even a tentative conclusion. You know how anxious I am to bring the whole prospect into the open and to make it extraordinarily attractive for you.

Faithfully yours,

The prevailing consideration in our decision not to accept was that the excitement of the social sciences at the University of Chicago— colleagues, students, the research environment—all of the elements that had attracted us in the first place were still there and only barely experienced. It was certainly too soon to leave.

Notes to Chapter X

1. John Drury, *Old Chicago Houses* (Chicago: University of Chicago Press, 1941). See also Jean F. Black, *Hyde Park Houses* (Chicago, University of Chicago Press, 1978).
2. William Michael Murphy and D.J.R. Bruckner, eds., *The Idea of the University of Chicago* (Chicago: University of Chicago Press, 1976), pp. 292-301.
3. Mortimer J. Adler, *Philosopher at Large, An Intellectual Autobiography* (New York, Macmillan, 1977).
4. Ibid.
5. Ibid.

WE WERE STILL LIVING in Cambridge, of course, when Hitler came to power. I remember our experiencing a feeling of near strangulation with the ruthless spread of fascism and Nazism, a gut fear of its spread through the world—Spain already the tragic battleground for the test war of the forces of fascism and communism. Lloyd was pinned to the radio listening to Hitler's fanatic harangues to the German people. I was at Lying In Hospital at the University of Chicago after Bill's birth in 1939, reading André Malraux's *Man's Hope,* when the news came of Barcelona's fall. Feelings were intense about aiding the Allies or striving to keep out of the war as the only goal—America First. We became active in the William Allen White Committee to Defend America by Aiding the Allies. I ran the speakers' bureau for our Hyde Park community, and Lloyd carried at least his share of the work. It was a time when, in any gathering of friends, every effort would be made to keep the conversation away from this most divisive subject.

At a meeting of the William Allen White committee Lloyd met Frank Smothers, foreign correspondent for the *Chicago Daily News,* which was noted for its prestigious foreign service. With his family Smothers had lived in many countries of Europe and in China. They were living in a western suburb but moved to Hyde Park. Soon after, Marshall Field started publishing the *Chicago Sun* and raided every newspaper in the country to gather a top staff, holding out the attraction of starting a new, exciting, bold enterprise. Frank became editor of the editorial page. He and his wife were able, intelligent, attractive. She had been raised as a Catholic and he had become a Catholic as a teenager and was, if anything, more doctrinaire than she and more knowledgeable of church ritual. We became close friends, often stopping to talk for a while in the evening. Lloyd was interested in talking about the Catholic Church, especially with Dode, who had been educated in a convent, and we all enjoyed politics. When Field changed policy and summarily fired most of the staff whom he had inspired to join him, Lloyd spoke to Frank Bane, head of the Council of State Governments, about putting Frank Smothers on his staff as editor of the council's yearbooks, and there he stayed until retirement. But once a newspaper man . . . He was in China at the time of the long march of Mao Tse Tung and his followers and described them as not so much communists as agrarian revolutionaries. He had no confidence in Chiang Kai Shek and thought of him as an exploitative seeker of personal power.

As the United States geared up to the production of war material for England, Lloyd and Bob Havighurst both felt that, as in World War I, Negroes would be recruited in the South for northern industry. As industry employed blacks and promoted them, their concern was for developing and maintaining a state of race relations that would avoid problems when blacks were put in supervisory positions. Burleigh Gardner had left the Soil Conservation Service to return to Western Electric; he then began teaching evening courses at the Business School of the University of Chicago and also free-lanced as a consultant. The idea for a Committee on Human Relations in Industry was largely his; Lloyd and Bob Havighurst joined the project as the medium they thought would put them in contact with management in studying and resolving the racial problems which they were anticipating.

The first focus of the committee was the study of the black when he entered the work situation, and it was realized that he could become a foreman or supervisor. No one believed that it was possible at that time. But with the research for *Black Metropolis*[1] in his background, Lloyd realized how the work situation would develop and was prepared for it.

Bill Dickson and Fritz Roethlisberger had published *Management and the Worker*,[2] their report on the Western Electric research, and then stayed in the counseling program there, joined by Burleigh, to help with development and research. They actually applied the findings of the Western Electric research in which Lloyd, working under Mayo, had so large a part. Their book had wide readership, and still does, so this type of research was familiar to many business leaders.

Burleigh's little group picked up some publicity, especially around its two University of Chicago professors. A call came from George Watkins, a loyal supporter of Lloyd's work and vice president in charge of development at the university. "Lloyd, what's this you are doing?" Then, "Walter Paepcke says it ought to be in the University." Walter Paepcke was a trustee of the university and president of Container Corporation of America. Discussions started that led to Burleigh's full-time appointment to the faculty of the Business School, which meant that there would be, to some degree, integration of the social sciences into the programs in the School of Business. George Brown, of the Business School (who later went to Ford, then the Bureau of the Census, later the Conference Board in New York) was delegated by the Business School to seek corporation involvement and support. The Committee on Human Relations in Industry was established with Lloyd, Burleigh, Bob Havighurst, Everett Hughes, Allison Davis, and Fred Harbison, who soon became involved with Lyle Spencer and Robert Burns in the organization of the Committee on Industrial Relations, also associated, but tenuously, with the School of Business.

I remember Lyle Spencer as an outstanding, bright student in the Social Science Division. Bob Havighurst remembers him when he asked the GEB for a grant to help him and Bob Burns in educational tests they were developing and in the publication of a scries of goal- and skill-oriented pamphlets. Bob had to refuse because the proposal was outside of the GEB program, but he saw Lyle go on to become head of a very success-ful publishing company, Science Research Associates, which later he sold to IBM. Upon his death in 1969, he left a foundation capitalized at $65 million. From the beginning, the Committee on Industrial Relations was a profit-making enterprise as contrasted with the Committee on Human Re-lations in Industry, which was closely associated with the university and research-oriented.

The first research grant received by Human Relations in Industry was from the Container Corporation. Sears Roebuck, where management had been impressed with the results of the Western Electric research and wanted to set up its own counseling program, came in. Howard Goodman, head of Goodman Manufacturing and a trustee of the university, and the American Restaurant Association both gave grants. The Committee brought in William F. Whyte, a student of Lloyd's at Harvard who got his Ph.D. there with his study of north Boston—*Street Corner Society.*[3] *Human Relations in the Restaurant Industry*[4] was Whyte's report on the Restaurant Association research.

Burleigh had published *Human Relations in Industry.*[5] He felt that the university system was limiting and departmental meetings a waste of time. He had enjoyed free-lancing and working with the Committee on Human Relations in Industry. So he proposed starting a consulting firm. Lloyd had long wanted to work through an organization to apply his ideas directly to business situations. Burleigh and Lloyd talked it over in our garden and set up a plan for a small consulting firm, with Burleigh doing the organizational work joined by Lloyd and Bill Henry as consultants and Buford Junker, Paul Lunt, and others as project workers. Lloyd and Bill Henry, a psychologist member of the Committee on Human Relations, had done a symbolic analysis of radio's daytime serial programs.[6]

Social Research Incorporated (SRI) did not become involved with government work, but Lloyd made trips to Washington when he was asked to work for various agencies. One invitation had such strong appeal that he seriously considered asking for leave from the university—to work with Bill Donovan in O.S.S. He was charged with ideas for it and did all he could with the time he had. Later another invitation almost won him from académe when James Webb took over the operation of NASA and asked Lloyd to join him in helping with organizational problems. But he always felt that there was not enough time to carry all of his research ideas to fruition; he knew that unless he steered a straight course, refusing diver-sions no matter how attractive, he would in the end be frustrated.

SRI had no capital and was forced to build its accounts from scratch without even a proper office. Harriett Moore, a psychologist doing work for her advanced degree at the University Clinics, and then in the Department of Education, worked with Bill Henry on the analysis of Thematic Apperception Tests (TATs)[7] administered to the executives and applicants for executive positions in large firms. Accounts came in from advertising firms who realized what it could mean to them to have symbolic analyses made of their products' acceptance by the market and know who comprised that market by class level and income. Information was collected systematically about the lives of mass-market women, their role in purchasing, their relationship to food products and to advertising, and their attitudes and behaviors. Much of this research was carried on by Earl Kahn, who was working for an advanced degree at the university while associated with David Moore at Sears Roebuck in personnel planning, trouble shooting, and studying employee attitudes; and by Leone Phillips, who was in from the beginning and did everything from typing to assembling cadres of interviewers all over the country. They trained to do market testing of specific types of groups. Much of the training was done using Lloyd's techniques of selecting samples representing different classes.

Burleigh became the businessman to attract accounts and promote the work. Everyone helped recruit bright people, especially part-time graduate students from the University of Chicago. Bob Havighurst feels that this system worked to the benefit of SRI and of the university since it gave students training in the application of theoretical knowledge. Burleigh talks of Lloyd's role as consultant, his attraction to the work because of the diversity of his interests, and recalls how, at Harvard, he brought his students in touch with the whole field of symbolic analysis, especially in language as in Ogden and Richards' *Meaning of Meaning*.[8] When Alfred Korzybski, the author of *Science and Sanity*,[9] came to Chicago Lloyd encouraged his students to go to the seminars given in his apartment near campus. Korzybski would have liked Lloyd to use influence in securing an invitation to join the faculty, but Lloyd felt that he was too much of a cultist, as indeed he had become, though students would have much to learn from working with him informally.

SRI was an extraordinary organization in the way its people stimulated each other, the work of each complementing the others', a single unit highly productive of a great variety of innovative ideas and theories and the techniques to carry them out. All of the different points of view were applied to understanding the given phenomena whether it was a television program or what was going on among the employees in a plant or out in the community.

The American Hospital Association was one of the first clients, then Sears Roebuck and the Encyclopaedia Britannica. As Sears' interest in TATs increased, Harriet Moore was asked to help Bill Henry and Bob Peck, also from Human Development, with the analyses. Burleigh and Bill

Harrison were counseling industrial management on organization and employee relations. The first marketing work, for the Gardner Advertising Agency, involved symbolic analysis in which Lloyd took part with Burleigh and Bill Henry. The Gardner Agency was so impressed with the results that they asked for TATs to be done on their executive personnel, abetted by guideline discussions of weaknesses and strengths. The Gardner account was very important to the development of SRI, opening up the world of advertising and consumer research. Burleigh had difficulty adapting the research he knew in the anthropological pattern, whereas Lloyd was able to make visible, obvious, and continuous efforts to comprehend survey techniques as opposed to participant-observer techniques and to understand something of the structure of sampling—to utilize interviews from various social-class levels. The research was entirely qualitative. But when more interviews were needed it was necessary to move from the personal observations and conversations to written questionnaires, which Lloyd helped to prepare—long, totally qualitative, no "yes or no, undecided" kind of thing.

For one account with Gardner, Sid Levy and Harriett Moore, both psychologists, began designing projective techniques that would discover the symbolic dynamics of the selection by the market of certain products as if they had been doing TATs. This moved the research away from the long interviews to a more economical approach but always with what was called classification data on the respondents—parents and grandparents, educational history, occupational history, plans for the future. This then had to be viewed in relation to communication, trying to get at mobility—past, present, anticipated—in order to evaluate advertising and interpretation of products. *Social Class in America*[10] was viewed by the research staff at Social Research as a bible.

Jim Worthy was head of personnel planning at Sears. Dave Moore, who was one of his three bright boys, knew Lloyd from the University of Chicago and was the contact with Jim on this and the work that had been done for Sears by the Committee on Human Relations in Industry. The development pattern was to diversify as people in SRI achieved the capabilities—TATs and other projective techniques, consulting for management organization, morale surveys, advertising, symbolic analyses, and studies of life style in relation to social class were among the early activities. Product research came in later. Examples of projects carried on: a sociological, psychological, anthropological analysis of consumer acceptance for the Tea Council, which hit the market like a bomb; and a background study of illnesses, what people think are good and bad illnesses, and the role of proprietary drugs for Miles Laboratories. All were in-depth studies. A landmark study was done for the *Chicago Tribune* on cigarette advertising—the purpose of the *Tribune* was to eventually sell more cigarette advertising, but the study was on people's attitudes toward smoking.

In all of these efforts, Lloyd's role was to contribute his knowledge and experience with research—to train researchers, give guidance, formally and informally, and then let people carry on. University of Chicago students continued to be fed into the firm, receiving invaluable field training as they worked for their advanced degrees, many of them staying on with SRI if there were openings for them. There was never a desire to expand; everyone involved realized the value of the close working relation, the interstimulation, of the small group—bright and quick to pick up on one another's ideas. Harriett Moore was the only one, for quite some time, who had not come from the Committee on Human Development.

One of the accounts was Crawfords, a large advertising agency in London that sent some of its people to this country after the war to look at various kinds of advertising agencies, research facilities, and some industries. They came to SRI through contacts at the University of Chicago. When Lloyd taught at Cambridge he was asked by SRI to meet with the Crawfords people from time to time to help with the accounts SRI had with them. This was fun for Lloyd. He always enjoyed London and found the people at Crawfords sophisticated, able, witty, and amusing. Lunches were always at a fashionable French restaurant with excellent food. Much as he enjoyed life at the university and his work there, the sessions with Crawfords were in a complete contrast and much enjoyed. I stopped there one day when I went to London with Lloyd and could easily understand his feeling. He loved the rapid give and take in conversation, in exchange of ideas; he liked working with quick and intelligent people who could pick up a point, develop it, and run with it.

Vance Packard was a frequent visitor, gathering material as the basis for *The Hidden Persuaders*,[11] which was considered at SRI to be such a bad book that no one really resented the lack of credits, though there was no doubt that most of his ideas came from Lloyd. However, it did give SRI a boost.

Projects were developed with transit systems that required much background research and staff discussions of segregation regarding public transit and capabilities of holding up in its present form. Paul Lunt undertook a study of the Capital Transit System on his own. And Lloyd became involved with a study of the Bureau of Standards.

It was at this time that SRI was engaged in large studies of the *Detroit Free Press*, the *Miami Herald*, the *Chicago Tribune*—studies of the newspapers, not circulation, and of how readers viewed the newspaper in relation to other newspapers. Of course the client's basic problem was always, how do we sell more? But that was not the orientation of the research. Robert R. McCormick was close to death, and the *Tribune* people were beginning to come out in the open with anxieties about the image of the *Tribune* and its total unacceptability to a large part of the community. Pierre Martineau, head of advertising, became a good friend of Lloyd's; he was a crazy, marvelous person and brilliant. In the course of SRI's study of the *Tribune* and its readership, the research people were having lunch at the Pearson, a rather staid hotel now replaced by the Ritz Carlton, when Pierre had one of his outbursts. "Jesus Christ, I don't know what's the matter with me, I spend all this money on you people and coddle you and coax you along and everything else to do a research for the *Chicago Tribune*, and there isn't a god damned person here that would be caught dead reading it." He and Lloyd worked on a book on consumer response to types of products. All of the research was complete, Lloyd had done much of the writing, when Pierre died, and Lloyd lost all interest.

No report by SRI ever had recommendations about how to sell more. They started with basic research. Yet the general development of market research—*consumer* research—was toward more actionable reports, recommendations. Apparently Burleigh was so committed to SRI's capabilities and resources that he would sell a job without truly realizing at the time how it would be accomplished. In a way this was excellent because it meant that the research had to be creative. Lloyd could pick it up, and he taught the research people as he developed the implementing ideas. Burleigh has often said that Lloyd taught through research, even going back to the days at Harvard.

Leone Phillips, who had started with SRI before it even had an office, had left to go to California but returned and was asked to come back. She recalls now how Burleigh took her to lunch, Bill Harrison took her to lunch, and both extolled the beauties and values of SRI. Then Lloyd took her to lunch and told her clearly, precisely that her job would be to hold hands. "Your job will be to see that there is some peace, some calmness in this organization, so that Harriett doesn't have a temper tantrum, Burleigh doesn't go wandering off in this direction or another." Nobody else had told her these things. "I will never forget as long as I live the way he outlined my job in a fabulous fashion."

One of SRI's early accounts was MacFadden, publisher of *True Story* and other journals, studying the composition of their readership. Rockford, Illinois, was used as a kind of laboratory for intensive research in the identification of social classes and their characteristics, making it possible for SRI to do intensive interviewing by social group. *Life* magazine got wind of the project and asked permission to do a photographic essay on the research findings. Margaret Bourke-White, the famous photographer and a person of great insight and intelligence who will long be remembered for her courage, came with a research team that included John Dille, assistant editor who later became managing editor. He and Bourke-White came to our house one afternoon to interview Lloyd before going to Rockford with their team. Lloyd and I were familiar with Bourke-White's work, beginning with her photographs of industry and of the concentration camps as she went into Germany with U.S. advance troops. She took seventy-two photographs of Lloyd that afternoon-evening; the one used with the article showed him speaking—as she said, projecting ideas verbally—a shot taken as we were all in discussion.

The *Life* team left for Rockford with some of Lloyd's people the following day, staying until they had the material for their story. The article described Lloyd's research and system of analysis, including the Index of Status Characteristics set out in *Social Class in America.* The subjects of the photographs were well chosen, and, through Bourke-White's camera, made an eloquent statement about the American way of life. With the help of Lloyd's trained field workers and the results of research completed, the *Life* team were able to put together the Rockford story in a few weeks. They were an interesting, highly trained, talented crew.

No one at *Life* ever knew when a story was going to be printed or pulled at the last minute because of a news break that might take priority. John Dille read the entire story over the telephone to Lloyd to secure his approval and clearance. Like most publishers, *Life*'s management was always concerned about possible libel. On the whole, we were pleased with the story and felt that the *Life* people had done a good job, very professional in every way.[12]

Then the mail began. One letter arrived airmail, special delivery, registered, from a couple in Florida who lived in a trailer community there and spent part of the year in a trailer in California. They expressed their indignation about the family in Rockford selected to represent the lower-lower class who lived in a trailer community. They sent us photographs of their elegant trailer and landscaping, in both Florida and California, and left no doubt that this was an ideal way of life admirably suited to middle-class values.

About 1952, Lloyd began to decrease his activity at SRI, feeling that it had begun to take too much time from his academic work. He decided that his name should not be used in connection with future researches, that he would go to the office from time to time for consultations with staff on specific projects but not on a regular basis. Later, after he went to Michigan State and *Big Business Leaders*[13] had been published, he resumed going to SRI on a once-a-week basis to be available to people who wanted to consult with him about their research, and he served in an advisory way on problems within the organization. Through his years of association he had much enjoyment and satisfaction, and the income was a help in paying tuition for preparatory school and college. We would have managed but it operated at that strategic margin.

1. St. Clair Drake and Horace R. Cayton, *Black Metropolis* (New York: Harper and Bros., 1945).
2. Bill Dickson and Fritz Roethlisberger, *Management and the Worker* (Cambridge: Harvard University Press, 1937).
3. William F. Whyte, *Street Corner Society* (Chicago: University of Chicago Press, 1943).
4. William F. Whyte, *Human Relations in the Restaurant Industry* (New York: McGraw Hill, 1948).
5. Burleigh B. Gardner and David G. Moore, *Human Relations in Industry* (Homewood, Illinois: R.D. Irwin, 1955).
6. *Genetic Psychology Monographs* 37: 3–71.
7. A projective method for the investigation and personality developed by Henry A. Murray and the staff of the Harvard Psychological Clinic. The protocol was later adapted to specific use with business executives by William E. Henry and Harriett Moore.
8. C.K. Ogden and I.A. Richards, *The Meaning of Meaning* (New York: Harcourt Brace and Co., 1938).
9. Alfred Korzybski, *Science and Sanity, An Introduction to Non-Aristotelian Systems and General Semantics* (New York: The Non-Aristotelian Publishing Co., 1933).
10. Kenneth Eels, Marchia Meeker, and W. Lloyd Warner, *Social Class in America* (Chicago: Science Research Associates, 1949; Gloucester: Peter Smith, 1957; rev. ed. New York: Harper Torch Books, 1960).
11. Vance Packard, *The Hidden Persuaders* (New York: McKay, 1957).
12. "A Sociologist Looks at the American Community," *Life* 27 (1949), photographs by Margaret Bourke-White.
13. W. Lloyd Warner and James C. Abegglen, *Big Business Leaders in America* (New York: Harper and Bros., 1959).

Formal portrait, 1950s

ABOUT THE TIME *Social Class in America* appeared in 1949, Lloyd received an invitation to deliver the Munro Lectures at the University of Edinburgh. These were honorary lectures in anthropology and prehistoric archaeology, and he was pleased with the invitation and encouraged by the University of Chicago to accept. The Rockefeller Foundation offered a travel grant to cover expenses. But he was reluctant to leave his research and his family. This made preparations difficult, and it seemed that he would never get it all put together. At the Englewood station, where he would take the train for New York, we were very much affected; I am not sure why this seemed different from previous trips, probably because he would be out of the country.

Then the letters started to arrive describing his feelings about leaving us and about how we had put our lives together as a family, around our home in Chicago, our place in the dunes. His letters were always written to all of us and signed "Lloyd and Daddy," sometimes "Lloyd, Daddy, and me." He had dinner with Flora in New York and she went with him to the boat the following day, for which he was grateful. They stopped first to buy books for the trip. Then he discovered that he was sharing a cabin with a former student from Chicago and commented "forever and ever I am a man who can go anywhere but who will always be kept in his place." It did seem to us that wherever we went, for whatever purpose, we always encountered people we knew or, rather, people who knew Lloyd.

He enjoyed the ship, the Cunard *Parthia*, and the excellent food. He shared a table with his cabin mate and Evans Pritchard, the anthropologist at Oxford who had been teaching in the United States.

The English on board he found their "usual nice decent selves, but something is gone from them, something I used to detest. They seem a little shocked; they've lost their supreme confidence, their superiority. It's too bad for they knew how to do it. The Americans are moving in, but they don't know how to do it. The English on board are largely upper-middle or upper. They're being wiped out, but you don't hear anyone complaining or so much as talking about it. When they go a major epoch of modern life will be gone, with the Russians and Americans the candidates to take their place and keep the world as decent as stupid humanity will permit it to be. I like Americans, but we don't have the seasoning nor the understanding. The Russians, of course, will happily escort us all to the security of a penal colony."

He commented that few dressed for dinner. The young Englishmen back from the war were too big and broad for old suits and unable to afford new ones, but the older people dressed as formerly. "Maybe it was swank and nonsense, but this and many other rituals nurtured by the English gave the outward forms of life a significance and well mannered charm that helped compensate for the ugly realities of being a human animal."

Many people were seasick but not Lloyd. He must have been born with a stabilizer. "Weather has improved, people are enjoying it though the ship is taking a more southerly route which will make arrival late." His anthropology companions were working, but he was enjoying a holiday and some rest. He looked forward to seeing a lot of Rex. "They say he is old and awfully egocentric and unmanageable for easy relations. I don't believe it. Old yes, still difficult, but easy." He then marks off the weeks until he will return to us.

A letter came for Bill, who had just turned eleven and was shooting up in height as Lloyd had done. During his father's brief absence he passed both of his sisters and then me, to his great delight. However, this turned to concern when, having passed us and his peers, he continued to grow. The letter played up to Bill's everlasting interest in geography and history and told him also about two Scotland Yard men on board, "very high up in the service, who have been to America on a big case, chasing crooks and seeing our F.B.I. Last night they came down in their uniforms looking very big, fierce, and smart. All of the good looking girls were duly impressed. So was I, but an American businessman who sat between them kidded them about socialism in England and refused to take them too seriously." He described the ship, the personnel and their responsibilities, drew a map of the route, and enclosed a news photo of the Order of the Garter ceremony at Windsor Castle, all of the things that would interest a youngster. He sent his love to all of us including Davida, our gentle, lovely live-in maid.

He landed in Liverpool on a bank holiday; it was raining and he was feeling stranded, lonely, low in spirits. What he did not know was that Ralph Piddington, who was expecting him in Edinburgh, had engaged a room in the North British Station Hotel. With his arrival there his spirits picked up. He found Edinburgh one of the most beautiful cities he had ever seen; his room had a view of the castle and, from a turret, he could see over most of the city. Service and appointments were superb. The first lectures in the series were prepared, and he was working on the closing lectures, which he found difficult since they were to be based on the unwritten Volume V of the Yankee City series. Although he had put much of it together in his mind, there was the problem of organization.

The following day a reporter from *The Scotsman* called to arrange an appointment, which Lloyd enjoyed because he learned so much about Scottish nationalism, the Covenant, the English, economics, and literature. Wilfred Taylor was "senior writer for The Scotsman, an independent conservative paper like the London Times and about as good or perhaps better." Taylor later took him to a meeting of the Edinburgh branch of the Scottish Convention, a non-party organization for Scottish control of Scottish affairs.

He saw a lot of the Piddingtons, who entertained for him and generally made the days in Edinburgh pleasurable. With all of his social and academic involvement there, he thought of sending a wire to each of his sisters on his mother's birthday.

The lecture schedule that had been worked out for him took him to the universities of Manchester, Birmingham, back to Manchester, Oxford, and London. He had been invited to Cambridge but felt it was too much and considered giving up Birmingham because of time. He had received the manuscript of a piece of Radcliffe-Brown's that I had forwarded to him. "Hope you read it. God what a sweet job he did on Pete Murdock." This was Radcliffe-Brown's reply to Murdock's analysis of the Murngin kinship system in which he claimed that Warner had failed entirely to understand the Murngin system. Radcliffe-Brown, though he did not publish to the degree that many would have liked, was well known for jumping into the fray on specific issues and, once in, not letting go, often to the embarrassment of his friends and admirers.

At home Lloyd rarely wrote a check or carried money. He found himself in Scotland with no blank checks and asked to have some sent on since he did not know the name of our bank. We did not have charge accounts until Ann and Caroline had gone off to college. Lloyd spent very little money and depended upon me to supply what he might need. He also wanted to know how to wash his nylon underwear; he liked nylon shirts, pajamas, and shorts because of their softness. Most of his students would have been astonished to think of Professor Warner washing his underwear, just as they could not imagine his working in the garden or cooking. They pictured him as abstracted from such mundane activities and did not realize that he made the best cheese omclette and loved to garden except when frustration stopped him because flowers did not grow the way they do in California, but weeds do. True, he liked to do such things at his choice, and he did not want the ongoing responsibility. But planning and planting a garden was a joy for him and he did it beautifully.

He was in touch with Radcliffe-Brown and expected to see him in Manchester, where he was lecturing for a term, in part to be near his daughter.

We had missed Rex when we first went to the University of Chicago; he was still in Yenching. A group of anthropologists had a memorable welcome home for him at a restaurant in Chinatown where we had an authentic Chinese feast, Rex ordering and presiding over the table and the serving of the rice wine he had brought back. He returned with so many thoughtful gifts for us. Then he left permanently to return to Oxford and, while there, took leave to teach at São Paolo from 1942 to 1944. Lloyd saw him in 1950—he had recently returned from two years in Alexandria. When he left Chicago he gave us a Medici print of Van Gogh's irises, which was beautiful in our living room, accenting the blues of the crysanthemums in our Chinese rugs. It was a lovely reminder of our close friendship.

Lloyd wrote: "Sir Stafford Cripps' budget speech has made no one happy and made 'the better classes' very angry. The government seems to decide everything here through their use of taxation and the control of private wealth. Those who might want to leave can't because they can't use their money beyond England. Maybe it's the medicine needed, bitter but good, but so far I don't like it. I'd be afraid to say decontrol everything, for it might mean a whole host of unpleasant results. The people I've talked to—high and low—complain but perhaps many of them still vote labor. I don't know enough from personal experience to say whether there has been real benefit to the lower groups. If they have really been helped (as I suspect) and Sir Stafford doesn't wipe out the great middle classes, who have given us the world's greatest culture, then I am willing to swallow the medicine and ask for more. But . . .

"I ought to say I like and enjoy this long holiday, and do, but I think a shorter one would be nicer because I could come home. My sentimental heart will never let me enjoy traveling by myself and away from my family any more. That was for yesterday, not now."

Lloyd had decided to deliver his lectures from notes rather than reading when he realized that his audience was having trouble with his American accent, and he found this made for better communication and a faster pace. The lectures were published by the University of Edinburgh Press as *Structure of American Life*[1] in the same sequence he presented them except for exchanging a chapter on the factory for a lecture on a political hero.

The course title for his lectures was "The Application of Social Anthropology to Contemporary Life," and the scope of the lectures is indicated by subjects of the ten lectures: The Study of Contemporary Society; Social Class and Colour Caste in America; The Family in a Class System; American Ethnic and Sectarian Groups; Education, Occupation and Social Mobility; Cultural Persistence and Personality Development; The Activities of Voluntary Associations; Sacred Ceremonies; Mass Media; and An American Political Hero.

Later, the University of Chicago Press published *American Life: Dream and Reality*[2] based on the Edinburgh book in large part with material added from lectures given at Occidental College under the auspices of the Haynes Foundation of Los Angeles, from the work-in-progress on Volume V of Yankee City, and from other sources. His British friends had urged Lloyd to add to the Munro Lectures for the Edinburgh book, feeling that because American books were so expensive in England this was an opportunity to represent a broader scope of his work.

In his lecture on mass media Lloyd alluded to the soap opera that he and Bill Henry had studied. *The Scotsman* reported it:

"Soap Opera"

In his Munro lecture, yesterday, professor Lloyd Warner of Chicago spent most of his time in a fascinating analysis of the social significance of "soap opera," the American day-time radio serials, to which it is estimated about 25 million housewives listen. In these programmes, he said, were to be found the present-day equivalents of the old folk-songs and ballads.

Although the "superior" people in the United States turned up their noses at "soap opera," declared Professor Warner, one ought to bear in mind the fact that when Negro spirituals and cow-boy ballads were first sung they were looked down on.

The audience was obviously completely absorbed as Professor Warner dealt with this American institution, and his many witty and informal asides drew frequent gusts of laughter. His pleasant, relaxed style of lecturing, which combines authority with informality, which can find a place for occasional slang instead of pedantry, which can be academic and intimate at the same time, makes him easy to listen to, although the subject-matter of his lectures is highly complex.

Understanding America

After the lectures one of the "voluntary" members of the audience remarked enthusiastically to us that they were the most interesting set of lectures to be given in Edinburgh for some time. We have met several others who have endorsed this opinion.

One of the things which has made them so refreshing is that it is unusual to hear a professor discoursing so freely on the structure of contemporary society. We are so accustomed to a cautious avoidance of the "century of common man" on the part of academic speakers that it is all the more exhilarating to find a professor going head on for that beguiling century. Quite apart from that, Professor Warner has given his large audience an insight into contemporary life in the United States which has done more to promote an understanding of the Americans than any number of films and books.

To-day Professor Warner gives his last lecture. He then goes on to Manchester and Oxford. He would have liked nothing better than to have an opportunity for informal discussions, but his time-table has not made that possible. Most of his listeners hope that he will be able to put into book form the material he has presented in Edinburgh. Dr. Ralph Piddington, Reader in Social Anthropology in the

University, who is himself shortly going to occupy a chair in New Zealand, is to be warmly congratulated on instigating and organising a memorable course of lectures.

On the day of the last lecture Lloyd wrote "I guess I am a terrific success—professionally and socially. I'm glad but tired . . . the last cocktail party was a beautiful one, but I felt too ghastly to enjoy it. Two days' rest have given me a big comeback. Have been invited to give a series of lectures at Cambridge, but wrote a polite no, and others also a polite no. Too much, too much. It seems a little crazy for *me* as I am to myself, telling the Royal Anthropological Society of Cambridge University and the University of Paris no, but it seems real and practical to the person living in this immediate world."

He enclosed two clippings from *The Scotsman* asking me to send them on to Frances and Kitch Jordan, our friends from Harvard, now at the University of Chicago, where Kitch had become editor of the University of Chicago Press. The clippings were about the Fourth Scottish National Assembly, to which Lloyd was invited by the National Covenant Committee through the instigation of Wilfred Taylor. He was in touch with Dorothea Mayo in London (Elton had died in England in 1949) and hoping to reach Aletta Lewis through Rex.

Cold, snow, winds off the North Sea almost defeated the spirits of this Californian. The degree of his homesickness was eloquently expressed in an envelope we received one night containing no written message—just dried chicken bones. Fried chicken was a family favorite and certainly a favorite of that son, once removed, of the South, and by chance we were having fried chicken the night his letter arrived. We were as lonesome for him as he for us.

Writing the last day in Edinburgh: "I literally received an ovation at the end of my last lecture. I've never experienced anything like it—they clapped, cheered, whistled—when I tried to leave they'd clap and yell some more. Ralph and Marjorie were terrifically pleased." He was about to leave for Manchester, where he would see Radcliffe-Brown.

At Manchester, one of the red brick universities as contrasted with Oxford and Cambridge, and located, of course, in the industrial Midlands, he would lecture on mobility among business leaders, based on his research with Jim Abegglen. From the *Manchester Guardian:*

A CHANCE TO RISE
How Much Reality in the "American Dream"?

The equal right of all men of a chance to get to the top—the very essence of what we call "the American dream"—was discussed by Professor W. Lloyd Warner, Professor of Anthropology and Sociology in the University of Chicago, in his concluding Simon Lecture yesterday at Manchester University.

In the United States, he said, there were two opposing social principles operating—the belief in the equality of all men and the belief in rank and status, but they were securely interconnected in this belief in equal opportunity. At the moment the principal "routes up" were by occupation, education and entrepreneurship, but for young men, occupation and entrepreneurship were no longer functioning in the easy way they once did.

Statistics showed that all over the United States the sons of "top" business men tended to be business men, too, and that the way up for "the man at the bottom" was not so easy as it once was. It was, also, much more difficult to start a small business in America than formerly, a position which Mr. Truman was trying to do something about through Federal aid.

For men who wanted to get ahead education was more and more taking the place of these former opportunities. But a very considerable proportion of lower class people never got very far along the educational route, and though a sufficient number did so, this was what he called "blocked mobility." Thus progress in the older occupations was blocked, or, at least, slowed down very considerably. But the newer occupations—radio, television, the aeroplane industry, and so on—were "open" and in them young men could rise very rapidly. Management, increasingly aware of this problem, was introducing training programmes within the plant to put the workers in, at least, a competitive position to rise.

But educators, too, had become increasingly aware of the position, and there was strong pressure to keep children from the lower social groups in school longer. The operation of educational and Government forces along a big front seemed to Professor Warner one of the great hopes for the future.

We always thought the *Manchester Guardian* was insightful. "A grand paper, liberal and sensible, not all out for Labor or for the Tories."

Lloyd saw Rex the first day in Manchester but would not see him alone until the day following. Max Gluckman, the anthropologist from South Africa—as were Harry Shapera and Meyer Fortes—had him to dinner, and he dined with Tom Pear, head of the Department of Psychology, and his wife. Other guests were a professor of American literature and Oxford English and his wife, a New York sculptor, who invited him to their place for drinks. Everyone very friendly, as always, but "Manchester ugly and squalid, the University very like it. The crowd I talked to yesterday hard to crack, but I got them and then it was fun."

But it was not like Edinburgh. These were the Simon Lectures: Status Systems in America, Child Development and the Family in America, Equal Opportunity and Social Mobility in America. Tom Pear was "in the chair" for the first lecture, then Max Gluckman, then Radcliffe-Brown. "I spent most of yesterday with Rex. We went off by ourselves and it was all like it used to be. Friendly, warm, and good conversation. He is obviously very fond of me, as I am of him. I took him to lunch—Rex called it the best he'd had since coming back to England."

Then to Oxford, where he stayed at All Souls. His letter was addressed to the children; "I am living at All Souls College built around 1440. The walls are four feet thick. A college here is where a group of scholars live. It is surrounded by high walls as if it were a monastery, as indeed it was in the old days. The walls of my room are heavily paneled like our dining room, quite beautiful. There are courts and quadrangles everywhere, lovely flowers and lawns and peace. A beautiful chapel where the dons of the college go for a beautiful service. I went Sunday night and said a few prayers for the good of my soul and those of my family.

"Night before last I dined at All Souls high table—the soup, fish, and main course in one room, lots of burgundy and claret, then to another dining room for port, fruit and dessert, and to the library for coffee and cigars. Had a long talk with the Archbishop of Canterbury, he in short knee pants (à la George Washington, a well turned leg), a short light purple jacket, set off with a large cross. Also talked with India's ambassador to Russia who cheered me up a lot about the future. Also with Sir Arthur Salton and seemingly everyone else of any importance in England. Lord Simon, the former Minister of War, there. This was to them an ordinary Saturday night. Last night I dined at Exeter College with Meyer Fortes— very lovely, same style. Very good food, well prepared, and beautiful. Tonight I dine with the Warden (President) of Nuffield College. He wants to talk to me about my research (Nuffield is the Ford of England). Tomorrow morning I go to London. I've talked with Chuck Baldwin by phone; will stay with them.

"My lecture here at Oxford very successful. Hope the others are. Fortes a charming, easy, nice human being. I like him a lot. . . .

"I feel more at home here than anywhere I've been. Evans Pritchard a very good host and everyone friendly and easy. Manchester, except for Rex, was a horror. I hated it. I'm writing in the library. The Duke of somebody is on the other side of my writing table talking about the dreadful socialists. Last night G.D.H. Cole, the socialist, gave America hell, very nicely, for trying to bring Germany back into the picture. Me, I'm a liberal, and liberals are a dying breed in England."

In London he saw Aletta Lewis and her husband, Dennis Dunlop, who had been through some rough times. "They were badly bombed, the houses around them knocked out, their own walls knocked in and all windows broken. Dennis away at the time, Aletta alone with the baby (a girl, Caroline, seven), she got to someone they knew, Dennis came home, found the house a shambles, no Aletta or child, but remains of a partly eaten meal and fifty houses down around them. He began his search at the rescue and identification station (hands with rings on them, a foot with a shoe etc.). Went on looking and after several days found them. Ghastly. Then the 'doodle bugs'—remember? Aletta at her mother's when one struck but did not harm them. Aletta then waiting to go to the hospital for a serious cancer operation. Miraculously successful. Painting very little, says she's not a success, but believes she's painting better than ever before. Dennis starting to do well again, architectural sculpturing, the London Clearing House, Queen Elizabeth Guild Hall, etc."

Lloyd had ordered suits and was waiting for fittings; he had bought cashmere sweaters for Ann and Caroline, was shopping for stamps for Bill, and had a Harris tweed for a coat for me. He was planning to go to Ireland for a few days but with some concern about finding old friends. "Until today the stores were closed for Whitsuntide, a Bank Holiday for the beginning of spring (the Holy Ghost descended when Jesus ascended). Asked everyone. No one knew. Asked the clergy after service at the Cathedral and was told. No one knows anything here. For a test asked a waitress the name of the river (the Thames). She did not know."

On the University of Edinburgh's publishing of his Munro Lectures: "It will take a little work on my part—and yours—after I return to make them [the notes] look pretty." He spent the first night in London with Chuck and Helen Baldwin. Then the last lecture, at the London School, was followed by a tea and a cocktail party at the American Embassy, which he found not much fun. "Chuck has risen rapidly, Santiago, Chile, Oslo, Trieste, now economic councilor at the London Embassy—third from the top counting the ambassador." He had gone with Helen to see Betty Squires—"she was Chris Squires' wife (Australia), now married to the vice president of a British American company and about to return to Sydney."

Feeling the need of a place on his own, he went to the English Speaking Union's Dorchester House, where he had made reservations and found it "filled with women and awful." So he did not stay and went to the Cumberland, "the Statler of London," where he was very comfortable. We had joined the English Speaking Union because a friend was president of the Chicago Chapter and we did think Dorchester House would be convenient. "No place for me. What a racket. Yet they can't care for 1/10 of 1/10 of one percent of those who apply."

He dined with Raymond Firth at the Atheneum and saw an American friend who was going English "and I told her she was a fool." In spite of the many attributes he liked and admired in the English, Lloyd was very much an American.

"Went to the Afghanistan Embassy to a cocktail party. Very diplomatique, London and Asia at once." He then went sightseeing in London—all of the traditional places, most of which we had seen together—and he had lunch at Simpson's on the Strand, where we often ate, and by chance met Helen and Chuck and they made plans to go to Hampton Court and to Windsor Castle together. "Had lunch with the head of Scotland Yard, went to Westminster Abbey for Evensong, and was pleased to see a plaque to President Roosevelt. On the trip to Windsor the Baldwins brought Rear Admiral Zacharias: Bill will remember his radio programs, true stories of secret service, called Secret Mission, I believe. He was at the top of our naval intelligence during the war. Very hush hush. On his way to Yugoslavia where he will see Tito.

"Gas rationing went off before Whitsuntide, first time since 1939. The English are filled with joy. I suspect the Labor Party is too. American capitalists, Standard Oil, were principally responsible. Chuck and his boss negotiated the deal from our end. But it may help Labor with the middle-class voters. The feeling continues to develop in me that Labor has lost confidence and faith in its own beliefs, not to give them up, but to feel less sure. There seems to be a carefully disguised retreat, a very slow one, but continuing, on the way. I expect to see them loosen up on their confiscatory taxation and, with that, dear old capitalism and the joys of risk taking will be back, Labor in power or not."

He had lunch with Dorothea Mayo, whose daughter Gail (Patty) had just married a young man who pleased Dorothea very much. He thought she looked smarter than he had ever seen her—and seventy-three! She was to leave that day for Australia and was dreading it—"The Australians are so naive and unsophisticated." The other daughter, Tony, in Paris "going with a raffish crowd." Very messy. She had married and had a child, and there was great difficulty getting them out of France after the German occupation. Gail had followed in Elton's profession and was being quoted as an authority, substituting for Elton. "Little said about him—he died last September in his sleep. Dorothea going over his letters since Australia, possibly for publication.

"I saw Mr. Roosevelt's statue in Grosvenor Square. There was a ladder for the cleaners—I almost climbed it, to touch him. But, after all, this is England and fifty years is very old for youth and spontaneity. On the four corners of the base are 1932, 1936, 1940 and 1948. From each corner runs a low wall on which are engraved Freedom from Want, Freedom from Fear, Freedom of Speech, and Freedom of Religion and at the base Friend of All Mankind—our guy, our guy, our guy. The aristocrat who was a common man, part of the mystery that makes America great and at times magnificent. Great and admirable as Mr. Churchill is, he lacks this basic and necessary and spiritual element which could make him the friend of all mankind. I left a few tears and then took a long walk, maybe as an act of contrition for the swine who come over here and tell the guides that the one thing they do not wish to see is that man's statue."

And he had an experience with a public school where they went to see the Baldwins' eleven-year-old son, like the one we had had earlier with the Mayos' daughter Ruth (now Tony) and later at a school in Newbury, England, where we stopped for lunch. Here the boys were six to twelve— like Newbury. "It was visitors' day for the parents. When they left all of the boys ran after the cars like little dogs who weren't allowed to do what they wanted. No tears, just quiet resignation. No hugs, no kisses, often not even a handshake. The parents might have been casual passersby who were saying a polite good bye to someone they had just met. Not for me. I remembered your description of Dorothea going to see the lonely little girl, Tony, and I thought maybe Tony is still a lonely child, no longer little, in Paris, telling her parents the story she could never put in words. Obviously kids must grow up to learn to be on their own, but their parents don't need to pitch them over a precipice to make this happen. Let them take their own good time and move along according to their own needs."

Before leaving London he took the Baldwins to see T.S. Eliot's *The Cocktail Party* and spent the last few days with them since they insisted if he did not they would consider that he did not like them. He had found them unbelievably generous and friendly and hoped that we would have an opportunity to entertain them here—and we did as they stopped off with us on their trips across the states. He had lunch with Midge and with Aletta and Dennis, and then set off for a last visit with people in Liverpool, where he would board the *Parthia*.

I had planned to meet him, and he had made reservations for us at the Biltmore. Due to arrive Sunday, "oceans of people to see, maybe we can leave Tuesday." He left the ship with a beautiful young woman, a recent widow returning from a trip around the world. She expressed surprise at finding his wife so attractive! We could not come home together because Marjorie Dawson, executive secretary of the Motion Picture Association, learning from Frances of Lloyd's imminent return, had arranged for him to address the members at a luncheon, so in addition to the appointments already scheduled he had this to do also. He felt that it would be a waste of time and was rather annoyed. He had not been able to communicate his ideas about visual and verbal symbols to motion picture people though he felt that it was a field that needed guidance through an understanding of symbolic behavior. And he wanted to come home. When I arrived I received an outstanding welcome from the children—who expected, of course, that they would be greeting their father.

Notes to Chapter XII

1. W. Lloyd Warner, *Structure of American Life* (Edinburgh: University of Edinburgh Press, 1952).
2. W. Lloyd Warner, *American Life: Dream and Reality* (Chicago: University of Chicago Press, 1953; Phoenix Books, 1962).

EXCEPT FOR AN initial period of loneliness, Lloyd had thoroughly enjoyed his stay in Scotland and England at the time he gave the Munro Lectures. So, when he was invited to Cambridge as visiting professor of sociology for the academic year 1954–1955, he was pleased, but he wanted his family to go. By that time Ann would have finished three years at Radcliffe, Caroline a year at Northwestern, and Bill his first year at Wayland Academy in Wisconsin.

Our big house in Chicago had been on the market for three years—the house and garden were too much for most people in the demands on physical and financial resources. We had had such bad luck renting that we did not want to try that again, so the house was a problem. Then we had good fortune: the broker produced a buyer just when our thoughts were darkest and we were wondering if we would have to divide the house in order to sell it, this house we loved so that we wept when we listed it for sale. We prepared for a massive move. Everything had to be labeled for destination—some things into storage for an anticipated apartment near campus, some to the Good Will and Salvation Army (how relieved I was to be rid of things that had been held together with nails and glue and concealed by slip covers) and the rest to the dunes. We explained to the mover what the dunes situation would be—especially in relation to our oversized Steinway grand—up thirty-two irregular flagstone steps. When we arrived we discovered that the men who actually did the work had not been told about the steps, so now, at the end of a day when they had already done a big job, they had what was in many ways the most difficult part of the entire task. Lloyd was furious at the injustice of their treatment, but they set themselves to the task with great good will and Lloyd and I arranged everything as it came in.

The house at the dunes was completely furnished, of course, but for summer living, so we had many adjustments to make. It was amazing how this log house, designed and built for vacation living, was made rather elegant by our antiques, books, and paintings. We did not expect to stay there indefinitely but knew that it would give us an excellent opportunity to try living in the dunes, with Lloyd's commuting to Chicago, and if we did not like it there was nothing lost. The sale of the Chicago house not only freed us of a responsibility, but also it helped our finances so that the children and I could accompany Lloyd to England. Had he thought this would not be possible he would not have accepted the invitation. The Edinburgh experience had taught him that he did not want to leave his family again.

I saw Meyer Fortes when he was teaching a semester at Northwestern University in 1978, and he recalled how Lloyd's invitation had come about. Meyer had been at the University of Chicago in 1950 teaching courses on South Africa. When he returned to Cambridge, there was much discussion of sociology—what to do about it—with a great deal of suspicion as to what sociology was about. A fund had been set up to develop social studies, social sciences—not adequate to finance a full-time chair but adequate to finance visiting professors who could acquaint Cambridge with sociology as a field of study. "Incredible how suspicious they were at that time. A professor of social anthropology discussed introducing sociology 'over my dead body only.' So the problem I had to face was—all right, let's have some visitors, but whom? I decided upon Talcott Parsons who, after all, was *the* theoretical sociologist, and I must say that Talcott, although he was impressive, did not succeed in persuading Cambridge. Next was George Homans, also a sociologist but acquainted with anthropological literature. That was the point, he had a foot in both fields. Third was Lloyd, who was an anthropologist. I personally selected Lloyd and the committee agreed because his was the kind of sociology that started from an anthropological base—and he was doing urban studies, which was the big thing they wanted: not theoretical but actual research in an urban community. It has taken the university another six to eight years to establish a chair of sociology. There is a kind of feeling that in a good deal of sociology they do nothing but calculate figures and do surveys rather than intensive studies—uninformative and bogus in a way. So Lloyd was asked to teach courses in sociology, but he also had a seminar in anthropology that was almost entirely for anthropologists. My secretary, very intelligent, attended all of Lloyd's seminars and, on the strength of that, applied for and was accepted as librarian for what became the Center for South Asian Studies, where she used the anthropology she had learned in the seminars in a very satisfactory way.

"You know professors in England are not as they are in America. There is one in a department, two at the most, and they are the top grade of things. So we make quite a business of taking the title of professor. Some people get the title for distinguished researches during their lifetime. I was a professor and so what one would call permanent chairman of my department, responsible for organizing the teaching programs and for hiring staff. There is a rule in Cambridge that everyone who is elected to a professorship (elected because there is a special committee who sits on the job and elects from a list of candidates), must be made a fellow of some college. Each college has a quota of fellows who are professors, simply elected as fellows because they are professors or for any other reason. There is a body of people called the fellowship electors who consider the newcomers every year. And Trinity said they would like to have Lloyd. I suppose Trinity regards itself as the most distinguished college in Cambridge—other people have other views—for example, we think King's is—but Trinity has always been very famous for its natural sciences, Nobel Prize winners, goodness knows what—and it did some sort of innovative things like—well, it was Trinity that took in Razinovitch and made him a fellow—most people would not touch him with a barge pole in Cambridge."

When our family gathered in New York for departure to England, we must have made an impressive sight, lined on the curb, waiting for taxis to take us to Holland America's pier in Hoboken. An unusually large number of pieces of standard luggage because of the period we would be gone, typewriters, dictaphone, the electric heater with thermostat like one we had used in the desert, electric blankets, and boxes and boxes of books and research notes for Lloyd's writing and lecturing. We had chosen the *Maasdam* because it was inexpensive, popular with students, and had a reputation for food and service. A young man on his way to the University of Edinburgh—his first trip away from home—attached himself to Caroline, so when we reached Southampton we had six. In England customs took one look at us and waved us through. The trainmaster disregarded our second-class tickets, took the label from a first-class compartment, and piled us in.

We stayed at the Cambridge Arms, which was not a cheerful introduction to food in England. The first morning Lloyd and I walked over to our apartment, passing a beautiful fish market on the way, and felt encouraged. Our apartment was at the end of Chaucer Road, near the Cam. Living and dining rooms, kitchen and breakfast room on the first floor with a bedroom and half bath; upstairs the master bedroom and bath and another bedroom for Bill. The rest of the second floor was a separate apartment occupied by a young couple with a baby. The phone required coins and was shared, and it was in the entrance hall, which made it necessary to wear coat, hat, and gloves for a call to the grocer.

A young man from the university arrived to explain things, introduce us to the best shops, and help us open accounts. There was a fruit and vegetable market in the square; on Saturdays it became a big general market with meats, crockery, and sundries. I managed our first shopping, which had to include equipment as well as food, by collecting it in the corner of a hospitable shop and taking a taxi home. I quickly learned shifts in vocabulary, which simplified ordering by phone. Fresh bread, very good because of the coarse flour, was delivered each morning. A large market that did not deliver had several special things, like wood pigeon. Vegetables left much to be desired, but we ate very well. Flavors were sometimes disturbing as I discovered when I tried to bring a needed touch of home with a chocolate cake, the recipe for which was so simple and so good that

Ann and Caroline had started making it when they had to use the seat of a chair as a table. But it tasted strange because the vanilla was different, the chocolate different.

The second night we were there someone came to the front door looking for the address across the street. She was Esther Newcomb, who was arriving to do graduate work in anthropology. When Lloyd returned he said, "Not Ted Newcomb's daughter?" She and her sister, who was at the University of Edinburgh, became our children's good friends. Her father was a professor of sociology at the University of Michigan.

And the young man from Edinburgh who had been planning to use this period for travel in the British Isles? Only when no other action was possible did he force himself to make the break from his surrogate family.

Sir Adrian was headmaster of Trinity. We were guests of honor at many dinners at masters' lodgings, but Trinity was by far the most formal. As usual, the guest list and seating plan were on the center table of the great hall as one entered. The menu and wine list were at each place, and there was a butler for each two guests. Dinner—which was very simple, beef and kidney pie and vegetable marrow for the main course—was served from a side table. Dinner at Trinity was the only occasion I have experienced where ladies were individually seated for coffee in the drawing room—usually there is some opportunity to move about a bit for informal conversation. One thing was memorable about Trinity, central heat, lovely warm air wafting about.

Lloyd liked his associates at Trinity although he had little contact with them, since he did not use his rooms and did not take dinner there except on feast nights, when his presence was expected. Most fellows almost live in their colleges, eating most meals there. Often I was invited to dinner with wives only.

Lord Adrian was knighted while we were there. A distinguished scholar, a winner of the Nobel Prize, he was a slender white-haired handsome person who rode around Cambridge on his bicycle in all kinds of weather. After retirement from Trinity at seventy-five he was succeeded by Lord Butler and became chancellor of the university. Lady Adrian was a delightful person, very active in governmental affairs.

It was a requirement of the university that a member of the faculty receive a master's degree from Cambridge, even if he is a visiting professor. Sir Henry Willink, the vice chancellor, performing the ritual in Latin, conferred the degree on Lloyd, who called the ceremony the laying on of hands but took it sufficiently seriously to want his family in attendance. Sir Henry was the master of Magdalene, at one time, I believe, Minister of Health, and a sophisticated person. At dinner in the masters' lodging I was at the right of the host, as frequently happened; on his left was the wife of a faculty member being welcomed on his return to Cambridge from Manchester. During the dinner, Sir Henry turned to this lady and said, "Well, now, it must be pleasant to be back. You must be enjoying your return to Cambridge?" When she replied with a firm no he was completely taken aback—harumphed a time or two and said, "Well, why not?"—still with surprise. She replied that Cambridge was no place for women, that the university retained the social organization of monastic days that permitted women no function. She was a member of an old Cambridge family and her brother, a well-known architect, was designing an addition to St. John's College; she was in a position to be familiar with the social order of Cambridge and what it was like for a woman to be part of the Cambridge community.

I have several memories of that dinner. One the centerpiece—a silver gilt chalice given to the college by Sir Walter Raleigh. Sir Henry said that it was the thing he would be most reluctant to give up when he left one day. Another was the delicious dinner—roast duck done to perfection and really great wines. The colleges pride themselves on their wine cellars and their silverplate, which are always used on ritual occasions. The third memory was our departure. I was first to leave, of course. Usually Lloyd quickly followed since he disliked long leave-takings, and often complained about my dallying over good-byes. The butler brought my coat from what must have been the deep freeze; as my arms went into the sleeves I began to feel a chill that increased—no chance of my body warming that coat. After seeming ages Lloyd appeared. Driving home I began to shake and continued shaking for another hour.

We have friends who think I did not like England because we were cold. First, we both like England and the English people, for whom we have great respect. The Parsons had had the house we occupied and had no complaints. We never became reconciled to a kitchen and breakfast room whose walls ran with condensation, a manorial dining room that would have been a joy had we been able to heat it but, instead, increased the distance between kitchen and living room where we ate—with a coal fire on one side and our Sears Roebuck electric heater on the other. Even so we rarely achieved temperatures above fifty-five degrees. The water in the toilets had a thin coat of ice each morning until I was forced to acknowledge reality and acquired paraffin heaters. I had never liked the smell of kerosene, but it became a heavenly scent. I discovered the principles of radiant heat since the temperatures outside were rarely freezing; it was indoors that one felt discomfort when the heat of one's body radiated to cold walls, ceilings, furniture.

Using the electric appliances that we had so confidently brought with us was made possible by the transformer lent to the university by the U.S. Air Force base nearby. The children had even brought a record player which was affected by the difference in cycles—but everything else was satisfactory, and the electric blankets, for everyone in the family, I do believe made life possible.

We were encouraged about our attitudes by our friends who exclaimed, "Why does the university always put Americans in a house that is impossible to heat!" They all had compact quarters with a heating unit in the center. Before we left a Cambridge professor came with his wife to look at our house because friends from the states were to live in it the following year. They were appalled and protested to the university, with the result that our neighbor across the street who had been so endlessly helpful to us was appointed by the university to serve in this capacity officially, helping visiting faculty to meet their needs, but first of all to find them comfortable housing. She had little sympathy with our being cold; she did her housework in a sleeveless sheepskin jacket with all the windows open. But she came to our rescue when Lloyd became ill with an infected tooth, which a dentist extracted before controlling the infection. His face swelled like a balloon, yet the dentist insisted that everything would be fine. But Mrs. Bergquist, who had for years been active in bringing refugees from Europe, especially dentists, who were most welcome in England (until recently they had been called dental barbers and still did not have medical status), took Lloyd to a dentist, a woman whom Mrs. Bergquist had helped to bring to Cambridge. She took care of him and cured him.

Having the children with us meant that we had young people around much of the time. Bill made friends with twin boys he met at the secondary school where he took courses in English. The headmasters of schools where we applied for his admission were horrified when they learned that we had taken him from a boarding school to bring him to England at the time when students were concentrating on the exams which would qualify them for entrance to Oxford or Cambridge—all studies were review. He was admitted to a preparatory school nearby that had only boarding students except for some sons of Cambridge faculty members, and there he had extra tutorial in French and mathematics. I tried to help him with both of these subjects as well. Meanwhile I was doing all of Lloyd's secretarial work and running the house. Occasionally I would get away—to Ely, for example, which I reached on a two-decker bus that looked awkward and strange on country roads—to indulge my love of cathedrals. But for the most part I was busy.

Relating to the lives of our young ladies was not always easy for Lloyd and me. They had been away at colleges with much more lenient rules than anything I had known certainly and more permissive routines than at home. At certain periods when there were no classes they stayed in bed until time to get up for a coffee date and from then on their days were filled with social activities. Although I was feeling burdened I did not have sense enough to realize the problems of our household and to try to do something about it. Lloyd did. First, he got a secretary. Then he assigned tasks to each of the children to relieve me of some of the household chores. We had a little family conference in which he said that because I was able I was put upon and that it was up to everyone to do his share. This all went very smoothly; he accomplished what I could not.

We very much enjoyed Jack Goody, a young tutor in anthropology. One night when he came to dinner he described his experiences in the war. He had been among those stationed along the channel coast to guard against a possible invasion. Five soldiers armed with rifles were grouped at half-mile intervals. It was an amazing tale, especially when one realized that very soon after there would be anti-aircraft batteries on the ground and Spitfires in the sky. Jack was Esther Newcomb's tutor; they were much attracted to each other, it was clear to see, and later married. They did field work in Africa and now have two children. Esther became a teacher in one of the women's colleges.

For Thanksgiving we invited the children of American friends: the Hugheses' daughter Helen (Cherie), the Parsonses' son Charles, and Esther, of course. We had a really great Norfolk turkey, cranberry sauce from Czechoslavakia, and sweet potatoes from Israel. Pumpkin could be had in London, but we settled for lemon cream pie. We started a fire in the manorial dining room in the morning, and it was pleasantly warm by early evening. There were still some roses in the garden. But the garden, which looked so promising when we first saw it, was all too often in fog. The young couple in the apartment put their baby out in a carriage near the house to nap, and it would disappear in the mist.

We were not sure that Helen Hughes enjoyed celebrating this thoroughly American holiday. With her Canadian background, she was quite an Anglophile and became more so. She lived with the Forteses at first and then moved to the home of an Anglican minister where I called just to be sure that everything was going well. She finished her academic work in the classics, I believe, at Cambridge, married, and remained in England.

At Christmas Lloyd took off for Malaga to get warm. Ann and Caroline went skiing in Austria with an Oxford-Cambridge group. Bill and I went to Paris and then on to Rome, where we met the girls. On our return we stopped in Paris again for a few days, arriving New Year's morning. In the Gare de l'Est, which we reached just before dawn, people on their way to work stopped at what looked like a coffee bar as they passed through. But it was a wine bar, where each person asked for red or white. How they did this early in the morning was a marvel; the statistics on alcohol-related accidents in industry answered the rest. We could not get a taxi to take us to the Hotel du Quai Voltaire, so we rode the subway to the

Place des Vosges and crossed the river on foot. The light was pale mauve, diffused in the mist hanging over the river, the street lights shining dimly through. We had to stop in wonder at the beauty. Of course we had to wait for our rooms, occupied late after New Year's Eve celebrations, and finally settled for less desirable rooms where we could clean up and rest after our all-night's journey from Rome.

Meanwhile, Lloyd had found the Hotel Bel Aire, a delightful place to stay in Malaga. On the flight down he met the football coach from Barcelona—football (soccer) had taken over in Spain as baseball had in Japan. The coach, who was greeted at the airport by a crowd of fans, invited Lloyd to go home with him and stay until his flight to Malaga. Lloyd had some concern about the luggage search because the books he had for his work during the long holiday included a copy of *Das Kapital.* The football coach made all of this simple—they went through customs with nothing being opened. Lloyd had beautiful service and excellent food at the Bel Aire, which overlooked the Mediterranean and was set in a grove of orange trees. Many English were in Malaga; Spain was popular because prices were low and the English were restricted severely in the amount of currency they could take out of the country. So Lloyd met a number of people he knew and thoroughly enjoyed his stay.

Before the long spring holiday we decided to buy a car. A friend in Chicago wanted us to bring back a Hillman for her, so we bought a Hillman from the export list. This was the only way one could get a car without a long wait. The steering wheel was on the left, of course, which made passing difficult but not a real problem—and in France and Spain it was an advantage. We had rented a car on a few occasions for special trips but had decided earlier not to buy a car because we felt that it would involve the children in family-oriented activities rather than going off on bicycle trips and excursions to London with friends.

Just before Lloyd was again to leave for Malaga we both became ill with a respiratory infection, but he took off anyway, convinced that the balmy climate of Spain would cure him. I became increasingly ill and realized that I had pneumonia. I was unaccustomed to respiratory infections and it took a while to recognize the symptoms. We were waiting for the car to arrive from the factory. Ann managed all the details. We needed to have the registration numbers of the tires before going into Spain and the factory refused to allow us to use the number of tires on a similar new car in Cambridge, which we would then put on our car when it arrived. With this sort of delay, I had time to recover from the pneumonia, with the help of our local Public Health doctor who was certainly most attentive. Also there were complications about Bill's bicycle trip to France since there would be a short interval between our departure and the date his friends could leave. I think he was delighted to be out from under the dominance of parents and sisters; he made no effort to conceal the fact that he had no intention of lugging our luggage around France and Spain and playing escort to us. On a number of occasions in Italy especially he had been quite indispensable—he was so tall, so visible, that Ann and Caroline were not pursued when he was with them.

We took the girls' friend Janet Ingram in Bill's place. She was a delightful Newnham student from Brighton, where Caroline had visited her family and found them charming. She was especially delighted with their little corgi, who played the piano and sang in mournful tones. Janet was a most observant person, a great help in following roads and maps, and expressed contagious delight in everything she saw. She was to travel on a student budget, so we all tried to do the same. Just before we left Lloyd phoned from Malaga, sounding terrible—but perhaps it was the connection? He assured me that he was all right, but he was set against our coming to Malaga. He would meet us in Barcelona. We had intended to cross the Pyrenees from Pau, go to Madrid for a few days and to the Alhambra before Malaga, returning up the Mediterranean coast, and pass through Barcelona. Lloyd and I could not reach agreement but closed the conversation with a firm promise from me never to drive at night (he had been warned by many of the hazards of our driving at all without a male) and an agreement that I would phone him again from a place in France where the route would divide to Madrid or Barcelona. We had a lovely trip with many pleasant encounters with rural and small-town French—exceedingly thoughtful and generous but not as astonished as the Spanish at four females in a car. When I called Lloyd from Argentan, from the combination bar, cafe, office of the little hotel, the bartender put the call through—he was quite excited about placing a call to another country. When Lloyd came on the phone everyone listened to my end of the conversation and had a hilarious time mimicking my querulous "Honeys." I was concerned about the way his voice sounded. We agreed on the Madrid route; I was determined that he would not come to Barcelona, and I became increasingly anxious to get on to Malaga.

When we arrived the staff of the hotel were obviously surprised and relieved. It seemed that he had been very ill indeed; they thought of him as alone, without family, and they cared for him with great thoughtfulness. He refused to have a Spanish doctor—no confidence. This was holy week when reservations were almost impossible, but the lady who owned the hotel building and grounds gave up her house to us. Breakfast was brought to us there; lunch and dinner we ate in the main dining room. The food was superb, like excellent French cooking and beautifully served. Lloyd and I walked on the beach and stopped in little bars where marvelous shellfish was served with excellent beer. The girls met many English friends and we let them use the car since we seldom needed it except to drive down to Torremolinos, which was then a small town with villas along the sea. We had friends renting one, with a cook-maid who did all of the shopping and was paid $125 a month. Spain had not yet been overrun and overbuilt. Much as we loved it we later had no desire to return—in fact Lloyd associated it with illness and would not even consider traveling there again.

So reluctant were we to leave Malaga that we allowed only five days for the return to Cambridge. Driving up the coast was an experience—even the short-based Hillman could not go around some of the curves without backing and turning; the road was narrow, with broken berms, we were on the outside lane and the sea was several hundred feet below. All kinds of animal and vehicle were on the pastoral sections—men carrying bundles of brush or sugar cane, herding goats, and pigs, driving burros, paying no attention to a car trying to weave its way in and around. We had automotive difficulty in Tarragona and learned that the sounds the engine emitted were much more eloquent to the mechanic than anything we could say. While he did the repairs we walked around that lovely town with its Roman aqueducts and amphitheater, its marvelous setting on the sea, and we decided that this indeed was a place where we would like to return. We really did not have time to spend in Barcelona but went on to Perpignan and then up through the mountains of Dome. By that time we were weary of curves and hills and longed for an alternate route similar to our trip down through the Bordeaux country with its broad highways. When we inquired of a woman selling gasoline from a curbside pump she replied that there was no such alternate route but that the road we were on was *très jolie*. This became a family expression to describe anything that was close to insupportable. Lloyd wanted to see Vichy and then Ann wanted to go back to Paris and join Esther, so we found a suitable hotel for her in Versailles that would allow her to take the train to Paris in the morning and us to avoid Paris traffic.

I do not know why we did not have the sense to stay in the charming hotel in Dover where we had stopped on our way down. No, we had to press on to get home. Not only the usual strong urge to complete the journey but concern about Bill, who was due to arrive at that time. Every place we stopped for food had just served tea and did not serve dinner until we found a place, just beyond the Thames estuary, that took pity on our weary, hungry bodies and made us some ham sandwiches and brought us hot water for our powdered coffee. When we reached Cambridge we found that the management had not turned on our water service (it would have frozen had it not been turned off in our absence), but fortunately we found the buffalo box and soon had water running.

We then called the Turvilles and learned that Bill was still in Paris—he had written to us, hadn't we received it?—that he was staying at the Palais Bourbon with the family of a girl the boys had known as a student in Cambridge. Her father was a member of the French Assembly. Soon we heard from Bill in urgent need of money to come home. Having anticipated this, we had arranged with Barclays to forward funds to their Paris bank for Bill's use should he need it. It had not been easy for us to let him go on a trip where we would be completely out of touch for so long. When he returned we learned that they had had such a good time in Paris that they did no traveling beyond, had to live in tents at the youth hostel, and had their first bath when the dorms at the Cité Universitaire made rooms available during vacation. Meanwhile Bill was also a house guest of Hélène's family, who had put up with his bathless state and soiled clothes! He had obviously had a wonderful time and was full of his own competence and maturity. He had had the good judgment to have his bike shipped from London by train.

When term was over and exams were on, Flora Rhind came for a tour of Britain that we had promised ourselves. We met her at Southampton, a weary, edgy lady who had just finished the agenda for the annual board meeting of the foundation before leaving and then found the Queen Mary (or Elizabeth) so ostentatious, the passengers so overloaded with money and its symbols, and the parties so sumptuous that she was in a deep depression. On our way from Cambridge, we stopped for lunch at Newbury to see the precursor of Newbury in Massachusetts. We were struck by the absence of visual similarity between the two towns. In fact, it is a marvel that so much fine architecture appeared at such an early date in the colonies—the classic salt box is a good example. We had spent the night in Winchester and misjudged the time, so we were late, which added to Flora's edginess, and this did not make driving simpler. We stopped at an inn for coffee that was, of course, terrible to an American palate, and then went on to Salisbury Cathedral and Stonehenge; with the beauty of the Salisbury plain we all began to relax.

We spent the night at Wells and were fascinating by swans nesting in a nearby stream against the wall of the cathedral. Then we went into Wales, Llandrindod Wells, where Flora adopted the Welsh pronunciation Cloyd. The innkeeper there, in describing our route, said that it would be a nasty, curvey road—no *très jolies* here—and it was foggy besides, but lovely scenery. We did some walking on the old Roman wall in Chester, which gives access to the second story of shops. But what we most remembered was a Pekingese puppy running towards us, his soft, beautiful coat shimmering in the sun, full of delight.

Arriving in Liverpool, where we would stay until the next night, waiting for the car ferry to Dublin, was grim. There had been a long dockworkers' strike which the workers had lost. They were bitter, aggressive — I had never had the experience of a bicyclist trying to ram a car.

Numerous accidents were reported. It was ridiculous to spend a night crossing the Irish Sea, but having the car made this necessary.

It was Sunday morning when we reached Dun Laoghaire and were greeted as old friends who had been away too long—we were welcomed home. There are few strangers in Ireland, especially after a Saturday night nipping on the job. We always loved Dublin and the Shelbourne, where we were amazed to discover almost a French cuisine, the young man at the table adjoining explaining the menu to his young lady with great pride in what Ireland could produce. On to Limerick and lunch with Paddy Meghen, a warm reunion in this town that had become industrialized in the war and changed by the Shannon airport nearby. Paddy was on the city council and seemed to run the town. We tried to avoid talking about the war, but that was impossible. He wanted to tell us how Ireland had suffered, had had to burn peat in their trains, endured many deprivations. We listened and did not mention the role they played in lighting the route for German planes to reach London, their refusal of food for England, and all the rest. It was of no use; the Irish will always hate the English. And we did not want to spoil our reunion.

Ennis had changed little; industry had not yet come to Ireland as it has now. We spent the night in a pleasant hotel in Galway where we tried the Irish coffee that Lloyd and Crawfords had invented for the John Jameson Irish whiskey account. It had become a great success and still is. Galway too had changed little and was still the market town for the Aran Islanders, who wore the same handmade sheepskin boots and wool skirts.

Flora's mother had been born in Armagh in northern Ireland, our next destination. Lloyd was an excellent navigator and found a road skirting the border on the south, a good road and shorter. We passed miles of stone wall bounding an estate and wondered whose it was. The wall was in poor repair—but what could one do when there was so much of it? Suddenly there was a car in the middle of the road, coming towards us. As we stopped the driver came to our car and asked our destination, which was Tynan, as I recall. He said that would not be possible since it was not a legal crossing, that we would have to turn back quite some distance to a legal crossing, and that if we proceeded much farther we would be shot at. So much for the IRA. Lloyd was quite put out since we had done so well on his route and had almost reached our destination. We asked about the estate and learned that it belonged to Sir Shane Leslie, whom we had met frequently at the Henns' in Cambridge. We had always considered him something of a fraud; for some reason he lacked validity. But indeed he was a member of the Irish gentry and indeed he had an enormous estate even though the main house, like the fence, perhaps was falling down. We learned that we were not alone in thinking Sir Shane Leslie had rather tiresome postures.

Armagh was a well-ordered, pleasant town. We found the cemetery with Flora's family plot; as usual people were most helpful. It is so difficult to think of what that town is like now after the civil battles. We proceeded to Belfast and found not a hotel room available. It was a busy, thriving, commercial city. We spent the night in a pleasant tourist home, went to the Anglican cathedral for services the following morning, and walked about. Then Lloyd had to return by air to Cambridge to resume teaching. Flora and I crossed to Scotland and drove on to Edinburgh, a city it is impossible not to fall in love with. Our journey down the East Coast back to Cambridge was pleasant except for the heavy lorry traffic resulting from a rail strike. It was my only encounter in England with aggressive drivers. We stopped at all of the famous cathedrals on our way, as we could not have done had Lloyd been with us. But we missed his companionship, his observations, and wit.

We found our household in one piece, the girls having cooked up a storm and invited friends into our kitchen who had never been in a kitchen. They had taken turns at baking that Warner cake.

When our friends at home learned that we were going to take the children to England, many asked if we were not concerned that our daughters would marry and live there. No, if we were so concerned we would not take them—we did not want our children or grandchildren living abroad. Two attractive American girls cut a notable swathe in Cambridge social life, where the ratio of male students to female was about seventeen to one. When there was a large social occasion the boys would ask girls to come up from London—as they asked New York girls to important dances at Harvard, rather than "cliffies"—and oftentimes our daughters would experience an effort on the part of these young ladies to put them down, which stopped when it was apparent that our daughters were not only beautiful but intelligent and quick-witted enough to take care of most situations. Also, the young men were there to intercede for them. I think that both Ann and Caroline were much attracted to particular young men both of whom we found charming—even Lloyd had to agree to this. But the deficiency was lack of motivation in their careers. One beau of Ann's was studying geology and was an ardent rockhound. He was going into the insurance business, by family arrangement. Apparently the prerequisite for the position was a degree from a status college at Cambridge or Oxford. He knew nothing of the insurance business and felt scornful toward it and indeed toward business in general. His goal was to have sufficient income to live comfortably, with sufficient leisure time to pursue his primary interest, geology. This both Ann and Caroline found troublesome; each wanted to marry a person really involved in a career. The status of women has changed since then, and each has a career of her own. But at that time they had reason to feel that their satisfaction would be a vicarious one, through the careers of their husbands.

Lloyd felt that a basic problem in the English economy was the lack of training of management personnel. The days of empire that could absorb many well-educated, generally able young men had passed. The business and industrial communities of the country needed executives with training in business administration. Not only were Oxford and Cambridge not preparing students in these fields, they were not even giving them the motivation to enter business and industry with respect for their functions and a desire to learn.

Soon it was time for the children to return to the states. They had wanted to travel on the continent during the summer, but we found that prospect too costly, and preferred that Ann and Caroline have summer jobs and that Bill catch up on courses missed that year by going to St. George's summer session. He insisted upon returning on a ship separate from his sisters and claimed the *Ile de France* as his.

Lloyd had a chapter to finish for a book[1] edited by Ed Mason, the Harvard economist. It was our plan to find a little fishing village on the coast of Devon or Cornwall and settle down for a few weeks of intensive writing. We spent the first night in the Boar's Head Inn in Aylesbury, one of our favorite spots even though the ancient rooms had ceilings too low for Lloyd to stand straight, but any objection was overcome by their superb ducks, superbly prepard, famous all over England. We went on then to the coast for a trip along the channel looking for a fishing village where we could settle down before our sailing date. We had to ferry across many estuaries—one having a bank so steep on the opposite side that our little Hillman, fully loaded, could not make it. So amidst much joking about his size the men asked Lloyd to leave the car and, with that, and their help, we got up the bank. We went through Mousehole and towns built up hillsides rising from the river with streets so narrow it was almost impossible for our Hillman to pass through. On the way we found a pleasant inn on Tor Bay, across from Torquay, and decided to settle there. It had been converted from a spacious home, each bedroom named after a famous English author, the food incredibly bad, but the views of the bay, the grounds, and gardens superb. As we took trips we found the little village we had been looking for—Blackpool—and we yearned for it even though it was not clear there would be a place to stay, nor was there time to make a change. We had that familiar feeling that we would never come back, that our opportunity to stay there would never return.

Lloyd finished his chapter and sent it off to Ed Mason just in time for us to go to London, where Lloyd would stay while I returned the car to Cambridge and settled our house accounts with the university. We had decided against bringing the car back. We phoned Aletta to ask her to find a hotel for us and learned, after she had tried for two days, that nothing was available because of a convention of ministers from all over the world and the opening of Epsom Downs. At this time Aletta was confined to bed completely. The doctors had wanted to try surgery, but she and Dennis both recognized this as an effort in scientific research that would not possibly benefit her and refused to let her be subjected to the procedure. She did find us a place in a rooming house near them, a pleasant room at the rear that had not been cleaned in years and years—if one dropped a couch pillow a cloud of dust rose. This is where I left Lloyd while I went to Cambridge. Returning to London, I must say I felt a big loss without the car. In those days it was possible to park almost anywhere, even near Trafalgar Square. We said our final farewells to Aletta, who was a marvelous person, of great courage. Dennis promised to keep in touch.

We had to wait endless hours at Southampton to board the *Staatendam* and when we finally reached our stateroom we found an immense box of flowers from the people at Crawfords—in such quantity and variety that we filled the room with vases of beauty. It was very dear and typical. We were then ready for a drink and dinner and discovered to our delight that they had Heineken beer on draft, of course—a Dutch liner. And dinner was excellent—simply a fine paté and roast chicken—and it need not have been prepared as well as it was to seem superb to us after those weeks at Tor Bay. The meals that followed were all excellent. We had not had food as good as this since Spain.

After we debarked at Hoboken and were on the bus to Manhattan, I suggested that we watch directional signs, as if we were driving, to compare them with the signs in England, which we always found deficient or led us to turn the wrong way. We agreed that we never would have found Manhattan.

Since we wanted to see the children before returning home, we had arranged with Frances to borrow her car. We had ordered coffee when we got up. In Tor Bay the maid had brought us morning tea before we dressed with a charge of a shilling a day. Our pot of coffee at the Biltmore was five dollars. This was the beginning of our own culture shock. Frances was to meet us there at twelve noon. We heard footsteps in the hall at twelve, and of course it was she. After a wonderful reunion, she had to return to Albany, and we ordered her car around to start for Newport to see Bill. In the trunk were a man's golf clubs, which made us wonder, since this was not Steve's car, and when we questioned the doorman he checked and discovered that indeed it was not Frances's car. So much for that touted American efficiency. Only good fortune had prevented our going off in someone's else's car and probably being stopped on the Merritt Parkway by the highway patrol.

We had a tour of Newport's "summer cottages" with Bill, talked to the headmaster, and felt satisfied with the decision to have Bill do this extra work. Putney seemed like a better choice than Wayland for his secondary school work since Wayland might seem parochial after a year abroad, and Putney was a stimulating school intellectually, had a good mix of students, and was interested in Bill's background and the essay he presented with his application.

We then went to Cambridge to see Ann. She had a summer job with Evon Z. Vogt, Jr., doing editorial work in which she excelled. E.Z., as we knew him, had been a student of Lloyd's at the University of Chicago; he had been a member of the research team doing the Morris study and one of the authors of *Democracy in Jonesville.* We enjoyed cooking dinner, shopping for live lobsters in the supermarket, and broiling them in Ann's tiny kitchen. We then went on to the Stevens's to return Frances's car, spent a pleasant evening, and took the train home the next day. We were met by the salesman with the new car we had ordered before leaving the previous year. When English people commented on how frequently Americans turn in their cars they do not realize the distances we drive. As soon as the English had freeways their cars began to break down under the greater demand; also accidents increased.

Caroline, who had been living with the Havighursts while she held her summer job, came home to Dune Acres, in fine spirits and pleased because she had been accepted at Pomona. She always felt scornful of Northwestern, perhaps because she was admitted with such ease. Pomona was the right place for her—intellectually stimulating yet relaxed, as Radcliffe was not, with a close relationship between faculty and students, and a highly creative environment.

Note to Chapter XIII

1. W. Lloyd Warner, "The Corporation Man," in Edward S. Mason, ed., *The Corporation in Modern Society* (Cambridge: Harvard University Press, 1959).

LLOYD WANTED to bring out a book on business leaders that would present readings by many representative authors. With Norman Martin, director of research of the Industrial Relations Center at the University of Chicago, he edited *Industrial Man*[1] using selections by authors as disparate as John Marquand and Peter Drucker. Their first intention had been to write the entire book, but further consideration swung them in favor of using the writings of others as well as themselves and contributing introductory material that would define the problems to be considered and set the stage.

The main purpose was to seek understanding of why business leaders are attacked. They are in large part responsible for our collective wealth and contribute to our material and spiritual well-being, to the advancement of learning, support of the arts, the church, civic improvement, and scientific advance, yet they are often the target of detractors, who are ironically often the beneficiaries of their munificence. Why?

Feeling that the answer lay not in a paucity of information about corporate men but in the great amount of information, too much for ready comprehension, they decided on a book that would bring together in one volume representative writings, organized by fields of knowledge and elucidated by introductory material.

While working on this book, they had undertaken with others the research for *The American Federal Executive*.[2] It was the last segment to be studied before undertaking the total society.

Just as *Big Business Leaders in America*[3] closely followed the Taussig and Joslyn research for *American Business Leaders*[4] in order to achieve comparison, this study followed that book as closely as possible. *The American Federal Executive* covered the military, civilians, and the civil service system. The research was financed by the Carnegie Corporation and sponsored by eminent leaders in American life: Chester I. Barnard, John Jay Corson, Lewis Douglas, Clarence Francis, and Otto L. Nelson, Jr. Government people were endlessly helpful in all stages of the research.

Because government people are usually paid less than their counterparts in the corporate world, it is often thought that they lack the ability for business or the drive and initiative for competitive position. Yet, "Despite the great diversity and heterogeneity in American society and the increasing division of labor, a growing integration of our regional life into a unified social system has tended to move ultimate authority toward the central government. All this has vastly added to the responsibilities, duties, authority, and power of the men who manage our nation," with "increasingly great impact of government and public affairs upon almost all aspects of American life," requiring "further attention to the crucial role of government executives," especially federal. "However, this role cannot be fully understood, much less carefully considered in terms of the future, without more knowledge concerning the social origin, education, mobility, attitude, and personality structure of those who occupy these positions of trust and responsibility. . . ."[5]

"The concept of representative bureaucracy is important to this study because it is concerned with the institutional consequences of the mobility process, particularly as applied to government."[6] How can vast civil and military bureaucracies be kept responsive and responsible to the people and their representatives?

The research defined its several purposes: to learn about the kinds of men and women in the highest civilian and military positions—their families, what they are like as individuals, their origins, to what degree they are representative of Americans generally. What were their career lines? Very importantly, a comparison was wanted between federal executives and big business leaders, which defined the structure of the research, and especially to show if there is greater opportunity to reach the top of the hierarchy in government than in business. The comparative data should show, for example, if higher education, so important in the careers of big business leaders, was equally important for federal executives and if they tended to go to the same colleges. If the study could learn the relation of social backgrounds and personalities of federal executives to their beliefs, values, and ideologies and whether they varied from those of other American leaders, then broad inferences could be drawn about the representativeness of the federal bureaucracy and, indeed, about the nature of occupational mobility and succession in the society as a whole.

The corpus of the research was 10,851 civilian executives: 7,640 in the career civil service, 1,269 foreign service, 1,865 holding political appointments, all in positions from Cabinet level to General Schedule grade level 14 or equivalent, and 77 unclassifiable. The 2,078 military ranged from admirals and generals to captains in the Navy and colonels in the Army, Air Force, and Marine Corps. Questionnaires, based on those used in the study of Big Business Leaders, were mailed, as a pilot study, to 240 government leaders in Washington and Chicago, and a number of civilian government leaders were asked if they would participate in a Thematic Apperception Test, as in the Big Business Leaders study. The response to this test mailing was encouraging since it showed eagerness to participate. Discussions were held with top government people and the questionnaire was revised. Press releases acquainted federal employees generally with the nature of the study, and stressed voluntary participation, the nonofficial role of the government, the interests and backgrounds of the re-

Dune Acres house designed by Richard Neutra, 1959

Borrego Springs, 1960s

searchers, and the financial support of the Carnegie Corporation.

A questionnaire communicating with people in many different departments that would also conform basically to that used in the study of business leaders was difficult to design. Comparisons of rank and position, organizational levels, and variations in function all had to be reconciled. Terms had to be used that had meanings sufficiently general to transcend all systems yet sufficiently specific to make realistic comparisons possible. The same questionnaire could not be used for civilians and the military.

A total of 15,601 questionnaires were mailed to civilians, with a return of 10,851, and 2,919 to the military with 2,078 returns—a total of 12,929 useable questionnaires returned. A total of 257 interviews, which included the Thematic Apperception Test protocols, were collected on civilian executives, one interview for every 42 executives in the sample, drawn at random.

Lloyd was the overall director; Paul Van Riper, professor of administration, Graduate School of Business and Public Administration at Cornell, concentrated on the military; Norman Martin of the Committee on Human Development, later professor of business administration at New York University, worked especially on the personality studies; and Orvis Collins, of the Committee on Human Development, worked with Van Riper and with the material on education and career lines.

To oversimplify the findings, although business executives differ in many respects from federal executives, in broad outline they are more alike than different in social and economic characteristics, including family and occupation as well as education. Both groups are highly educated, but government men are significantly more often college graduates with higher degrees. ". . . American society is not becoming more caste-like; the recruitment of business leaders from the bottom is taking place now and has been slowly increasing for the last quarter century . . . . Our society, although much like what it has been in past generations, is more flexible than it was . . . ." However, "men born to the top have more advantages and are more likely to succeed than those born farther down."[7]

Variations were found among the groups composing the study, but all possess lofty aspirations, have strong achievement goals for which they mobilize inner resources, yet often feel inadequate. Bill Henry, of the Committee on Human Development, assisted with the study of personalities.

When the research was about in midstream, Lloyd received a call from Michigan State University expressing an interest in his work and asking if he would come to talk with the dean and other key people. Lloyd's reaction was mixed. The only time we had visited Michigan State was long ago when Sol Kimball was on the faculty, and we visited him and Hannah for a football weekend. Our recollection was of an agricultural college, girls currying horses, that sort of thing. Then Dave Moore phoned and gave Lloyd some background. He felt the university would make a very attractive offer that Lloyd might very well wish to consider in view of the fact that he would reach the mandatory retirement age of sixty-five at Chicago in four years; Dave was quite sure Michigan State would offer him an appointment that would allow him to have active status well beyond that. We accepted the invitation to visit. Because Dave was so involved in the proceedings I would like to recall his career.

Dave had received his bachelor's and master's degrees in sociology from the University of Illinois and was looking for a job in the field when he was told that the only place that would hire a sociologist was Western Electric. There he became acquainted with the Harvard research and met Burleigh Gardner. Dave was at Sears Roebuck when the Committee on Human Relations in Industry, in which Lloyd and Burleigh were both active, was doing a number of studies there. Dave introduced Burleigh to Jim Worthy, director of planning and research, with whom Dave worked as assistant. This was the beginning of a long and effective association with Sears that led to their setting up an organizational survey based on the Westen Electric and Yankee City research. It was applied anthropology, studying various morale problems and situations within the organization, an application of some of these ideas to the solution of morale problems, and it culminated in a series of lectures in which Lloyd presented his interpretation of social class and the relationship between the attitudes and values of the developing community and of industry and business.

Dave received his Ph.D. in sociology at the University of Chicago, working primarily with Lloyd and Everett Hughes, and then went to Michigan State. There Alfred Seelye, dean of the College of Business Administration, told Dave that he had an opportunity to make a university professorial appointment and that he would like to get the best person in the behavioral sciences in this position. Dave said there was only one person who could possibly fill the position, and Al Seelye asked him to call Lloyd. "He responded with some interest but not all that much—it was an interesting possibility, and he was willing to explore it."

We had been at the University of Chicago for twenty-five years and felt very close to it, had strong friendships, and were most reluctant to make a change at this time in Lloyd's career, a change we might regret. Moreover, we were building a house in the dunes—designed by Richard Neutra, a famous architect whom we had met long ago through Frances. He was a genius in designing a house for the special interests of the people who would live in it, and we were excited.

But we went to East Lansing, where we stayed in a suite at the Kellogg Center and of course found a greatly changed university. As we came over a rise we saw the campus spread out over hundreds of acres. The faculty, we quickly learned, were quite international; the university has so many programs in foreign countries in every part of the world that the faculty has to be forty percent larger than that on campus. Lloyd was much attracted by John Hannah, the president, who had had a background in poultry before coming to Michigan State and marrying the president's daughter. Lloyd commented to Paul Miller, the provost who was an anthropologist from the University of Chicago and worked with Sol Kimball at Columbia, that what he liked about Michigan State is that they take former chicken pluckers and make fabulous administrators out of them! The Hannahs were quite rigid in their ways, never served liquor, were very low key, disliked ostentation. Mrs. Hannah, daughter of the previous president, had lived all of her life in the president's house. John Hannah had a distinguished career as a scholar, administrator, and public affairs activist. He was a member of the Human Rights Commission, of which Father Hesburgh was chairman and, after retiring, became head of AID.

Al Seelye had arranged a large dinner for us—a banquet, really— where we met all of the people we were supposed to meet. I was interested that so many of them assumed we would come. Dave described Al Seelye as a super salesman with great respect for ability, who had decided that Lloyd was exactly the person he would like to have at Michigan State and was prepared to do whatever was necessary to attract him. The following day Al took Lloyd around the university while his wife, Katherine, took me to see possible places to live. Things were moving very fast. Serious discussions took place between Al and Lloyd that made a possible move to East Lansing very attractive. The appointment would be directly under President Hannah, with no administrative responsibilities. Since the professorship had only recently been created by the board of trustees and Lloyd would be the first incumbent there was freedom of definition, and Al Seelye had the authority to negotiate for the university. Lloyd wanted very much to continue living in Dune Acres. I felt that this was totally unrealistic, that it would involve basic compromises of position that would not be feasible. Lloyd quietly replied that it was time I entered the present world where communication made almost anything possible; he did not consider this a hurdle. And of course he was right.

A decision was reached that Al Seelye would summarize in a letter his understanding of their agreement and Lloyd would comment or make alterations. The title of the chair was still under discussion. It was to be The University Professor "designed only for exceptionally distinguished people of international stature," which would allow appointments to be made anywhere within the university. Both Al and Lloyd felt that it had to be more closely defined, and both were inclined to the name The Émile Durkheim Professorship of Social Research. As Lloyd said, "This would announce our broadest interest to every variety of social scientist. The name Durkheim carries the highest theoretical and research connotations among social anthropologists, sociologists, social psychologists, and all other behavioral disciplines."

The salary offered was fifty percent higher than the salary at the University of Chicago with an annual ten-percent increase. Since both of our daughters had finished college, our financial needs were greatly diminished and our long-established living style was not demanding. He would be on active status until age sixty-eight and, as a distinguished professor, until seventy if physically and mentally able. This was very attractive—a five-year extension of productive life. We had seen people like Fay-Cooper Cole continue their careers after retirement by taking visiting professorships at various colleges; they had no productive base, no continuity which was especially important for someone involved in large research projects. Lloyd's would be a research appointment with no teaching or administrative responsibilities. He would have a secretary and research secretary, a research director, and three part-time research assistants. "We will schedule your teaching assignments in any manner you desire so that you are free to be on the campus one or two days a week and spend the rest of your time in Dune Acres." He would be in residence fall and spring quarters when his teaching assignments would actually be research seminars. When involved in a research Lloyd liked to have a forum for discussion of ideas, but he was no longer interested in the kind of teaching he had done all of his life—he certainly felt an urgency to develop as far as possible research as his primary interest.

We decided to accept.

Bob Havighurst knew of course about these proceedings, but Lloyd wrote him a formal letter once the decision had been made. "The real decisive factor, however, is the point on retirement, with all that it means in terms of continuing career and security but with a very positive feeling that there is real opportunity and time at the new place to start a whole new career." Dave Moore had first said this to Lloyd, and it had made an impression, lifted his spirits in anticipation. "Perhaps it is not nice of me to say it, but I do feel very much at ease and very happy now that the decision is made. Nevertheless, I, being the kind of person I am, with my deep liking for friends, will find it very difficult to pick up my things and leave Judd Hall." The association with Bob Havighurst in Human Development had been a long and satisfying one.

Lawrence Kimpton, president of the University of Chicago, said, "What are they offering you that you don't have here? You pretty well write your own ticket. You are not here winter term. You have all the research facilities you want. I feel confident that within the next few years mandatory retirement will be changed—if you stay I am sure we can work things out." He had already offered Lloyd a salary to match Michigan State. This was troublesome because Lloyd had never used offers from other universities to bargain with the University of Chicago and now he realized that for many years he had been undercompensated. About retirement, Kimpton was undoubtedly speaking sincerely, but within two years he had left to go with Standard Oil of Indiana.

As Lloyd wrote to Al Seelye formally accepting the appointment, he wrote to Kimpton, formally resigning from the University of Chicago, and to Chauncy Harris, dean of the Social Science Division. Chauncy Harris had joined Kimpton in efforts to persuade Lloyd to stay at Chicago. In his reply Harris wrote, "It brings a touch of sadness at the University at losing a distinguished and productive scholar and a thoughtful and gracious gentleman. From our side we are delighted at the years of our association, at the many contributions which you have made to scholarship and to numerous programs within the University. We rejoice in this fruitful and happy collaboration. . . ." Chauncy Harris is a fine person Lloyd greatly appreciated. Larry Kimpton wrote, "I felt sure that you would go, and I must say it is heart-rending so far as I am concerned, but I know how much thought and anguish has gone into your decision. The best of luck, Lloyd, and I think you know how much affection exists for you throughout this University, and in the person of the Chancellor." Kimpton had told Lloyd that if, at the end of a year, he did not like his new post, he should get in touch with him about returning to Chicago.

The research on federal executives was not yet completed; writing had begun. The entire project and the funds had to be moved to Michigan State. Eppley Center, a new building for the College of Business, a project of Al Seelye's, had recently been completed and the faculty was in the process of moving there. The Dean's old offices in Morrill Hall were given to Lloyd—marvelous offices with high ceilings, spacious rooms, a board table in Lloyd's office where he could hold research meetings, and cool—the windows shaded by large trees. At one time every variety of tree suited to the climate zone was planted on the campus. It is the most beautiful campus I have ever seen, really gorgeous in spring, and most beautifully maintained with immense pieces of equipment, the flowers labeled, rotated, a large rose garden, a pool of waterlilies, a joy to walk through. But immense. While we were there campus traffic became unmanageable and vehicles had to be banned, parking provided for students on the boundaries, with buses.

It had been agreed that Lloyd could bring Alice Chandler as his research secretary. She had been with him almost from the beginning of his days at Chicago; she is a wonderful person beyond being intelligent and efficient and knowing exactly how Lloyd wanted things done, able to keep people working happily. Moving to East Lansing would not be simple for her since she had a husband and son. She went over, hired a cab, and asked to be shown the various residential reas of the community, including those for Negroes. It was a very smart thing to do, but it led to her realization that she could not bring her youngster there for it was completely segregated. Not the university, the community. We have remained close, but her leaving was a great loss. Lloyd then had a series of secretaries through the years, an experience made more difficult because he had no preparation for it. He had had a first-rate secretary at Harvard—only one.

It is fortunate that Alice did not leave the University of Chicago. She was sharing her time with Lloyd and the Committee on Human Development when we left. Then the Behavioral Sciences were included in her responsibilities. When John Wilson became interim president, Alice was asked to be his administrative assistant, the capacity in which she later served Hannah Gray.

Though Lloyd's appointment was under President Hannah, he was placed in the College of Business for fiscal purposes, actually in the Department of Personnel and Production Administration, of which Dave Moore was head.

A position was arranged for Orvis Collins so that he could continue his work with Federal Executives, and a place needed to be found for his wife, June, as well. Lloyd and I went to East Lansing to make arrangements about his work and for me to look for an apartment. Al Seelye had a graduate student, John Komines, a charming and able young man, do the preliminary hunting and together we saw what he had found. We were not accustomed to apartments, and I was discouraged. But this young man learned what I thought we would like and later found it. The provost of the university offered June an appointment at Oakland College, a kind of elitist small college in the state university system. This infuriated her; and she let all concerned know it. Lloyd was disturbed since he felt that the university had done very well, but she felt that an inferior position had been offered her because she was a woman.

Leaving East Lansing that night, very tired, we agreed with the Collinses to meet on the way home at a restaurant in Marshall, Michigan, that Dave had recommended. It was a lovely, warm, welcoming place, just what our weary selves needed. But the Collinses did not arrive for quite some time, obviously delayed by serious and controversial discussions. Eventually they went to Southern Illinois University before the writing of the Federal executives book was completed, which, once again, left Lloyd with the task of meeting someone else's responsibility.

Darab Unwalla, a graduate student in Human Development, wanted to come to Michigan State to continue working on the Federal Executives research. Lloyd wrote to Dave about him, saying that the research would pay him, but that the university might wish to avail themselves of Darab's ability in the field of statistics: "He is a parsi from India with a higher degree in sociology, one in law, and one in industrial sociology. He has taught at the University of Bombay, has written a couple of books, is a swell guy." Darab did come and played an active role. He had trouble writing precise English, so I had to work with him closely to be sure that he was saying what he intended. He was orderly in work habits in contrast to Orvis, who was something of a dreamer, which had charm but often caused problems in organization.

It had been agreed with the respondents to the Federal Executives questionnaires that all material would be destroyed when the writing was completed. Lloyd and Darab did this at the University's incinerator and had a photograph made as evidence.

Darab did receive a faculty appointment. Later he went back to India to marry the young lady who was in the right relationship to him and brought her back, beautiful, charming Nellie, who had been waited on all of her life. Darab did the shopping and cooking while teaching her.

There were delightful, friendly people on the faculty we enjoyed knowing even though we saw them infrequently. On alternate weeks we would drive and I would clean the apartment and restock the freezer. At those times I usually had lunch with Katherine Seelye or Ellen Louhi, wife of the assistant dean of the College of Business Administration. Both are intelligent and able people. Other weeks Lloyd took the train from Valparaiso. We went to the fall gathering of faculty and sometimes to the annual reception for the faculty at the president's house. When John Hannah retired he was succeeded by Clifton Wharton, international agricultural economist of the Rockefeller Foundation. His wife, interested in the arts, hung the work of students and faculty in the president's house, which added to its beauty and gave recognition to the artists. She knew our daughter Caroline and her husband, John Hightower. When John became director of the Museum of Modern Art he had Wharton on his board.

In moving to our new house in Dune Acres, Memorial Day weekend 1959, we stored the furniture we could not use. Discipline is a characteristic of Neutra's architecture that brings excitement as well as composure to his designs but does not allow intrusions. So little of our furniture could be used—the piano, a secretary, a coffee table that had belonged to the Lorado Tafts, some lady chairs. The rest went into storage and furnished our East Lansing apartment. This new place would have the things which had the longest associations and the greatest sentiment for us.

When Caroline was married in 1964 to John Hightower, director of the New York State Arts Council, almost everyone who would be involved was in New York and it seemed ridiculous to bring them to the Dunes, where we had no church affiliations. Ann and Michael offered to have the reception and John and Caroline decided on a side chapel of St. Thomas's for the ceremony, which pleased us since we liked the Episcopal ritual and had confidence in it. Michael and Ann put us up at the Algonquin as their guests—the Algonquin having sentimental associations for Michael because of his father and for Lloyd as well going back to early days in New York. It was a beautiful ceremony, the minister urging Ann to bring the children and make it a family affair. The reception Michael had agreed to provided it would not be disruptive; Ann managed so well that she and I had lunch before the service. Once again a beautiful daughter was a beautiful bride and none of our friends or family was there except Jane Olson, whom we invited to the reception, Peter Robeck, Flora Rhind, and others, but most of the guests were New York friends of John and Caroline and of Ann and Michael.

Lloyd had to be in East Lansing the preceding week, so we decided to take a New York plane from Detroit. At first I thought I would leave the suitcase with our wedding outfits in the car, in the parking lot of the apartment building, but decided against this, concerned about dampness. When I went down the following morning with enough time to get the connecting plane in Lansing, there was no car. I looked around the parking area in disbelief and wondered if I could have left it on the street. Then I went up and told Lloyd, who phoned his secretary to notify the police and call us a cab. At the airport we received the message that the car had been found. Not until we reached New York did we learn the details; that a new manager of the building, seeing Indiana plates on our car, thought it was illegally parked and had it towed away. We had seen the tire tracks. When we returned he called on us and Lloyd told him in detail what he had done and what he thought of him for not having checked the tenants in the building first. Lloyd could be so coldly scathing that it was hard not to feel sorry for the object of his derision.

Notes to Chapter XIV

1. W. Lloyd Warner and Norman H. Martin, eds., *Industrial Man: Businessmen and Business Organizations* (New York: Harper and Bros., 1959).
2. W. Lloyd Warner, Paul P. Van Riper, Norman H. Martin, and Orvis F. Collins, *The American Federal Executive* (New Haven: Yale University Press, 1963).
3. W. Lloyd Warner and James C. Abegglen, *Big Business Leaders in America* (New York: Harper and Bros., 1955), pp. 1–2.
4. F.W. Taussig and C.S. Joslyn, *American Business Leaders* (New York: Macmillan Co., 1932).
5. *The American Federal Executive*, p. 2.
6. Ibid., pp. 4–5.
7. Ibid., p. 22.

BEFORE *The American Federal Executives* was published, Lloyd was involved in the next project, the beginning of the long-planned study of large-scale organizations. Norman Martin had been approached by the Carnegie Corporation to do a research on a large industrial organization, for which he had chosen Corn Products since he had associations there. He then suggested that this be one of the large-scale organizations of the research on the Emergent American Society. Lloyd wanted the first volume of this series to represent the most important large-scale societal structures as studied by experts in each field. When he discussed the book with Jane Olson, his editor at the Yale Press, she said that, of all such books planned, most had not been completed because it was almost impossible to get individual contributors to produce on schedule. Lloyd felt confident that he would succeed. Each chapter was to be based on original research for which the author was paid. Funding came from the Carnegie Corporation and from Michigan State University.

The first casualty was Norman Martin who, because of his involvement with New York University and other researches, could not do the study of Corn Products. Fortunately George Downing, chairman of the Department of Marketing at Arizona State, and a top executive for many years of the General Electric Company, agreed to write a chapter on the organization of that company, which was well suited to the study because of the degree of autonomy given to individual divisions within the company. Keeping such a system operating as a unit is the great challenge.

Bob Havighurst was ideal for the education chapters. Not only did he agree to undertake the work, but when the plan for his chapters was changed after he had finished most of the work, he cheerfully adapted and met the deadline for the altered chapters.

Bill Henry, also a long-time friend, colleague in Human Development, and collaborator, agreed to do the work on business executives, a field in which he had specialized and for which he and Harriett Moore had designed a Thematic Apperception Test for executives based on Harry Murray's protocol.

Desmond Martin, of the University of Cincinnati, was a student of trade associations and undertook the chapter on that subject in collaboration with Lloyd and Frank Nall of the faculty of Southern Illinois University, who had experience in national associations. June Collins of Oakland College, later of Southern Illinois University, wrote the chapter on labor unions; and Darab Unwalla, whose specialty was statistics, collaborated with Lloyd on the chapters on corporations. John Trimm, of Michigan

State, later of the University of Arizona, was one of the first to join the research staff. An able and pleasant person, he quickly took charge of office routines, selection and purchase of equipment, and of procedures vis a vis the university administration. He had worked on *The American Federal Executive* and was well qualified to collaborate on the big government chapters. So much did he and Darab contribute to the total undertaking that their names appear as coauthors. Many able graduate students made large contributions. Some of these were financed in part at least through a grant of $25,000 given by the Ford Foundation to the President's Fund of the University of Chicago for Lloyd's use. It was not solicited and had almost no restrictions; the grant could be used for travel, writing, research, for students, as he wished. Some of his students were young veterans, married with families, working for advanced degrees. When the GI bill was passed many university people were concerned about the quality of students it would support. In Lloyd's experience these young men were intelligent, mature, serious, dedicated, and great to work with. They became recipients of much of the grant.

Lloyd was pleased that Gibson Winter, professor in the Divinity School of the University of Chicago, agreed to do the research and writing on religious organizations.

Only recently I have learned that the Ford grant was made as part of a plan to give unrestricted funds to a selected number of behavioral scientists to learn whether they could be productive of significant contributions to the field.

From Volume I:

During the last fifty years big corporations, big government, and other large-scale organizations have proliferated in the United States and in European and other civilized countries, and their power and importance have become problems of conscious concern and debate. Since the rise is clearly associated with vast increases in population, technological advancement, and growing complexities of modern life, it is often assumed that these and other contemporary conditions are sufficient to explain and understand the nature of big organizations. In many respects this is too simple an assumption. It is sometimes far from the truth, although often it is part of it; but taken too literally it injures our scientific understanding of what these organizations are and what they do in this society. One needs to ask about the different kinds of demographic, economic, technological, and social worlds in which large-scale organizations exist. When and where do they not exist? Under what conditions do they flourish? When and why do they develop?"[1]

Simple typologies to compare and contrast human societies are based ultimately on some division of social labor, of varying degrees of complexity. Three types of adaptive systems can be distinguished—the technology and economy, the social organization (moral order), and the sacred symbol systems, each of which relates the society to a given environment. No society is so simple that it has no division of labor, no social differentiation. Some simple hunters and gatherers—for example, the Australian aborigines and some western American Indians—have little division of social and economic labor, and most activities are based upon biological differences; whereas the United States has an elaborate economic and social division of labor, economic differentiation, specialized occupations, which are ranked but do not rank the worker, as in feudal systems.

A principal characteristic of our moral order is the partial interrelation of the elaborate hierarchies of ranked status with the general social classes that arrange most people in orders of superiority and inferiority, in which social mobility is prized and is in the spirit of the system itself. Social differentiation has such flexibility that individual autonomy and free social movement of individuals in the general status system and within the various hierarchies are not only permitted but encouraged.[2]

It is the high degree of differentiation and specialization and their high numbers that distinguish between large-scale organizations in our society and others less complex, rather than their structures. Large organizations often seem more rigid than they, in fact, are and respond adaptively to changes that occur in the larger society. Ours is an open system, with mergers, growth, and innovation creating new corporations, new government agencies, new professional and trade associations, new hierarchies. These are a necessary part of the social system. The problem of coordinating relations and activities to allow men to work together for common purposes requires the superimposition of general social goals over individual action.

As our national society becomes more and more a primary social and economic community, as place and time are less limiting in face-to-face interaction, and as simultaneity of coordinated action over great distances becomes more frequent and more diverse, large organizations are increasingly used to order and maintain the national, primary action system. . . . All sizes and varieties of organization exist and function successfully in this rapidly developing primary national community. Millions of small businesses, millions of families, hundreds of thousands of small associations, and many thousands of local schools, churches, and government, with varying degrees of success, make up the small fiber of the life of 190 million

Americans! Yet given the newly expanded territorial and biological basis of our society and its need for coordination of adaptive behavior; given the vast new elaborations of industry and the enormous growth in productivity; and given the increasing heterogeneity of ideas, beliefs, values and behavior, the need for the small territorial units is decreasing, and more reliance is being placed on big, widely extended hierarchies.[3]

The first plan was for two volumes, the second to be one on the emergent American society itself, the emergent processes related to the realignment and centralization of power in various kinds of nationwide hierarchial institutions. But as the research developed on big farmers, as one of the large-scale organizations, it became clear that it would require a separate volume.

Unlike Lloyd's other researches, most of the material would be historical, derivative. Material was clipped, organized, and annotated, to fill a four-drawer file. Paul Lunt returned to Newburyport to gather comparative data on the current period as compared with the earlier research, especially on shoe factories. The *Encyclopaedia Britannica*, Bureau of the Census, journals, and Historical Statistics of the United States were among the sources. But the research on big farmers and ranchers, once the contacts were established that made it possible to gather original data on a large body of big farmers, became all-demanding, shunting aside the work that had been done on the general volume, even though much writing had been completed on the general concept.

Notes to Chapter XV

1. W. Lloyd Warner, Darab B. Unwalla, and John H. Trimm, *Large-Scale Organizations*, The Emergent American Society, Vol. I (New Haven: Yale University Press, 1967), pp. 14–15.
2. Ibid., pp. 17–18.
3. Ibid., p. 20.

THE TREMENDOUS amount of data on big farmers and ranchers had been analyzed by computer and organized into over 200 tables on the basis of multivariate criteria, and Lloyd had started writing. We took this vast quantity of research material with us when we went to Borrego Springs for the winter of 1969–1970. We had a competent typist there, and Lloyd intended to continue sending dictabelts back to East Lansing for typing as well.

We both became ill soon after moving into a new house we had rented. When I realized how sick I was I forced myself to a doctor; it was a Saturday morning and by chance he was there working on correspondence. He realized that I required prompt treatment, and when I told him that my husband was more ill than I he returned with me and diagnosed pneumonia and congestive heart failure. He wanted to get Lloyd to Scripps but was afraid to risk a trip over the mountains to the coast, even in an ambulance with oxygen. So he decided to treat him at home, hoping to achieve recovery sufficient to travel. We rejoiced when this was accomplished. At Scripps we met Dr. Carmichael, a well-known and almost unreachable cardiologist, who was waiting for us. He questioned Lloyd intensively, had a nurse take him to a room, ordered oxygen and digitalis, then turned to me, "We have a lot of very ill people in this hopsital, but of them all he is the sickest. If he lives he will be here at least two weeks. I will do everything possible for his recovery. He is a most remarkable person—I think the most remarkable person I have ever met. Ill as he is he sat there and gave me a consistent history, answered all of my queries. Only with great will to live could he do this. I will do everything I can to save him."

When I went to his room I found Lloyd introducing himself to the nurse and asking her name. He refused to tolerate the depersonalization of hospitals, insisted upon being recognized and treated as a person, and wanted to recognize the personnel working there in the same way, all but the lab technicians whom he considered too far gone to try to reach. He deeply resented their cold, technical behavior.

In two weeks he was ready to go home. I had a long conference with the dietician and received a list of acceptable and interdicted foods; I have heard people talk about low-sodium diets but I have never heard of one as strict as this. It was limited to 1,600 calories a day, two or three ounces of meat, chicken, or fish, two eggs a week, one teaspoon of unsalted margarine a day, two ounces of alcohol. I was surprised at the number of vegetables high in sodium, but fortunately almost any kind of fruit was allowed. With a few innovations we could eat quite well; sometimes when Lloyd was enjoying a meal particularly he would feel that it was surely not permitted and had to be reassured. Dr. Carmichael had told him that the most important person in his life was sitting beside him, that it would be my responsibility to see that the diet was followed. It included seven slices of bread or other cereal, which was far too much for our way of eating; actually we consumed only about 1200 calories, and both lost weight until I think Lloyd was really too thin to have the energy he needed. But he could take walks, extending them gradually, and could swim although he never really enjoyed it again. And as he regained strength he began to work on the Emergent American Society, was delighted to be doing again what he had thought he might never be able to do. One day when he had been working on a complex interrelationship he found the solution and exulted.

Dr. Carmichael brought up the possibility of open heart surgery and Lloyd promptly said no—no more operations. It was not known really what caused the heart failure; it was assumed that it was occlusion of the aortic valve, but only an exploratory would disclose what it was. Lloyd said why find out if that would only indicate the type of surgery required and he was not going to have it. Dr. Carmichael was relieved. He had assured us that he would get Lloyd to the best person in the field and suggested Massachusetts General. But as we talked he referred to a study made of the recovery rate from open heart surgery and acknowledged that Lloyd would have about a ten-percent chance of leaving the operating table alive. It was a pointless discussion. All that Lloyd wanted to do was to be at home, work as long as he could, try to finish his current projects, and do his best to live with the restrictions.

When the weather warmed sufficiently in Chicago, Dr. Carmichael gave us permission to leave. He gave us the name of Dr. Oglesby Paul, chief of staff at Passavant Hospital in Chicago and a famous cardiologist. But first Lloyd wanted to see Dr. Phelan, out of regard for him, even though there was a delay in getting an appointment. He wanted Dr. Phelan to release him as a patient. To our amazement he refused to do so and spoke of his associates in cardiology at Presbyterian-St. Luke's; they were all surgeons. So I called Dr. Paul, found that the nurse had Dr. Carmichael's letter and had been expecting us to call; she gave us an appointment three weeks hence. I replied that it would probably be too late. So he saw us within a few days.

I shall never understand what happened then. I fully expected that he would hospitalize Lloyd, digitalize him, and give oxygen that had had such beneficial effects in La Jolla, but he let us go home, wanted the diet continued but fortified somewhat for strength, and prescribed mild exercise. It is frustrating that only nitroglycerine is available to relieve the pain. It was worst at night; sometimes he would not go to sleep until dawn. If he napped in the afternoon and awakened late enough to have a drink before dinner, one of those two ounces he was allowed, he felt cheered since it was among the few things that relieved the pain—that and the ministrations of an electric massager which I used on his back.

We resumed trips to Michigan State so that Lloyd could keep in touch with the tabulation of the research data. The university gave him half-time status, after which by mutual agreement his appointment would terminate.

As spring came to the dunes he took such joy in watching the changes, the beauty and excitement, from the comfort of a glassed porch. We have a sunburst locust adjoining a glass wall that he adored—its new leaves are its blossoms, as beautiful as any flower. We had time to talk— often at breakfast, which he usually had in bed, as he had for many years. Like Winston Churchill he used his bed as a desk and when he did get up would continue to work in a dressing gown until lunch, by far the most productive period of his day.

So much is said about the loneliness and isolation of the dying person, that no one will listen to him if he wants to talk about dying because no one wants to acknowledge reality. But Lloyd had the courage to face reality as he saw it and hoped that others would do the same: he realized that he was growing weaker and that this would be a continuing process. We talked about dying, and he said that he wanted to be cremated and no services. But I said the University of Chicago and Michigan State would both want memorial services and he made no objection. He wanted his ashes on Coyote Mountain in Borrego Springs, a lovely mountain that rises in gradual slopes from the desert floor. We had taken a jeep and driven around to the far side one day and were enchanted by the beauty, the silence, hummingbirds feeding on the blossoms of a pale verde growing in a wash—that was all. But he did not want me to try to do something too difficult and suggested that I ask the Barbers to go with me. Matt and Susie are lovely people, our dear friends, and oh so resourceful.

We had an appointment at Passavant. Dr. Paul was sure that no one was reading the blood pressure correctly, and they had a new way of testing in the blood stream. When the appointment was made I said that we would have a wheelchair, that we should probably be in an ambulance, and that we should be met. Dr. Paul and an assistant were waiting for us and we went immediately to the lab. Again, one of those amazing procedures. Why bother with the blood pressure of someone so ill? Why not directly help him? When we returned to his office Dr. Paul said that he thought Lloyd should be in the hospital for a few days. The next day I brought him books and pajamas and found that they were giving him tap water, not distilled water, and no oxygen, which would at least have made him feel better. Dr. Paul and an assistant came at supper time and insisted upon lifting him higher in bed so he could eat. I had not dared touch him because of the pain. After they left he put his head back on the pillow and said wearily, "All I want is to be left alone."

Not long after I reached home Dr. Paul phoned to say that Lloyd had gone into a coma, that he was in intensive care, that he did not expect him to regain consciousness, and urged me not to come, that he would not know I was there. I accepted that because I did not trust myself to drive back into the city. I stayed at the phone all night and heard from Dr. Paul early in the morning that he had died.

The University of Chicago had a memorial service bringing people from all over, many former students who are close friends, Lloyd's sister, our children, and dear Old Hyde Park friends, and Mrs. Clifton Wharton, wife of the president, spoke for Michigan State. The tributes were warm, appreciative, and loving—spoken with care not to come too close to things that would upset me—by Bob Havighurst, Allison Davis, Lloyd Fallers, Everett Hughes, and Burleigh Gardner.

I had arranged for an autopsy, wanting to know some answers and feeling that the people who had worked so hard at Presbyterian-St. Luke's should know, if possible, the cause they had been seeking for the anemia. It was not there. But they found the occlusion in the coronary artery and also a small clot in the heart. Dr. Paul had helped me find a mortuary that would agree to no embalming, no elaborate casket before the cremation. And they held the ashes until the desert would be tolerably cool. Our daughter Caroline came from New York to join me in Chicago for the trip West. We stayed with the Barbers the following day and went to Borrego, where Matt borrowed a jeep to drive into the desert. As we went around the far side of Coyote Mountain he would ask here?—here?—but I was waiting until the mountain turned. And there we climbed to huge overhanging boulders and placed the ashes among them with rosemary we had brought from the Barbers'. I took photographs so that I can always return and find the spot. There in his desert, on the mountain he loved, silence, peace.

Snapshot, 1964

	Personal	Academic positions and activities
1898	Born Redlands, California	
1913–17	Colton and San Bernadino High Schools	
1917	Enlisted in U.S. Army	
1918	Discharged from U.S. Army	
1919	University of Southern California	
1919–22	University of California, Berkeley; disqualified because of political activity in December and readmitted	
1922	Married Louise Overfield and separated	
1922–23	University of California	
1923–24	University of California; withdrew in the fall to go to New York City; readmitted	
1924–25	University of California; received A.B. degree	
1925–26	University of California; graduate work in anthropology	
1926	Withdrew from University of California to study with Earnest Hooton at Harvard	
1926–29		
1929		Harvard University as instructor and tutor in Department of Anthropology
1930		
1931	Summer in Ireland	Assistant Professor, Harvard University

Research activities   Publications

Field work on Australian Murngin under
direction of A. R. Radcliffe-Brown

Yankee City research (1929–50)

Project with Elton Mayo at Hawthorn Works
of Western Electric (1930–33)

Harvard Irish survey (1931–33)

	Personal	Academic positions and activities
1932	Married Mildred Hall; spent summer in Ireland; moved to Newburyport in fall	
1933	Daughter Ann Covington born; moved to Cambridge in fall	
1934	Father died	Hanover Conference of General Education Board
1935	Daughter Caroline Hall born; spent summer in Berkeley	Visiting professor at University of California during summer session; Associate Professor of Anthropology, University of Chicago
1936	Spent summer in New York	Visiting professor, Columbia University
1937	Moved to 5714 Dorchester Avenue in Chicago	
1938		
1939	Son William Taylor born	
1940		Member of Committee on Human Development, University of Chicago; full professor, University of Chicago
1941	Spent academic year in Santa Monica	Visiting professor at University of California at Los Angeles
1942		Founder of Committee on Human Relations in Industry, University of Chicago
1944–45	Bought vacation home in Indiana Dunes	
1946	Cofounder of Social Research Inc.; spent winter months with mother in California	
1947	Mother died	
1949		

Research activities	Publications
Deep South (1933–36)	
	A Black Civilization, A Social Study of an Australian Tribe
Black Metropolis (1938–43)	
	Preface, *Family and Community in Ireland*
Jonesville Community Research (1941–49)	*The Social Life of a Modern Community.* Yankee City Series: I
Research on American Indians (1942–46)	*The Status System of a Modern Community.* Yankee City Series: II
	Who Shall Be Educated? and *The Social Systems of American Ethnic Groups.* Yankee City Series: III
Rockford, Illinois (1946–48)	"Radio Daytime Serial: A Symbolic Analysis"
	The Social System of the Modern Factory. Yankee City Series: IV
	Social Class in America and *Democracy in Jonesville*

	Personal	Academic positions and activities
1950	Spent winter in Redlands, California; spent spring in Scotland and England	Gave Munro Lectures at University of Edinburgh; gave lectures at Oxford, Manchester, and London School of Economics
1951		
1952		
1953	Winter in Borrego Springs; moved permanent residence to Dune Acres, Indiana	
1954–55	Cambridge, England; consulted in London for Social Research Inc.; trips to Spain	Visiting Professor of Social Theory, Trinity College, Cambridge
1956	Spent winter in Mexico	
1957	Daughter Ann married to Michael Arlen	
1958	Spent winter in Borrego Springs (to become winter residence)	Resigned from University of Chicago as of 1959
1959	New house in Dune Acres	University Professor of Social Research, Michigan State University
1960	Assisted in Kennedy campaign for presidency	
1961		Ford Foundation Lectures at New York University
1963	Daughter Caroline married to John Hightower	
1965	Resigned from Social Research Inc.	
1967		
1969		Worked half-time at Michigan State University
1970	Died May 23 in Chicago	

Research activities	Publications
Kansas City	
	Structure of American Life
Big Business Leaders in America (1953 – 54)	*American Life: Dream and Reality* and *What You Know About Social Class*
	Big Business Leaders in America and *Occupational Mobility in American Business and Industry*
The American Federal Executive (1958 – 62)	
	Industrial Man and *The Living and the Dead*
	The Family of God and *The Corporation in the Emergent American Society*
The Emergent American Society (1963 –)	*The American Federal Executive* and *Yankee City* (abridged edition)
	Large-Scale Organizations. The Emergent American Society: I

Books by Warner and (where noted) collaborators

Abegglen, James C., and Warner, W. Lloyd. *Big Business Leaders in America.* New York: Harper and Bros., 1955; rev. ed. Atheneum, 1963; Tokyo: Diamond Publishing Co., trans. 1955.
————. *Occupational Mobility in American Business and Industry.* Minneapolis: University of Minnesota Press, 1955.
Adams, Walter A.; Junker, Buford; and Warner, W. Lloyd. *Color and Human Nature.* Washington, D.C.: American Council on Education, 1941; New York: Harper Torchbooks, 1967; Westport, Conn.: Greenwood Press, 1970.
American Life: Dream and Reality. Chicago: University of Chicago Press, 1953; rev. 1962; Phoenix Books, 1962.
A Black Civilization, A Social Study of an Australian Tribe. New York: Harper and Bros., 1937; reprinted 1958; rev. ed. Harper Torchbooks, 1964.
Collins, Orvis; Martin, Norman H.; Van Riper, Paul P.; and Warner, W. Lloyd. *The American Federal Executive.* New Haven: Yale University Press, 1963. Paperback ed. 1963. Reissued Westport, Conn.: Greenwood Press, 1975.
The Corporation in the Emergent American Society. New York: Harper and Bros., 1961.
Eels, Kenneth; Meeker, Marchia; and Warner, W. Lloyd. *Social Class in America.* Chicago: Science Research Associates, 1949; Gloucester: Peter Smith, 1957; rev. ed. New York: Harper Torchbooks, 1960.
The Family of God. New Haven: Yale University Press, 1961; Westport, Conn.: Greenwood Press, 1975.
Havighurst, Robert J.; Loeb, Martin B.; and Warner, W. Lloyd. *Who Shall Be Educated?* New York: Harper and Bros., 1945; Tokyo, 1956, trans. Takako Mori.
The Living and The Dead. Vol. 5. New Haven: Yale University Press, 1959.
Low, J. O.; and Warner, W. Lloyd. *The Social System of the Modern Factory.* Vol. 4. New Haven: Yale University Press, 1947.
Martin, Norman H., and Warner, W. Lloyd. *Industrial Man.* New York: Harper and Bros., 1959.
Srole, Leo, and Warner, W. Lloyd. *The Social Systems of American Ethnic Groups.* Vol. 3. New Haven: Yale University Press, 1945.

Structure of American Life. Edinburgh: University of Edinburgh Press, 1952.

Trimm, John H.; Unwalla, Darab B.; and Warner, W. Lloyd. *Large-Scale Organizations.* The Emergent American Society. Vol. 1. New Haven: Yale University Press, 1967.

Warner and Associates. *Democracy in Jonesville.* New York: Harper and Bros., 1949; Harper Torchbooks, 1969; Westport, Conn.: Greenwood Press, 1976.

Yankee City. New Haven: Yale University Press, 1963. Paperback edition, 1963.

Yankee City Series, 5 volumes:

Lunt, Paul S., and Warner, W. Lloyd. *The Social Life of a Modern Community.* Vol. 1. New Haven: Yale University Press, 1941.

Lunt, Paul S., and Warner, W. Lloyd. *The Status System of a Modern Community.* Vol. 2. New Haven: Yale University Press, 1942.

Articles and chapters by Warner and (where noted) collaborators

Abegglen, J. C., and Warner, W. Lloyd. "Equal Opportunity and American Business Leaders." *Michigan Business Review* (March 1956).

———. "Executive Careers Today: Who Gets to the Top." *The Management Review* 45: 83–96.

———. "Individual Opportunity—A Challenge to the Free Enterprise System." *Identifying and Developing Potential Leaders.* New York: American Management Association. Personnel Series #127.

———. "Successful Wives of Successful Executives." *Harvard Business Review* (March–April 1956).

"American Caste and Class." *The American Journal of Sociology* 42: 234–37.

"An American Sacred Ceremony." In *Reader in Comparative Religion: An Anthropological Approach,* by William A. Lessa and Evon Z. Vogt. New York: Harper and Row, 1965.

"The American Town." In *American Society in Wartime,* edited by William F. Ogburn. Chicago: University of Chicago Press, 1943.

"Anthropology." *Britannica Book of the Year.* (1941) pp. 48–50.

"Birth Control in Primitive Society." *Birth Control Review* 15: 105–07.

Burton, Rev. F. W.; Radcliffe-Brown, A. R.; and Warner, W. Lloyd. "Some Aspects of the Aboriginal Problem in Australia," Notes on Addresses to the Society, March 13, 1928. *The Australian Geographer.*

"The Camp Life of the Murngin." *Hobbies* 11 no. 6.

"The Corporation Man." *The Corporation in Modern Society.* Edited by Edward S. Mason. Cambridge: Harvard University Press, 1959.

Davis, Allison, and Warner, W. Lloyd. "A Comparative Study of American Caste." *Race Relations and the Race Problem.* Edited by Edgar T. Thompson. Durham: Duke University Press, 1939.

Davis, Kingsley, and Warner, W. Lloyd. "Structural Analysis of Kinship." *American Anthropologist* 39 (1937) 291–313.

"Discussion of Fred Eggan, 'Culture Change Among the Tinguian of Luzon.'" *Proceedings University of Chicago Seminar on Racial and Cultural Contacts, 1935–36.* (1936) pp. 34–41.

"Discussion of Philleo Nash, 'Nativistic Religious Movements.'" *Proceedings University of Chicago Seminar on Racial and Cultural Contacts, 1935–36.* (1936) pp. 5–9.

"Education for Cultural Unity." *Seventeenth Yearbook, California Elementary School Principals' Association* (1945).

"Educative Effects of Social Status." *Symposium on Environment and Education at the 50th Anniversary of University of Chicago: Supplementary Education Monographs* 54: 216–29.

"Educative Effects of Social Status in Environments and Education." *Human Development Series* 1 (1942), University Department of Education Supplementary Educational Monographs #54.

Eels, Kenneth; Meeker, Marchia; and Warner, W. Lloyd. *Social Status in Education.* Phi Delta Kappa 30: 4.

Eggan, Fred, and Warner, W. Lloyd. "Obituary for A. R. Radcliffe-Brown." *American Anthropologist* 58: 544–47.

"The Family and Personality in the Social Organization of Modern American Communities." *Parent Education* 3 (1937) no. 5.

"The Family and Principles of Kinship Structure in Australia." *American Sociological Review* 2 (1937) no. 1.

"Formal Education and the Social Structure." *The Journal of Educational Sociology* (1936) pp. 524–31.

Havighurst, Robert J., and Warner, W. Lloyd. "Should You Go to College?" *American Job Series.* Chicago: Science Research Associates, 1948.

Henry, William E., and Warner, W. Lloyd. "Radio Daytime Serial: A Symbolic Analysis." *Genetic Psychology Monographs* 37: 3–71.

Howells, W. W., and Warner, W. Lloyd. "Anthropometry of the Natives of Arnhem Land and the Australian Race Problem." Harvard University, *Papers of the Peabody Museum of American Archaeology and Ethnology* 26 (1937) 1.

"Introduction: A Study of Caste and Class. In *Deep South,* by Allison Davis, Burleigh B. Gardner, and Mary Gardner. Chicago: University of Chicago Press, 1941.

Introduction to "The Man in the Middle: Position and Problems of the Foreman," by Burleigh Gardner and William F. Whyte. *Applied Anthropology* (special issue) 4 (1942) no. 2.

Introduction to *Social Mobility in China*, by Yung-Teh Chow. New York: Atherton Press, 1966.

"Kinship Morphology of Forty-one North Australian Tribes." *American Anthropologist* 35: 63–66.

"Life in Suburbia." *Saturday Review* 29: 26.

"The Living Stone Age of Australia." *Harvard Alumni Bulletin* 32: 656–59.

Low, J. O., and Warner, W. Lloyd. "The Factory in the Community." In *Industry and Society*, edited by William F. Whyte. New York: McGraw Hill Co., 1946.

Low, J. O., and Warner, W. Lloyd. "Yankee City Loses Control of Its Factories." In *Perspectives on the American Community*, by Roland L. Warren. Chicago: Rand McNally and Co., 1965.

"Malay Influences in the Aboriginal Cultures of North East Arnhem Land." *Oceania* 2: 476–95.

Methodological Note in *Black-Metropolis*, by Horace Cayton and St. Clair Drake. New York: Harcourt, Brace and Co., 1945.

"A Methodology for the Analysis and Interpretation of the Meanings and Functions of a Primitive Religion: A Study of Social Logics." *The Society for Social Research Bulletin* (1935).

"Methodology and Field Research in Africa." *Africa* 6 (1933) no. 1.

"A Methodology for the Study of the Development of Family Attitudes." *Social Science Research Council Bulletin* 18 (1933).

"A Methodology for the Study of Social Class." In *Social Structure*, edited by Meyer Fortes. New York: Oxford University Press, 1949.

"Morphology and Functions of the Australian Murngin Type of Kinship, Part I." *American Anthropologist* 32: 207–52.

"Morphology and Functions of the Australian Murngin Type of Kinship, Part II." *American Anthropologist* 33: 207–52.

"Murngin Warfare." *Oceania* 1 (1931) no. 4.

"New Look at the Career Civil Service Executive." *Public Administration Review* 22: 188–94.

"Obituary for A. R. Radcliffe-Brown." *Anthropology Tomorrow* 4: 67–68.

"Opportunity in America." *Journal of Business, University of Chicago* 23: 141–53.

"Personality Formation." In *Culture and Personality*, edited by Franz Alexander. *American Journal of Orthopsychiatry* 8: 592–96.

Preface in *Family and Community in Ireland*, by Conrad Arensberg and Solon T. Kimball. Cambridge: Harvard University Press, 1940.

"Procrustean Bed of the Social Sciences." *Annual Proceedings of the Associated Harvard Clubs* (1938).

"Profiles of Government Executives." *Business Topics* 9: 13–24. East Lansing: Michigan State University Press.

Redfield, Robert, and Warner, W. Lloyd. "Cultural Anthropology and Modern Agriculture." *Yearbook, U. S. Department of Agriculture, Part V* (1940), pp. 983–93.

"Significance of Caste and Class in a Democracy." National Conference of Social Workers (1955), pp. 289–301.

"Social Anthropology and the Modern Community." *American Journal of Sociology* 46: 785–96.

"Social Class." *Nelson's Encyclopedia*, 1951.

"A Social Configuration of Magical Behavior: A Study of the Nature of Magic." *Essays in Honor of Alfred Louis Kroeber.* University of California Press, 1936.

"Social Science in Business Education." *The Challenge of Business Education.* University of Chicago 50th Anniversary of the Founding of the School of Business. Chicago: University of Chicago Press, 1949.

"Social Stratification." *Review of Sociology: Analysis of a Decade.* Edited by Joseph B. Gittler. New York: John Wiley & Sons, 1957.

"The Society, the Individual, and His Mental Disorders." *American Journal of Psychiatry* 94 (1937): 275–84.

Warner, Mildred Hall, and Warner, W. Lloyd. *What You Should Know About Social Class.* Chicago: Science Research Associates (monograph), 1953.

——. "New Light on Lateral Entry." *Journal of the Society for Personnel Administration.* "The Careers of American Business and Government Executives; A Comparative Analysis." In *Social Science Approaches to Business Behavior,* edited by George B. Strother. Homewood, Ill.: Dorsey Press, Inc., 1962.

Warner, W. Lloyd, and others. "Women Executives in the Federal Government." *Journal of the Public Personnel Association* 23: 227–34.

——. "New Light on Lateral Entry." *Journal of the Society for Personnel Administration* 26: 17–23.

"White Australia." Chicago Council on Foreign Relations: *Foreign Notes* 19 (1942): 5.

Emergent American Society research, 201–204, 206
Emile Durkheim Professorship of Social Research (Michigan State), 195
Encyclopaedia Britannica, 156
England. *See also* British tour
  auto purchased in, 182, 188
  life in, 171–173, 177–181, 184, 187–188
  professorship in, 176
  return from, 188–189
  visits to, 63–64. *See also* Munro Lectures
Engle, Carl, 107
English Speaking Union, 171
Ennis, Ireland. *See* Harvard Irish Survey; Ireland
equal opportunity. *See* American dream
Ericson, Eric, 127

faculty wives
  at Harvard, 142
  at University of Chicago, 141–142
Fallers, Lloyd, 208
Family and Community in Ireland (Arensberg & Kimball), 75–76
family life
  in Chicago, 143–145
  in England, 177–181, 184, 187–188
Family of God, 126
Faris, Ellsworth, 112–113
Farmer, Frances, 10–11, 49–50, 110
farmers research, 204–205
Fatigue Laboratory (Harvard), 43–44
Faust, Clarence, 120
federal executives research, 191–193, 197–199. *See also* Business leaders
FERA, 91, 120
Fermi, Enrico, 150
Field, Marshall, 153
financing of projects, 91–92, 98, 150. *See also* *specific foundations*
Firth, Raymond, 22, 171
Fisher, Fred, 11
Fisher, Mary, 106
Flint, John [pseud.]. *See* Junker
Ford Foundation, 202
"Formal Education and the Social Structure," 95
Fortes, Meyer, 20, 169–170, 176
Fortson, Stokeley, 10
Fortune, Reo, 22, 59
Francis, Clarence, 191
Frank, Lawrence K., 106, 127
Freeman, Jenny Y., 9
Friedman, Eugene, 129
Friendly, Helen, 36
Friends in Council, 120, 142
Fund for the Republic, 132

Gaelic language, 69, 73
gardening, 165
Gardner, Burleigh, 50–51, 76, 93–94, 97–98, 114–115, 125, 128, 130–131, 154, 156, 159, 194, 208
Gardner, Mary, 91, 93–94, 97
Gardner Advertising Agency, 157
Gay, Edwin F., 107–108
genealogies, 26–27
General Education Board (GEB), 106, 120, 127, 154–155
General Electric Company, 201
Gifford, Edward W., 2–3, 12
Gillis, "Bossy" (Newburyport mayor), 85, 87
Gluckman, Max, 168–1169
Goddard, Amory, 65
Goodman, Howard, 155
Goody, Jack, 181
Goro, Fritz, 38
Granet, Marcel, 89
Green Goddess, The, 10

Halbwachs, Maurice, 45–46
Haldane, J. B. S., 63–64
Hale, Albert, 79
Hale, Mrs. Albert, 79–80, 82
Hall, Radclyffe, 63
Hannah, John, 195, 199
Hanover Conference, 103, 107–108, 127
Harbison, Fred, 154
Harper, Dr. (University of Chicago president), 146
Harper, Mrs., 142
Harrington, Gwen, 51
Harris, Chauncy, 197
Harrison, Bill, 157, 159
Harsborough, Mrs., 32
Hart, C. W. M., 22
Hartshorne, Hugh, 107
Harvard Irish Survey, 57–77, 102
Harvard University, 19
  Department of Anthropology, 108
  extension courses at, 111
  Graduate School of Business Administration, 43
  social sciences at, 107–108
  teaching fellowship at, 41–42, 49
Haughton, Bess, 51
Havighurst, Robert, 107, 127–132, 153–154, 156, 196, 201, 208
Hawthorne Works, 44–47
Hencken, Hugh O'Neill, 65
Henderson, L. J., 51, 53–56, 76, 114, 119, 121
Henry, Bill, 155–156, 193, 201
Hidden Persuaders, The (Packard), 158
Hightower, John, 199–200
Hogbin, H. I., 22

W. Lloyd Warner: Social Anthropologist
was typeset by Ira Ungar and produced by the
Publishing Center for Cultural Resources.
The Publishing Center is a nonprofit organization
founded in 1973 to help nonprofit educational
institutions and associations become
effective publishers. Its services, which
now extend to over 150 organizations
throughout the United States, are made
possible by grants from public agencies and
private foundations and corporate contributions.
The Publishing Center is located in New York City.

6. ✓

--

1988.

1